"Novick provides a new paradigm for teaching Christians about Judaism. Traversing both the shared heritage between Jews and Christians and the distinctive elements of the Jewish tradition, this book is an invaluable resource both inside and outside the classroom."

—*Daniel Joslyn-Siemiatkoski*

director of the Center for Christian-Jewish Learning, Boston College

"Tzvi Novick has produced an engaging account of Judaism, designed for a Christian audience, particularly Roman Catholics, but of interest to all. Novick guides the reader through three thousand years of Jewish history, explaining key practices and beliefs, identifying similarities of and differences between Christianity and Judaism. The book is commendable for its clarity and accessibility. It includes a brief bibliography at the end of each chapter enabling further reflection. I recommend this book to all those who wish to learn more about Judaism and the key concerns of Jews today."

—*Ed Kessler*

founder president of the Woolf Institute (UK), chair of the advisory board overseeing the unification of Reform and Liberal Judaism

"This is an insightful, comprehensive and simpatico presentation of Judaism from which both Christians and Jews will benefit. The author writes from a modern Orthodox perspective but often presents the range of denominational views respectfully. This book combines meaningful instruction on Jewish religion with a remarkable parallel presentation of Christian conceptions of Judaism in historic context. Thus what has been called 'the teaching of contempt' tradition in Christianity is presented without anger or 'guilting.' This allows Christians of good will and Jews who want a better future for Jewish Christian relations to leave hostility and misrepresentation behind—a signal achievement. This book will be most useful to Christians of deep faith who seek to continue on the path of healing between Jesus's family and the faith in which he grew and their covenant faith which brought the Gospel to the farthest reaches of the earth."

—*Irving Greenberg*

president of the J. J. Greenberg Institute for the Advancement of Jewish Life, senior scholar in residence at the Hadar Institute, author of *For the Sake of Heaven and Earth: The New Encounter of Judaism and Christianity*

"In this book, Tzvi Novick provides an amazingly comprehensive and accessible introduction to the Jewish people's history, texts, traditions, and practices. Written with a Christian audience in mind and drawing on his classroom experience, he constantly offers comparisons and contrasts to Christianity with great insight, knowledge, and sensitivity. Indeed, readers of any or no religious background, including Jews, will benefit from this book's judicious and nuanced presentation of Judaism and its theological and historical relationship with Christianity."

—*Philip A. Cunningham*
director of the Institute for Jewish-Catholic Relations,
Saint Joseph's University

"Novick has authored a most welcome and highly readable guide for understanding the richness and diversity of Jewish religious thought and practice. Well researched and written by a modern Orthodox Jew, this is a valuable read for both Jews and Christians. One of Novick's strengths is the ability to give the reader a feel for the inner spirit of Judaism and its practices. This volume may be used effectively as a classroom text or as a helpful companion to an interfaith dialogue group. This illuminating, well-balanced text offers a fresh set of Jewish eyes to explore the theological story of Judaism. I highly recommend this book."

—*Marvin R. Wilson*
emeritus professor of biblical and theological studies, Gordon College

"Novick's *Judaism* is a succinct and yet comprehensive account of Judaism for the general Christian reader. The key elements of Jewish/Christian relations as well as Jewish thought and practice are covered with frankness and generosity. This is an excellent volume for study and reflection whether in the college or seminary classroom or the priest or pastor's office. I commend it with enthusiasm."

—*John E. Phelan Jr.*
emeritus president and dean, North Park Theological Seminary

Judaism

A Guide for Christians

Tzvi Novick

William B. Eerdmans Publishing Company
Grand Rapids, Michigan

Wm. B. Eerdmans Publishing Co.
2006 44th Street SE, Grand Rapids, MI 49508
www.eerdmans.com

Published 2025

Book design by Leah Luyk

Printed in the United States of America

ISBN 978-0-8028-8432-9

Library of Congress Cataloging-in-Publication Data

A catalog record for this book is available from the Library of Congress.

Dedicated to the memory of Ophir Agassi (1977–2022)

בצל א-ל היית עומד

Contents

Preface

THE ORIGIN OF THIS BOOK LIES IN AN UNDERGRADUATE course that I have taught in numerous iterations at the University of Notre Dame, both at the main campus in South Bend and at the university's Jerusalem campus. When I first arrived at Notre Dame, I taught an introduction to Jewish theology as a stand-alone course. But I came to appreciate that within the framework of a Catholic theology department, it was important for there to be an undergraduate course that introduced Jewish theology in conjunction with the history of Christian teaching about Jews and Judaism. That is the goal of this book: to conjoin, in an organic and synergistic way, a survey of Christian teaching about Jews and Judaism to a survey of Jewish theology that is attentive to the assumptions and questions with which a Christian might approach Judaism, and to opportunities for comparison. Although the book's origin at a Catholic university lends Catholicism a certain salience in the book, forms of Protestant Christianity will figure importantly at a number of points. The book is meant for the general reader—Christian, Jewish, or otherwise—as well as for classroom use. I have included a section at the end of each chapter called "Further Inquiry." This section identifies the scholarly sources on which the chapter draws, as well as additional works of scholarship that the interested reader might pursue. It also frames thought questions that are related to but not directly addressed in the chapter.

There are, of course, innumerable and profound disagreements within the field of Jewish theology. In some cases I have found it possible to describe a range of views. In other cases I focus on what I take to be the mainstream view in the tradition. Inevitably, however, there is a measure of idiosyncrasy in my account of Judaism. Put differently, my account, while seeking to be descriptive, is necessarily also constructive. In the context of my Notre Dame course that underlies this book, I assign students the task of locating and interviewing a "Jewish leader" from their hometown to obtain his or her views on Judaism. The purpose of this assignment is not only to make Judaism personal for students and to seed the possibility for future interactions but also to enable them to hear a different perspective from the one that I present in class. I invite the readers of this book, likewise, to seek out other perspectives.

Some notes on terminology, texts, translations, and transliterations: when the book refers to "the church," the reference can be either to the Catholic Church specifically or to the Christian community in general, depending on the context. "Israel" can refer either to the people Israel, that is, the Jewish people, or to the state of Israel, depending on the context. The scholarly convention is to speak of the Jews of the biblical period as "Israelites," and as "Jews" only for the period after the Babylonian exile (at the earliest); I generally follow this convention, though sometimes I find it easier to use "Jews," anachronistically, for the biblical period. Biblical quotations generally depend on the New Revised Standard Version translation (updated edition), but sometimes diverge, often in the direction of the New Jewish Publication Society translation. Every other primary text not originally written in English has been translated by me, unless otherwise indicated. For rabbinic texts I use standard printed editions but sometimes modify on the basis of manuscript witnesses. In transliterating Hebrew words, I use *h* for ח, *ts* for צ, and *q* for ק, but for words that appear commonly in English, I use the conventional English spelling. I also use an apostrophe for both א and ע, except when they are word-initial, in which case they are not transliterated.

I owe a great debt to the Notre Dame students who took the course underlying this book for their questions, observations, and engaged attention. I am grateful beyond measure, also, to my colleagues in the Department of Theology, from whom I have learned, to the degree that I have, how to think theologically. A special thanks to my colleague David Lincicum, who read a draft version of chapters 2, 3, and 5, and offered wise and encouraging comments. Two colleagues at St. Joseph's University—Phil Cunningham and Adam Gregerman—likewise provided very helpful feedback on the first six chapters, and my friend Robert Erlich did the same for the whole manuscript. The fingerprints of the capable hands of the editorial team at Eerdmans are present everywhere. To my children, Aiden, Caleb, Eve, and Maya: thank you for the joy that you bring me through your marvelous selves, a joy that accompanied me in the writing of this book and that accompanies me always. If you read the book, I hope you will find in it the love of Judaism and of open inquiry that I have sought to impart to you. No words of gratitude will convey my debt to my wife, Rachel, or to my parents, Etta and Isaac Novick. All the more so to God, who graces human beings with insight, and teaches mortals understanding.

— *Chapter 1* —

Starting Points

In mid-March of 1943, the Vatican received a request on behalf of the Jewish community in Slovakia, which at that point numbered some twenty thousand and was slated for deportation to Nazi concentration camps in Poland. Could the Holy Father intervene with the head of the Slovakian government, a (Nazi-allied) Roman Catholic priest named Jozef Tiso, to enable one thousand Jewish children to emigrate to Palestine? The request found its way to the desk of Monsignor Giuseppe di Meglio in the Vatican's Secretariat of State, who produced a report on the immediate question within the framework of a general reflection on the Jews and Palestine. Di Meglio noted in his report that, until the war, Jews had in general been reluctant to emigrate to Palestine. He offered this explanation: "Now it is known that most Jews are mainly dedicated to industry and, for the most part, commerce. This commerce remains quite profitable for them when they find themselves living among Christians. If, on the contrary, *all* and *only* the Jews come together, one has an enormous gathering in of . . . swindlers, while lacking those to be swindled. Therefore, most Jews had no desire to migrate to Palestine."[1] He added that the Holy See had a consistent position opposing a Jewish state in Palestine, and that diverging from it "would mean offending the religious sentiment of all Catholics and all those who . . . call themselves Christian."

Di Meglio's portrayal of the Jewish people in this report depends on a long history of Christian anti-Judaism, refracted through modern antisemitism. In the prevalent Christian view, which crystallized in antiquity and persisted into the twentieth century, the Jews were the people who responded to Jesus's

1. Quoted from David I. Kertzer, *The Pope at War: The Secret History of Pius XII, Mussolini, and Hitler* (New York: Random House, 2022), 275. The ellipsis is in the original document.

coming with arrogance and willful blindness, who rejected him and killed him. They were condemned by God to inhabit a dead-end existence, in exile and subject to the church triumphant, until Christ should return, and the Jews should finally accept him. Di Meglio's Jews, following along these lines, are of low character, enemies of Christians and indeed of all gentiles (non-Jews). They have no place in Palestine, where they might control Christian holy sites and escape the subservience that is their due punishment.

No element of such characterizations remains part of the teaching of the Catholic Church today. The person who conveyed the request on behalf of the Slovakian Jews, Archbishop Angelo Roncalli, then papal delegate to Turkey, would come to preside, as Pope John XXIII, over the first sessions of the Second Vatican Council or Vatican II (1962–65), which marked the beginning of a sea change in the relationship of the Catholic Church to Jews and Judaism. Driven most immediately by the Holocaust but shaped as fundamentally by the revolutionary intellectual forces that we call modernity—the scientific worldview, historical-critical consciousness, secularism—the Catholic Church now regards the Jewish people as beloved of God and affirms the eternal persistence of God's covenant with them. God's relationship with the church binds it in a fundamental way to the Jewish people, not only as a matter of ancient history but also in the present and into the future.

Consider in this light more recent remarks on Jews and Judaism, from the very beginning of Pope Benedict's encyclical letter on love, *Deus Caritas Est*, published in 2005.[2]

> "God is love, and he who abides in love abides in God, and God abides in him" (*1 Jn* 4:16). These words from the *First Letter of John* express with remarkable clarity the heart of the Christian faith: the Christian image of God and the resulting image of mankind and its destiny. In the same verse, Saint John also offers a kind of summary of the Christian life: "We have come to know and to believe in the love God has for us."
>
> *We have come to believe in God's love*: in these words the Christian can express the fundamental decision of his life. Being Christian is not the result of an ethical choice or a lofty idea, but the encounter with an event, a person,

2. For the full text of the letter see, https://www.vatican.va/content/benedict-xvi/en/encyclicals/documents/hf_ben-xvi_enc_20051225_deus-caritas-est.html.

> which gives life a new horizon and a decisive direction. Saint John's Gospel describes that event in these words: "God so loved the world that he gave his only Son, that whoever believes in him should . . . have eternal life" (3:16). In acknowledging the centrality of love, Christian faith has retained the core of Israel's faith, while at the same time giving it new depth and breadth. The pious Jew prayed daily the words of the *Book of Deuteronomy* which expressed the heart of his existence: "Hear, O Israel: the Lord our God is one Lord, and you shall love the Lord your God with all your heart, and with all your soul and with all your might" (6:4–5). Jesus united into a single precept this commandment of love for God and the commandment of love for neighbour found in the *Book of Leviticus*: "You shall love your neighbour as yourself" (19:18; cf. *Mk* 12:29–31). Since God has first loved us (cf. *1 Jn* 4:10), love is now no longer a mere "command"; it is the response to the gift of love with which God draws near to us.

According to Pope Benedict, we find in the Old Testament two love commandments: the command to love God, in a verse from Deuteronomy 6 that Jews recite in their daily prayer, and the command to love one's neighbor in Leviticus 19. Jesus "united" these commandments into a "single precept," and transformed them from commands into "the response to the gift of love with which God draws near to us."

How much warmer the image of Jews and Judaism is in this letter than in di Meglio's report! A Jew who gives expression to his Jewish faith in prayer is "pious." Christianity's profession of the centrality of divine love represents, according to the Pope, an inheritance from Judaism. And yet, other elements of the paragraph paint a less flattering picture. If Christianity gives Israel's faith "new depth and breadth," then such depth and breadth must be absent from Judaism itself. Israel has only a "mere 'command'"—"mere" presumably because commanded love can only be superficial—or more precisely, two disconnected commands. These commands cohere only in Christianity, and shed in it their status as command by becoming instead a response to God's love. One might infer that such love is unknown in Judaism, though in the continuation the Pope complicates this inference. Perhaps most strikingly, Pope Benedict speaks of Judaism in the past tense. He says that the pious Jew "prayed" Deuteronomy 6:4–5, even though religiously observant Jews in fact continue to pray these same verses today. The assignment of Judaism to the past is consistent with the gist of Pope Benedict's paragraphs. For if Christianity provides a more coherent, a more organic version of Judaism, what room is there now for Jews? Or to put the point differently, precisely insofar as Christianity recognizes its roots in Judaism, it is naturally led to find lacking in Judaism the boon that it attributes to Jesus.

The excerpt from Pope Benedict's letter teaches us two important and deeply interrelated lessons at this early stage, and while they become visible here in the context of the Catholic Church, they hold for other forms of Christianity that have taken similar directions. First, even after the great turn precipitated by the Second Vatican Council, the Catholic Church's perspective on the Jewish people remains fraught; we cannot by any means speak of an uncomplicated embrace of the Jewish people or wholesale affirmation of Jewish theology. Nor should we expect such things. The aim of Christian-Jewish dialogue, or of Christian reflection on Judaism, should not be to produce a formulation of Christian theology that yields the least friction with Judaism. What is sought, rather, at least in the first place, is precision, and the position adopted by Pope Benedict in this paragraph is a sound expression of current Catholic teaching on Judaism, minus the implicit relegation of Jews to the past.

The second lesson that the excerpt from *Deus Caritas Est* teaches us is that Christianity's understanding of itself is deeply bound up with its understanding of the Jewish people and of Judaism. The topic of Pope Benedict's letter is, after all, love, not Judaism, and yet he deems it important to begin with Jews and Jewish theology, and for good reason. In this respect, Christian reflection on Jews and Judaism is categorically different from Christian reflection on other religions, such as Islam or Buddhism. Because Christianity can be said in significant ways to originate in Judaism, it cannot theologically account for itself without giving a theological account of its relationship to the Jewish people and their faith. The existence of other religions raises important questions for Christianity, but a systematic Christian theology can proceed very far before it need address them.

This book has two interrelated aims. The first is to describe the development of Christianity's theological understanding of Jews and Judaism, with a special interest in Catholicism. We will examine major milestones from antiquity to today, devoting particular attention to contemporary theology and to unsettled questions. The book's second aim is to present the foundational features of Jewish theology, while taking care along the way to observe similarities to and differences from Christian theology. The second aim follows from the first: the corollary of the church's new perspective on the Jewish people is that Christians should understand Jewish theology. After all, if Christians take themselves to have, in some sense, a common destiny with the Jewish people, then they should know who these fellow travelers are. This consideration in fact supports Christian study not only of Jewish theology, but of Jewish history and culture more broadly. Even further, and bearing more specifically on Jewish theology, if the church is committed to the notion that God's covenant with the Jewish people endures, then Jewish responses to God can in principle be an important source of theological insight for Christians themselves.

This book adopts, in the first instance, the perspective of a Christian approaching Judaism. The opposite perspective, that of a Jew approaching Christianity, will figure only occasionally, mainly in chapter 9 amid discussion of Jewish perspectives on other religions, including Christianity. The marginal presence of the Jewish perspective on Christianity in this book is not, in the main, a matter of the book's intended audience. It reflects, rather, the basic asymmetry of the Christian-Jewish relationship. As a matter of ancient history and theological principle, Christianity depends on Judaism, while Judaism does not depend on Christianity. Christianity's origins lie in Judaism, while the foundations of Judaism long precede the emergence of Christianity.

This asymmetry is a matter of *ancient* history because Judaism as we know it today has been importantly shaped by continuous dialogue and debate with Christianity. As importantly, the remarkable shift in the church's perspective on the Jewish people over the last few decades has been met by some Jewish theologians with real theological curiosity. Amplifying some voices from the premodern and early modern periods, they ask: Could Jews in fact assent to the notion that they share a destiny with Christians? Does the deeply troubled history between Christians and Jews in fact conceal a common bond through which the kingdom of God can emerge? These questions are a topic for another book, but they will receive some attention in this book.

In a famous teaching from the mid-1980s, Krister Stendahl, a bishop of the Church of Sweden, offered three rules for interreligious dialogue, three maxims to keep one from caricaturing the other's religion. First, let the other speak for herself. Ask the other about her religion rather than seeking information from people outside of and potentially hostile to it. Second, compare best with best. Be careful not to compare the worst aspects of the other's religion with your best. Third and finally, leave room for "holy envy"; that is, find something in the other's religion that you find worthy of imitation, something that seems absent from or more marginal in your own religious tradition. To Stendahl's strictures we may add an observation by the great German Jewish philosopher Franz Rosenzweig. Reflecting in 1923 on certain apologetic works about Judaism that engage in comparison with Christianity, he warned that "one could not do a greater injustice [to Christianity] than to present it in terms of its own catechism. It is the first duty of theoretical neighborly love . . . that we never forget to ask ourselves about each opinion that we form about another person: can the other, if he is as I here depict him, still—live?"[3]

While aspiring toward Stendahl's and Rosenzweig's ideals, I myself, as a modern Orthodox Jew, inhabit only Judaism as a living tradition. Moreover, while in this book I offer a more or less systematic account of Judaism, on the Christian side I focus on Christianity's perspective on the Jewish people, a perspective burdened by a hateful and violent past. Thus, the book falls short of the aim of comparing best with best. But because the presentation of Jewish theology does occur within a comparative framework, we will have occasion to engage with other theological commitments of Christianity besides its teachings on Judaism. And even if, *pace* Rosenzweig, we will sometimes, for these purposes, make use of the Catechism of the Catholic Church, I hope ultimately to be able to arouse holy envy in both directions. Or more precisely, in all directions. For while the book's foundational perspective is Christian, and while it surveys Jewish theology systematically, my intention is that the book speak to readers of any religion, or none.

The first part of the book surveys the history of church teaching on the Jewish people and the consequences of such teaching for Christians' behavior toward Jews. The survey begins in the continuation of this opening chapter with a description of the emergent commitments of the early church (in the first and second centuries CE) that established the boundary lines—the lines separating orthodoxy from heresy—within which the church would forever

3. The translation is by Paul W. Franks and Michael L. Morgan, in Todd M. Endelman and Zvi Gitelman, *The Posen Library of Jewish Culture and Civilization*, vol. 8: *Crisis and Creativity between World Wars, 1918–1939* (New Haven: Yale University Press, 2020), 541–42.

after think through its relationship to the Jewish people. In chapters 2 and 3 we examine the writings of the New Testament and the early church fathers, especially Augustine, that initiated the Christian discourse of anti-Judaism. Chapter 4 surveys the violent expressions of Christian anti-Judaism from the Middle Ages into the modern period, culminating in the Holocaust. Chapter 5 describes the new perspective on Jews and Judaism that emerged from the Second Vatican Council and elsewhere in certain modern Christian contexts.

The second part of the book is an introduction to Jewish theology. The last section of this chapter, below, sets the stage for this part by giving some basic answers to the question: What is Judaism? As we will see, Judaism as we know it today is almost exclusively rabbinic Judaism, that is, the form of Judaism that crystallized in the first few centuries of the Common Era. Chapters 6–12 offer an account of the foundational theological commitments of rabbinic Judaism, with periodic comparative forays into Christian theology. Chapters 13–15 explore key developments in Jewish theology from the medieval and modern periods.

In the third and final part of the book, I put the two main areas of the book into direct conversation around the topic of Zionism and the state of Israel. Chapter 16 situates the emergence of Zionism in the encounter between Judaism and modernity, surveys Jewish theological responses to Zionism at the time of its emergence, and explores the implications of a modern Jewish state for the conceptualization and practice of Judaism. Chapter 17 addresses Christian and Jewish theological approaches to state power in the Israeli context, with particular attention to questions implicated by the conflict between Israel and the Palestinians.

What came, in the end, of the petition that Archbishop Roncalli brought to the Vatican, seeking its support for spiriting Jewish children to Palestine, away from the threat of Nazi deportations in Slovakia? How did the Vatican receive Monsignor di Meglio's opposition to this move? In its reply to the petition in May of 1943, the Vatican urged Fr. Tiso not to allow the deportation of Jews from Slovakia, but, in line with di Meglio's reservations, it refrained from calling on him to facilitate the children's emigration to Palestine. We begin now, in the next part of chapter 1, to lay the groundwork for understanding the theological considerations motivating the various actors in this episode. By the end of the book we will complete the picture through our survey of Christian views on the state of Israel.

Christianity's Self-Definition in Relation to Judaism

In roughly the first hundred years after Jesus's ministry, the resolution of two momentous theological conflicts, one after the other, set the terms for the emergence of what would become orthodox or mainstream Christianity. The resolution of the first and earlier conflict, between Christ followers who were "of the circumcision" and those who were not, established the principle—though they could not have put it in these words—that Christianity is different from Judaism, that it is not just a form of Judaism that happens to recognize a person named Jesus as the long-awaited messiah. The resolution of the second and later conflict, between Christian groups that we may reductively call proto-orthodox and Gnostic, affirmed the notion that the God of Christianity is the God of Judaism, and that the Jews' sacred texts are also sacred to Christians. The church that emerged from these conflicts thus saw Christianity as something new in relation to traditional Judaism, but as belonging to the same story as Judaism. Let us now elaborate on these developments.

Jesus was a Galilean Jew of the early first century CE who preached to Jews and won his first followers among them. He was crucified in Jerusalem as the purported king of the Jews. The earliest circle of Christ followers—the nucleus of the church—was a group of Jews whose beliefs and practices could in no way be distinguished categorically from those of other Jews. But within a few decades after the Easter events, the church came to be a majority-gentile institution, even an overwhelmingly gentile institution. The figure most associated with this development is the latecomer apostle, Paul.

We will have much to say about Paul in the continuation, especially in chapter 5. For now, it suffices to note that his letters, together with the book of Acts, represent an intervention in a great debate among early Christ followers over what gentiles who wished to attach themselves to Christ should do. There was no doubt that they must renounce their gods and worship the one creator God—the God of Israel, the God of Jesus—but some felt that they must do more. Some Christ followers believed that they must become Jewish, that they must convert to Judaism through (in the case of males) circumcision. "Unless you are circumcised according to the custom of Moses," they said, "you cannot be saved" (Acts 15:1).

Such a view would have been perfectly natural at the time. If a gentile had committed to worshiping the God of Israel alone, should he not also join the people of Israel? The Christ followers who took this position—Paul calls them "those of the circumcision" (Gal. 2:12)—evidently reasoned, likewise, that Jesus was the *christos* (Greek for "anointed," i.e., the king anointed with sacred oil), the prophesied descendant of King David, come to gather in the dispersed Jewish communities and restore the kingdom of Israel, God's kingdom, in Jerusalem. It stood to reason that a gentile who had subjected himself to the king of the Jews should become Jewish. Again, Jesus preached an imminent final judgment, and a prevalent line of thought among Jews of the time was that non-Jews, the gentiles, would be condemned in this judgment, because of their hostility toward Israel and their wicked ways. The laws that God commanded the Jewish people to follow—observance of the sabbath, the dietary laws, the laws of ritual purity, and so forth—represented, by contrast, the best way of life, a holy way of life. Surely a gentile concerned with surviving God's judgment should adopt these practices as his own.

Other Christ followers, first among them Paul, disagreed. They believed that gentile Christ worshipers need not and indeed should not convert to Judaism. To do so would be to misunderstand who Jesus was. Jesus was the prophesied Davidic king, yes, but he was not *just* that. Yes, his coming would soon solve the problem of Israel's suffering: its subordination to foreign peoples, its exile, its dispersion. But if this was all that Jesus was supposed to do, then he would have done so directly and immediately. If he had not yet done so, and if instead he died on the cross and was resurrected, then his person must be more exalted and his purpose more profound. Gentiles who took on the law out of the assumption that Jesus is chiefly to be conceived as the Jewish messiah were, for Paul, gravely in error.

This latter position became definitive for the future of Christianity. It is because Paul's position won the day that his letters figure so centrally in the Christian biblical canon. The perspective on Jesus articulated by Paul and his allies would mark Christianity as something different from traditional Judaism. I will call this proposition, that Christianity represents something new in relation to Judaism, the first "bookend," the first boundary line within which the church would ever after think through its relationship to Judaism. The terms I am using here are not those of Paul himself; as we will note in chapter 5, Paul did not have a concept of "Christianity" as something distinct from Judaism. What I am describing, instead, are the consequences of the victory of Paul's position for the future of the church.

In the decades after Paul, some Christian theologians went to radical lengths in distinguishing Christianity from Judaism. A key starting assumption for these thinkers was a categorical opposition between spirit and matter, which corresponded in turn to the opposition between good and evil. From this starting point, the creation of the world posed an insoluble problem: Why should God have created the material world, and thus entombed spirit in carnal bodies? In fact, they posited, it was not God who created the world, or at least, not the true and highest God. The creator god was a lower divine being, indeed a maleficent being, an ally of body and an enemy of spirit. Having imprisoned Adam's spirit in matter, the creator sought to prevent Adam from discovering his true spiritual identity by forbidding him from eating from the tree of knowledge, and it was only the emissary from the highest God, the serpent, who gave Adam the courage to eat from the tree and gain some inkling of his true, spiritual self. Christ was another such emissary, sent from the highest God to enable human beings to achieve knowledge (in Greek: *gnōsis*) of themselves, and thus become mentally liberated from their bodies.

The understanding of Christianity that follows from this approach, which is often labeled "Gnosticism," puts Christianity entirely at odds with Judaism. For Gnosticism, the books of the Old Testament contain important historical information, but they are certainly not holy. On the contrary, they must be read against the grain in order to expose the truth. The Jewish god, on the gnostic approach, is an evil god, and his laws, preoccupied as they are with blood and flesh, are evil laws. Christ's mission was to defeat Judaism and its god, through his teaching and through the exemplary crucifixion of his flesh.

Emergent orthodox Christianity came to define itself against this available understanding of Christianity, which it labeled heretical. Along a line of argumentation that one can trace already in the Gospel of John, what would become mainstream Christianity conceded the superiority of spirit over matter, but without demonizing matter. There was no higher God than the creator God of the Old Testament, and it is that very God whom Christians worship and to whom Christ belongs. The mark of the victory of this perspective over the gnostic one is the inclusion of the Old Testament in the Christian Bible; for gnostics, the Old Testament could in no way be called sacred Scripture.

Here, then, is the second and opposite bookend, the other conceptual boundary that defines the space within which Christianity would reason about Judaism and about its relationship to it. Yes, Christianity represents something new, something different from traditional Judaism, but it is also continuous with it. The God of Christianity is the God of Judaism. The God who chose Abraham, who led his descendants out of Egypt, who gave them their laws at Sinai, is the very same God whom Christians worship; there is no such thing as a "God of the Old Testament" and a "God of the New Testament." Christianity teaches something different from Judaism, but it incorporates the story of the Jewish people.

Now, the fact that emergent Orthodox Christianity defined itself by contrast to "those of the circumcision," on the one end, and to the gnostics, on the other, does not mean that those positions ceased to be relevant in the subsequent history of Christian thought. On the contrary, the boundary markers represent forbidden temptations and polemical cudgels: positions that beckon to the theologian by the power of their radicalism, and labels that can be used to attack an opponent in theological debate. It is probably fair to say that throughout most of the history of Christianity, Gnosticism has represented the temptation, and those of the circumcision, the cudgel. Today, in the wake of Vatican II, perhaps the opposite is the case. In any case, the point is that these positions figure prominently in the history of Christian thought precisely because they are recognized as bookends, as boundaries. An orthodox Christian cannot ultimately reject the God of Genesis; after all, the creation story is there in the Bible, alongside innumerable New Testament passages that cite it as Scripture. Nor can an orthodox Christian embrace the view that Christianity is nothing more than a waystation for gentiles toward Judaism; Paul is right there in the Bible, saying (in retrospective terms) very much the opposite.

These bookends represent not the end but the starting point for Christian reflection on Jews and Judaism, both theoretical and practical. How should Christian theology make sense of its Jewish roots? If the ritual laws—commanding observance of the sabbath, forbidding pork and shellfish, and so forth—were given to Israel by the one true God, why should Christians not observe them? Or perhaps Christians *should* observe them in some form? Can Christians accept Jewish approaches to their Bible as legitimate even when they diverge from Christians' own understanding? If everyone is saved through Jesus, then why did God, prior to Jesus's coming, choose a particular people, Israel? And now that Jesus has come, is Israel still God's chosen people? Does God still have a distinctive relationship with the Jews? If God does, then how should Christians relate to them? Among other things, should Christians support the restoration of the Jewish people to the land of Israel? We will explore all of these questions in the chapters that follow.

Some Basics of Judaism

We speak nowadays of "world religions": Christianity, Islam, Buddhism, etc. Is Judaism a world religion? If the term describes religions of world-historical importance, then Judaism must count as a world religion. True, it has many fewer adherents than Christianity or Islam, but it is also the foundation, in different ways, for both of these religions. But if by "world religion" we mean a religion that offers itself to the world, a religion that "aspires," as it were, to be the religion of the whole world, then Judaism cannot count as a world religion except in a qualified sense, to be detailed below. The reason is that Judaism is the religion of the Jewish people. This is not an incidental feature of Judaism; it would be misleading indeed to say that, just as most Irish people are Catholic by religion, so most Jews are religiously Jewish. Rather, Judaism is the religion of the Jewish people *essentially*. The Jewish people, defined by genealogy and by family relationships, is a foundational category in Judaism. It is the theological significance of the Jewish people in Judaism, and by extension in Christian approaches to it, that compels us to identify this book's first topic as "Christian approaches to Jews and Judaism," alongside other similarly clunky formulations, to capture the combination of religion and ethnicity.

The notion of Judaism as the religion of the Jewish people immediately raises certain questions. First, what does Judaism think of gentiles? If Judaism is the religion of the Jewish people, then does it simply ignore non-Jews? We will devote chapter 9 to this topic, but the short answer is no, Judaism does not ignore gentiles. Since Judaism conceives of Israel's God as the only God, and as the creator of the whole world, all people are bound to recognize Israel's God as God. Judaism affirms that a gentile can be in right relation with God and gain eternal life in the afterworld by adhering to a small number of obligations that boil down to two: worship of Israel's God and moral conduct. Gentiles should thus attach themselves to the God of Israel *as* gentiles—that is, in the particular ways that Judaism envisions as appropriate for gentiles. It is in this respect that one might be able to call Judaism a world religion in the fullest sense, in that it articulates a religious vision in which everyone in the world finds a place, albeit not the same place: Jews should worship God as Jews, and gentiles as gentiles.

If this is so, then what becomes of conversion? Can a gentile convert to Judaism? The topic of conversion will arise at multiple points in the continuation, but the brief answer is yes, traditional Judaism recognizes the possibility of a gentile converting to Judaism by formally and publicly accepting the obligations of Judaism and immersing in a ritual bath. A male convert, in addition, must be circumcised. A convert to Judaism (m. *ger*, f. *giyoret*) is understood to have joined the Jewish people, as by adoption. However, because traditional Judaism defines a place for gentiles as gentiles in relation to God, it does not especially encourage conversion.

In the other direction, if Judaism is the religion of the Jewish people, then what is its perspective on a Jew who does not practice or believe in Judaism? According to tradition, Judaism asserts the matrilineal principle: A person born to a Jewish mother is Jewish from birth and has this status even if he is not raised in the Jewish faith, even if he is raised in a different faith, and even if, having been raised in the Jewish faith, he afterward abandons it. A Jew who was born and raised within an entirely secular framework and then becomes religiously observant, or who had converted to Christianity (for example) but then decides to return to Judaism, is classified as a penitent (*ba'al teshuvah*), not a convert.

Judaism is thus a hybrid of religion and ethnicity. Or, put differently, Judaism indicates the religious practices of an extended family. Because Judaism incorporates ethnicity, it assigns theological significance to phenomena characteristic of ethnic groups. When we think of an ethnic group—the French, for example—we think of a language, a land, and a culture. Likewise, Judaism has a language, a land, and a culture. The language is Hebrew, which Judaism deems sacred. The land is Israel, likewise sacred, and imagined as the once and future homeland of the Jewish people. And cultural practices often acquire religious significance; many important religious laws in Judaism are in fact customs without a biblical basis, whose authority derives from the impulse to preserve the ways of the ancestors.

Although Christianity in its most general form does not theologize ethnicity—I bracket out the crucial exception of Jewish ethnicity, which we take up in detail in chapters 2 through 5—local expressions of Christianity can, and insofar as they do, they approach closer to Judaism as a hybrid of religion and ethnicity. Thus, for example, Roberto Goizueta suggests that among a certain generation of Hispanics in America, one can discern a distinctive form of Catholic theology rooted in their experience as an exiled and alienated minority community. According to Goizueta, this experience encourages them theologically to conceptualize community as prior to and constitutive for the individual self.

The form of Judaism that prevails across the world today is rabbinic Judaism, so called because it was decisively shaped by the rabbinic movement that emerged in the first century CE. The roots of this movement lie in the Second Temple period, especially in the Pharisaic sect, famous from the New Testament. Between the first and seventh centuries, the rabbis produced a set of legal and homiletical texts that became canonical for their followers. What we call Judaism today—rabbinic Judaism—has, then, a dual canon. The first part is the "written law" that is, Scripture, or the Jewish Bible, roughly corresponding to the Christian Old Testament, which in Hebrew is called the *Tanakh* (an acronym: *T* for *Torah*, the five books of Moses; *N* for *Nevi'im*, the prophets, like Isaiah and Jeremiah; and *K* or *Kh* for *Ketuvim* or "writings," meaning the other books, like Psalms and Esther). The second part is the "oral law," the aforementioned corpus of texts produced by the ancient rabbis, the most important of which is the Babylonian Talmud.

Besides rabbinic Judaism, other forms of Judaism have existed, and some of them persist until today. The Samaritans emerged as a distinct group near the beginning of the Second Temple period, around the fifth century BCE. They take the five books of Moses (along with the book of Joshua) as their sacred writings, but accept no other books. In Jesus's time, and long before and after, the Samaritans were thought of as a people connected to but different from the Jews; this understanding animates the famous parable of the Good Samaritan (Luke 10:25–37). The Samaritans still exist in very small numbers in Israel/Palestine and continue to perform sacrificial rites at their altar on Mount Gerizim, near modern-day Nablus. Another historically important non-rabbinic Jewish group is the Karaites. This group coalesced in the early medieval period, in reaction to the ascendancy of rabbinic Judaism. It rejects the rabbis' oral law and accepts only the Tanakh as authoritative. Karaites attained to considerable prominence in the medieval world, and exerted a lasting influence on rabbinic Judaism, but their numbers are very diminished today. In addition to the Samaritans and the Karaites, one could consider Christianity itself a form of non-rabbinic Judaism. While Christianity has moved much further away than rabbinic Judaism from the range of forms of Jewish life in the Second Temple period, it preserves better than rabbinic Judaism some prevalent aspects of Jewish theology of the Second Temple period, especially apocalyptic motifs.

Divisions within rabbinic Judaism have developed over the course of time. Perhaps the most significant is that between Sephardic and Ashkenazi Jews. This division traces to the medieval period. At that time, most Jews lived under Islam: in the Near East (e.g., Iraq, Syria, Palestine), in North Africa (e.g., Egypt, Morocco), and in Spain (Hebrew *Sepharad*). When Christian rulers completed their reconquest of Spain in 1492, the very large and deeply rooted Jewish community there, that of the Sephardim, or Spaniards, was expelled. Many Sephardim moved eastward, to communities throughout the Mediterranean and the Near East, where they exerted a strong cultural influence. Thus, the Jewish communities that historically inhabited these areas—places including Morocco, Tunisia, and Syria—came to be called, loosely, Sephardic. A broader term for such Jews is *Mizrahi* ("eastern," or oriental). Depending on the community, a Mizrahi Jew might traditionally have spoken Ladino (a Jewish dialect of Spanish), Judeo-Arabic, or Judeo-Persian, among other Jewish dialects.

A much smaller number of Jews in the Middle Ages lived in Christendom, both in the Byzantine Empire and further west. The most historically prominent of the medieval Jewish communities in these lands were situated in western Germany and northern France (Hebrew *Ashkenaz*). The Jews of western and central Europe, known collectively (allowing for some overgeneralization) as *Ashkenazim*, migrated eastward over the centuries, to countries like Hungary, Lithuania, Poland, and Russia, and there they grew to become the largest community of Jews in the world in the pre-Holocaust era. But they retained as their native language the Jewish dialect of German that had emerged in German lands. This language is Yiddish, which literally means "Jewish."

By the early modern period, then, two main expressions of Jewish life existed: the Ashkenazi one, concentrated in Eastern Europe, and the Sephardic or Mizrahi one, concentrated in the "Orient." The earliest Jews in the Americas were mainly Sephardic, but economic hardship and antisemitism led Ashkenazi Jews to emigrate to America, first in relatively small waves during the middle of the nineteenth century (mainly from Central Europe) and then in massive numbers from the late nineteenth century to the early twentieth century (mainly from Eastern Europe, especially Russia). As a result, most Jews in America today are Ashkenazi. The contemporary Israeli Jewish population, by contrast, is Ashkenazi and Mizrahi in roughly equal parts, drawing on immigration both from Europe (Ashkenazi) and from North Africa and the Near East (Mizrahi). As a combined result of the Holocaust, which decimated European Jewish communities, and the emergence of the state of Israel, which became a magnet for Jewish communities in Muslim lands (Morocco, Egypt, Syria, Iraq, etc.), most Jews today live either in North America (especially, by far, the United States) or Israel, though important Jewish communities remain in many other countries, including Argentina, England, and France.

The differences between Ashkenazi and Mizrahi Jews are chiefly ethnic and cultural. Mizrahi Jews tend to look more "oriental," and their culture (cuisine, music, etc.) has a distinctively Mediterranean character. Ashkenazi Jews, by contrast, are more "western" in appearance and culture. There are numerous small differences in religious practice between Ashkenazim and Mizrahim, from prayer formulas to the scope of the prohibition against consuming leaven on Passover, but these communities recognize each other as fully legitimate Jews, and today, especially in Israel, intermarriage among them is prevalent.

In the nineteenth century, following on the advent of modernity in Christian Europe in the form of the Enlightenment and its aftermath, Ashkenazi Judaism in western and central Europe fragmented into distinct religious movements (which I will call, following the convention, "denominations," even though the notion of mutual recognition that the word "denomination" can imply does not unproblematically hold in this case). Communities that modified traditional practices and beliefs in accord with contemporaneous conceptions of ethics, decorum, and universalism, became the nucleus of Reform Judaism. More traditional Jews coalesced around the banner of what we now call Orthodox Judaism. The center ground between Reform and Orthodox Judaism came to be occupied by Conservative Judaism, which sought to modernize traditional Judaism but in more limited and measured ways than Reform Judaism. When European Ashkenazim emigrated to America, they eventually brought their denominational structures with them. These structures, like large Jewish institutions in general in America, are weaker today than they were in their heyday in the middle of the twentieth century. But they remain important, alongside other, smaller denominations and emergent non-denominational institutions.

From a sociological perspective, the critical boundary in America today is between Orthodox Judaism, where in-group marriage is the norm, and non-Orthodox Judaism, where intermarriage is widespread. The prevalence of intermarriage among non-Orthodox Jews has led the Reform movement in America to take the momentous step of abandoning the traditional criterion for defining a Jew, the matrilineal principle. Instead, for American Reform Judaism, a person is Jewish if either of her parents is Jewish, so long as she actively identifies with the Jewish people.

In theological terms, it may be possible to distinguish Orthodoxy from non-Orthodoxy today by the readiness of Orthodox Judaism to accept the possibility of a genuine and irresolvable conflict between what one takes morality to demand, and what God, as interpreted through the framework of the Jewish legal tradition, is understood to demand. In such a case, the former must yield to the latter. Non-Orthodox Judaism, by contrast, tends to insist that if, upon deep reflection about the apparent moral demand and the apparent demand of the tradition, the conflict still obtains, the conclusion to be drawn is that the tradition has evidently gone wrong in interpreting God's word and must be modified in light of our moral understanding. Relatedly, the non-Orthodox denominations center their Jewish identity strongly around moral principles, especially social justice and (from the late twentieth century to today) equality across genders and sexual identities, while for Orthodox Jews, the foci of identity are Jewish law and the Jewish people. One advantage of an analytical distinction between Orthodoxy as a sociological phenomenon and Orthodoxy as a theological phenomenon is that it recognizes the possibility of individuals who are sociologically Orthodox but theologically non-Orthodox.

Among Orthodox Jews, there is an important though often blurry line between modern Orthodoxy and ultra-Orthodoxy. While all forms of Orthodox Judaism insist on the obligatory character of traditional Jewish law, modern Orthodoxy also embraces humanism and the scientific worldview. It typically educates its children in Jewish private schools, but often sends them off to secular universities. Ultra-Orthodoxy, by contrast, approaches the modern world as in the first instance a threat to traditional religious life, and organizes itself in relatively insular communities. Within ultra-Orthodoxy we must distinguish between *Haredi* ("trembling," i.e., God-fearing) Jews, on the one hand, who accept "value-neutral" elements of contemporary society—the vernacular language, (modest) dress and hair styles, even organized sports—and, on the other hand, *Hasidic* ("pious") Jews, who generally preserve Yiddish as their mother tongue, and conduct themselves in altogether distinctive ways. (There is terminological variation. The word *Haredi* can be used to describe the ultra-Orthodox population as a whole, in which case the first group goes under the rubric *Lithuanian*, after its original geographic center, or *yeshivish*, indicating its commitment to Torah study in the *yeshiva* or study-house.)

The denominations that emerged in Europe and migrated to America did not become established among Mizrahi Jews. Both because of the greater prominence of Mizrahi Jews in Israel, and because the logic of denominational Judaism was determined by the circumstances of Jewish life in Western diasporic communities, the denominational structures never struck deep roots in Israel. Religious observance in Israel tends instead to take more traditional forms. Aside from the very large secular (*hiloni*) population on one end of the spectrum, and the ultra-Orthodox on the other, Israeli Jews will identify as "religious" (*dati*) or "traditional" (*masorti*). Put differently, rather than recognizing multiple, ideologically distinct and mutually incompatible formations of Judaism, Israeli Jews tends to think of Judaism as a single thing, to which one can choose to conform oneself fully, partly, or not at all. But this tendency is changing, especially as the growing dati camp—some one-fifth of the Israeli Jewish population, according to a 2014 poll—has begun to fray into a variegated spectrum.

Needless to say, the above generalizations all require further nuancing, and do not in any way capture the immense variety in Jewish religious life in the past or today. The overview of Jewish theology and practice in chapters 6–12, insofar as it aims to describe the traditional commitments and expressions of Judaism, finds its fullest realization today among Orthodox or dati Jews. Subsequent chapters will elaborate, to different degrees, on Hasidism, denominational differences, and the history and contemporary state of Jewish religious expression in Israel.

Conclusion

Having set out some foundations for Christian theologies of Judaism and for the category of Judaism as such, we are in a position to broach some intersecting questions. Thus, for example, if Judaism is a hybrid of religion and ethnicity, then how does Christianity tend to process this hybrid? Does it lean toward a more religious interpretation of Judaism, or toward a more ethnic one? Insofar as Christianity is a religion, it instinctively processes Judaism in its own image, as a religion. But to the degree that it does so, it must confront the challenging differences between Christianity's interpretation of the Bible and that of Judaism, while a focus on the Jewish people as an ethnic category does not pose the same problem. And so, as we will see, there is a countervailing tendency among modern Christians to embrace the Jewish people more closely than Judaism qua religion. In this respect, Christianity has an interesting bedfellow in Zionism, since, as we will also see, Jews who are religious and Zionist tend to assign greater weight to the ethnic element of their Judaism than do religious Jews who are not Zionist.

Intersections of this sort follow from the intrinsic connection between the two topics of this book: Christian theological teaching on Jews and Judaism, and Jewish theology itself from a comparative lens. In the chapters that follow, the reader will encounter other intersections of this sort. Each of the book's two topics is large enough to merit a book unto itself, indeed many bookshelves, but what we must inevitably lose in comprehensiveness, we will, I hope, gain in the form of such intersections.

Further Inquiry

On Krister Stendahl's strictures, see Mary C. Boys, "Turn It and Turn It Again: The Vital Contribution of Krister Stendahl to Jewish-Christian Relations," *Journal of Ecumenical Studies* 51 (2016): 280–93. On the two heretical "bookends" that define the ways in which orthodox Christianity positions itself in relation to Judaism, see, on the one hand, Joshua D. Garroway, "The Pharisee Heresy: Circumcision for Gentiles in the Acts of the Apostles," *New Testament Studies* 60 (2014): 20–36, and, on the other, David Brakke, *The Gnostics: Myth, Ritual, and Diversity in Early Christianity* (Cambridge: Harvard University Press, 2012). Robert Goizueta works out his account of Hispanic Catholic theology in his *Caminemos Con Jesús: Toward a Hispanic/Latino Theology of Accompaniment* (Maryknoll, NY: Orbis Books, 1995). For a recent sociological overview of the contemporary American Jewish landscape, see Jack Wertheimer, *The New American Judaism: How Jews Practice Their Religion Today* (Princeton: Princeton University Press, 2018), which nicely supplements Jonathan D. Sarna's magisterial history of Jews in America, *American Judaism: A History* (New Haven: Yale University Press, 2019). See also now Joshua Leifer, *Tablets Shattered: The End of an American Jewish Century and the Future of Jewish Life* (New York: Dutton, 2024), which takes up, among other things, the past and present status of Zionism in American Jewish self-identity, a topic to which we will turn in the last two chapters of the book. While, as noted above, the Sephardic Jewish encounter with modernity did not result in fragmentation into denominations, Sephardim were by no means sheltered from modernity; for some of their religious responses to it, see Norman A. Stillman, *Sephardi Religious Responses to Modernity* (New York: Routledge, 1995). On differences in belief and practice within the Religious Zionist community in contemporary Israel, see Yair Ettinger, *Frayed: The Disputes Unraveling Religious Zionists* (New Milford, CT: Toby Press, 2023).

●

1. Think about the relationship between Christianity and Judaism in comparison with the relationship between Islam and the other Abraham religions. Just as Christianity takes itself to be part of the same story as Judaism, so Islam takes itself to be part of the same story to which Judaism and Christianity belong, hence the appearance of figures like Abraham and Jesus in the Qur'an. And yet, while Christians adopted Judaism's Bible as their own, Islam's scriptural canon contains only its own holy book, the Qur'an. What are the ramifications of this difference? We will take up this topic briefly in chapter 9.

2. Elias Canetti (1905–1994), one of the great humanists and men of letters formed by the cosmopolitan world of Europe before the Second World War, was born into a community of Sephardic Jews in Bulgaria. In *The Memoirs of Elias Canetti* (New York: Farrar, Straus and Giroux, 1999), 7–9, he describes his community thus. "The loyalties of the Sephardim were fairly complicated. They were pious Jews, for whom the life of their religious community was rather important. But

they considered themselves a special brand of Jews, and that was because of their Spanish background. Through the centuries since their expulsion from Spain, the Spanish they spoke with each other had changed little. . . . With naïve arrogance, the Sephardim looked down on other Jews; a word always charged with scorn was *Todesco*, meaning a German or Ashkenazi Jew. It would have been unthinkable to marry a *Todesca*, a Jewish woman of that background, and among the many families that I heard about or knew as a child in Ruschuk, I cannot recall a single case of mixed marriage." As a young adult, Canetti found the clan loyalty of his mother, whose intellect and good taste he greatly admired, to be mystifying. And yet he came later to realize that he was "exactly as she was," only he transferred his loyalty to humankind as a whole: even as he recognized and wrote about all of their flaws, he embraced them as his own. "There is almost nothing bad that I couldn't say about humans and humankind. And yet my pride in them is so great that there is only one thing I really hate: their enemy, death." Canetti's remarks raise some interesting questions. First, how might Jewish peoplehood be conceived as a coherent category in the sort of social circumstances that Canetti describes, in which different groups of Jews will not marry each other? Second, Canetti seems to suggest that clan loyalty and a universalist concern for humanity are not necessarily opposites, as we often think, but can be understood as two expressions of the same instinct. Is his view plausible?

— *Chapter 2* —

Supersession and Sin

The doctrinal disputes among Christ followers of the first centuries of the Common Era committed the church to the notion that Christianity is continuous with the story of Israel but that it also represents something new. Against this background, and especially once the church became an overwhelmingly gentile institution, the most straightforward way of positioning Christianity in relation to Judaism was to posit that God's relationship with Israel endured until the coming of Christ and then, with Christ's coming, it shifted to the gentile church. Scholars today describe this position as "supersessionist," because it envisions the church as superseding or supplanting Israel, so that there is no future for Israel as God's people after Christ.

Analytically, we can distinguish between two common ways of conceptualizing supersession (or, between two expressions of supersessionism). Punishment supersession, which is the focus of this chapter, is the notion of supersession as punishment for Israel's sins, first and foremost deicide: God's covenant with Israel came to an end because Israel killed God's son. The next chapter concerns economic supersession. "Economy" means literally the management of the household. God's economy is the way in which God runs God's household, the world; in short, it indicates divine providence. Economic supersession is the view that it was God's intention from the beginning to maintain a covenantal relationship with Israel only until the time of Christ. With Christ's coming, that relationship was dissolved to make way for a different sort of relationship between God and the world, through the vehicle of Christ and the church.

One might easily assert punishment and economic supersession together by treating the dissolution of God's relationship with Israel at Christ's coming as overdetermined. It was part of God's plan from the first, but it also found expression as punishment for Israel's freely chosen rejection of Christ.

Dual causation of this sort is a theological commonplace. Think of the Joseph story, which depicts the transformation of Joseph from Canaanite shepherd to Egyptian vizier as the result both of God's plan, manifested in dreams and apparent coincidences, and of the self-serving choices of a range of human actors, from Joseph's brothers to Potiphar's wife. And in fact, some of the texts below, as we will see, move easily between claims of punishment and economic supersession. Nevertheless, I treat these two supersessionist frameworks separately because it is possible to reject punishment supersession but maintain economic supersession. A Christian could deny the notion of any collective Jewish sin meriting the termination of God's covenant with Israel, but still insist that this covenant came with a providentially predetermined expiration date.

This chapter works through some of the texts from the New Testament and from the early church that articulate a doctrine of punishment supersession, or that later theologians who taught this doctrine could or did draw on for support. These texts are the foundation of a tradition of theological hostility to Judaism that goes under the rubric of *adversus Judaeos* ("against the Jews") literature, or, in Jules Isaac's term, the "teaching of contempt." At the conclusion of the chapter we consider the current position of the Catholic Church with regard to punishment supersession.

"You Are Forever Opposing the Holy Spirit"

One of the most rhetorically powerful works from Christian antiquity is a Greek homily for the Easter season, "On *Pascha*," attributed to a certain Melito, likely the same Melito who served as bishop of Sardis during the second half of the second century CE. Sardis, situated near the western coast of what is now Turkey, was home at this time to a substantial Jewish community. Archaeologists have uncovered a synagogue the length of a football field and its two end zones, a testament to the Jewish community's power and influence, but its relevance for contextualizing Melito's homily is limited by uncertainty about the period in which the structure came to be used as a synagogue. The evidence of the homily itself correlates with what another source explicitly claims, that Melito's community celebrated Easter according to the Jewish calendar, on the fourteenth of the month of Nisan, the date of the Jewish

Passover festival. (Christians who did thus were called Quartodecimans, or Fourteen-ers.)[1]

The festival of Passover (in Hebrew, *Pesach*) recalls the exodus of the people of Israel from bondage in Egypt. More specifically, it commemorates how the Israelites, following God's command, slaughtered a lamb or kid and placed its blood on their doorposts to protect their families from the plague of the firstborn, which was God's final blow against the Egyptians. Melito in his homily works out an analogy: the Passover sacrifice is to Jesus as a sketch is to a completed work. The blood of the Passover, in saving Israel, was a "first draft" of the ultimate source of salvation, Jesus, so that with Jesus having come, the Passover sacrifice is now defunct. "When the thing comes about of which the sketch was a type, that which was to be, of which the type bore the likeness, then the type is destroyed, it has become useless, it yields up the image to what is truly real. What was once valuable becomes worthless, when what is of true value appears." Although at the time of the exodus from Egypt "the slaughter of the sheep was of value, now it is worthless because of the Lord's life." Along the same lines, the people of Israel and their law became worthless once they were realized, respectively, in the church and in the Gospel: "Thus the people was a type, like a preliminary sketch, and the law was the writing of an analogy. The Gospel is the narrative and fulfillment of the law, and the church is the repository of reality."

The above words express the notion of economic supersession: when the church arrived, it was time for Israel to leave the stage. But Melito proceeds further, into punishment supersession, when he rebukes Israel for killing Christ: "You killed your Lord at the great feast" (i.e., the Passover festival). Just as the Jews performed the Passover sacrifice in Egypt, so they killed Christ in his day. In doing so, says Melito, the Jews manifested inexplicable ingratitude, for it was Christ who had formed Israel and done her countless kindnesses, from the exodus from Egypt itself to Jesus's healing miracles. Drawing on a traditional etymology that interprets the Hebrew word "Israel" to mean "one who sees God," Melito charges that "you were not Israel. You did not see God. You did not perceive the Lord, Israel, you did not recognize the first-born of God." The

1. See Alistair Stewart-Skyes, *On Pascha: With the Fragments of Melito and Other Material Related to the Quartodecimans* (Crestwood, NY: St. Vladimir's Seminary Press, 2001), 1–2. The translations of the homily quoted in the continuation come from this work. I quote from sections 37, 40, 44, 79, 82, 99.

result is the disownment and death of Israel: "You disowned the Lord, and so are not owned by him. You did not receive the Lord, so you were not pitied by him. You smashed the Lord to the ground, you were razed to the ground. And you lie dead, while he rose from the dead, and is raised to the heights of heaven."

We see in Melito's homily how the charge of deicide does not stand in isolation, but rather represents the linchpin of a broader characterization of Israel. Israel killed Christ because they did not recognize who he was, and this failure to recognize him is a manifestation of Israel's fundamentally bad character. The same line of reasoning is evident in assorted New Testament passages. Melito's homily has much in common, in particular, with Stephen's reflection on Israelite history in Acts 7. Stephen dwells on Israel's obstreperousness, which was on display even before the exodus, in the story of the two Israelites who rejected Moses's rebuke with the words, "Who made you a ruler and a judge over us?" (Acts 7:27, 35, citing Exod. 2:14). The same refusal to be governed became manifest, for Stephen, in the sin of the golden calf (Exod. 32) and beyond. Stephen's speech culminates in this summary condemnation: "You stiff-necked people, uncircumcised in heart and ears, you are forever opposing the Holy Spirit, just as your ancestors used to do. Which of the prophets did your ancestors not persecute? They killed those who foretold the coming of the Righteous One, and now you have become his betrayers and murderers. You are the ones who received the law as ordained by angels, and yet you have not kept it" (Acts 7:51–53).

From Criticism to Contempt

The immediate impetus for the critiques voiced by the book of Acts and by Melito is the fact that most Jews did not recognize Jesus as the messiah. Seeking an explanation for this great mystery, that Jesus's own people generally rejected him even as many among the gentiles acknowledged him, they posit a set of flaws in Israel's character. But their line of thinking also owes a deep debt to a much earlier source.

> You have been rebellious with God from the day that I came to know you.

> I know your rebelliousness and your stiff neck.

> For the children of Israel and the children of Judah have done only evil in my eyes from their youth.
>
> They and their fathers offended, and they did not heed your commands, and they refused to obey.

These statements come not from the New Testament or from early Christian theologians but from the Hebrew Bible (respectively: Deut. 9:24; 31:27; Jer. 32:30; Neh. 9:16–17).

These verses are typical examples of the Hebrew Bible's great tradition of prophetic rebuke. The prophets of Israel, from Moses forward, convey God's condemnation of Israel for its sins and urge the people to turn from their evil ways and obey God. How does the discourse of Christian anti-Judaism differ from the tradition of prophetic rebuke on which it draws? The prophets of the Hebrew Bible are social critics. As Michael Walzer cogently argues in his book, *The Company of Critics*, an essential element of social criticism is the critic's identification with the society that he critiques. True, the critic's posture demands that he distance himself to a certain degree from his society—this is what we call "critical distance"—but the critic's motivation comes from a sense of being bound to his society, and the hope that his critique will make it better.

Another important dimension of social criticism is familiarly expressed within the framework of comedy in the distinction between "punching up" and "punching down." When the target of a joke has more power than the comedian, then he is punching up, and the joke can serve the function of social criticism. Not so when the target has less power, when the comedian is punching down, because then the joke aligns with and reinforces existing social structures. The paradigmatic prophet of the Hebrew Bible—an Amos or a Jeremiah—is a social critic because he aims his barbs at the powerful: at kings and his society's economic elite.

The Hebrew Bible itself already obscures the character of prophetic rebuke as social criticism in a couple of ways. First and foremost, prophets speak in the voice of God, who stands outside Israelite society, rather than in their own voice. Second, the Bible constructs Moses, especially in Deuteronomy, on the model of the prophet as critic, even though Moses is Israel's leader. But the revoicing of prophetic rebuke in Christian anti-Judaism transforms this tradition altogether, so that it no longer constitutes social criticism at all. This transformation occurs in two ways. First, with the parting of the ways between Judaism and Christianity—the transformation of Christianity from a group of Christ-following Jews and others into a group categorically distinguishable from and indeed opposed to Judaism—the Christian theologian or homilist who wields the prophets' rebukes against Israel is targeting an Other. He does not identify with the Jews whom he condemns, nor, typically, does he even speak to them; he speaks *about* them, in the presence of fellow Christians. Second, with the phenomenon of Christendom—that is, the joining of Christianity to prevailing political power—the dynamic of anti-Jewish teaching no longer involves punching up but punching down. It means not speaking truth to power, but attacking the marginalized.

These processes that transformed the praxis of prophetic rebuke from seeds of reconciliation to expressions of hostility—first, the parting of the ways between Christianity and Judaism, and second, the ascent to power of Christianity—occurred to different degrees at different times in different places, a fact that we must bear in mind in understanding the words of Melito and the book of Acts in their original contexts. On the matter of power and punching, it matters that the community of Christ worshipers in the circumstances in which Acts was written, and in which Melito delivered his homily, was very likely inferior in power and social status to the community of non-Christ-worshiping Jews. It matters that, across the Roman Empire in general at the time, the community of Christ worshipers was substantially smaller and much more precarious than the community of non-Christ-worshiping Jews. We must remember that Melito and the author of Acts were punching up.

On the process of the parting of the ways we will have more to say in chapter 5, but the important point to keep in mind for our immediate purposes is that this process was at most only incipient for the author of Acts. The first recorded reference to the word "Christian" in fact occurs in Acts (at 11:26 and 26:28, or perhaps these just postdate the occurrence in 1 Pet. 4:16, the only other instance in the New Testament), but the author of Acts did not conceive of Christianity as something separate from Judaism. Rather, the church consisted of Jews who worshiped Jesus, along with gentiles who did the same. Melito, likewise, could not have thought of himself and his community as categorically apart from the Jewish people in the same way that a European bishop in the high Middle Ages would have. A canon law for the

Greek east written even after the time of Melito prohibited bishops and other clerics from celebrating Jewish holidays with the Jews, or accepting from them (presumably on Passover) unleavened bread, which suggests that some Christians did these very things.[2] At the same time, it is clear that Melito's homily does not address non-Christ-worshiping Jews. The targets of his critique are different from the audience to whom he speaks.

For Acts, then, and even for Melito, the transformation from social criticism to teaching of contempt had only just begun, but within a couple of centuries this transformation would be complete. Now, it is also the case that, because the church thought of itself as the new Israel, Christian theologians and homilists could and did also take on the voices of Israel's prophets in addressing their own Christian communities. In a manner fully continuous, mutatis mutandis, with the tradition of prophetic rebuke, they upbraided and exhorted fellow Christians to improve their ways. But insofar as Christian leaders also adapted the prophetic tradition to condemn the Jewish people, they put the prophets to work in a new way, to ground punishment supersession.

Augustine on Cain and Abel

The great father of the church, Augustine of Hippo, flourished toward the end of the fourth century and the beginning of the fifth. By this time, Christianity had achieved a very large following in the Roman Empire, and had indeed, by many measures, become the religion of the empire. In this chapter and the next we will examine selections from Augustine's *Contra Faustum*, likely written around the year 400. I postpone discussion of the work as a whole to the next chapter; here we will focus on one passage: book 12, sections 7–13.[3]

In the context of this passage, Augustine seeks to demonstrate that implicit references to Christ occur throughout the Old Testament. His method of

2. On this law, see Amnon Linder, *The Jews in the Legal Sources of the Early Middle Ages* (Detroit: Wayne State University Press, 1998), 463.

3. The translation is by Richard Stothert, from Philip Schaff, ed., *Nicene and Post-Nicene Fathers*, First Series, Volume 4 (New York: Christian Literature Company, 1887), with occasional minor modification.

exegesis is allegorical and Christological: allegorical, because it reads the biblical text as encoding a concealed layer of reality, and Christological, because that layer of reality revolves around Christ. Augustine begins at the beginning, with Genesis 1. We pick him up at Genesis 2:24, where the Bible tells that, as Adam found a partner in Eve, so "a man leaves his father and his mother and clings to his wife, and they become one flesh." Augustine uses assorted passages from Paul's letters to decipher this verse so that it describes not just the institution of marriage, but the advent of Christ in the world. Adam is a figure of Christ (Rom. 5:14), and thus the man of the verse should be identified with Christ. Paul quotes Genesis 2:24 itself in comparing the husband-wife relationship to that between Christ and the church (Eph. 5:31–32), and so, straightforwardly, the wife in Genesis 2:24 can be construed as the church. In Philippians 2:6–7, Paul says that Christ emptied himself from his equality with God to assume the form of a servant; thus, the father in Genesis 2:24 is God, whom Christ left by taking on flesh.

Augustine relies on Paul in this way to identify the man, the father, and the wife: Christ left God to cleave to the church. But who is the mother? "And so, too," says Augustine, "He left His mother, the synagogue of the Jews which cleaved to the carnality of the Old Testament, and was united to the church His holy bride, that in the peace of the New Testament they two might be one flesh." Strikingly, Augustine cites no verse from the New Testament to support the identification of the mother with "the synagogue [i.e., assembly] of the Jews." Here we see how the sharp opposition between the church and the synagogue is largely foreign to the New Testament itself, and represents the product, instead, of a parting of the ways that occurred gradually over the first few centuries of the Common Era. Taking this opposition as a starting assumption, Augustine engages in subtle exegetical reasoning: If there are two women in the verse, and one is the church, to whom Christ clings, then the other must be the Jewish people, whom Christ abandoned because they clung to something else.

And what is this something else to which the Jews clung? If Christ and the church are united as "one flesh [Latin: *in carne una*]" according to Genesis 2:24, then the Jews' clinging, too, must be fleshly, or carnal, but with a negative valence: the Jews held fast to the "carnality" of the Old Testament. Augustine thus links the opposition between Judaism and Christianity to the opposition between the Old Testament and the New. As we will see in the continuation, although these oppositions undoubtedly serve to delegitimize Judaism and to demote the Old Testament, in neither case does Augustine designate the negative pole for absolute oblivion.

The next passage clarifies what Augustine means when he refers to the carnality of the Old Testament. Here Augustine takes up the story of Cain and Abel in Genesis 4. The story begins with Cain, the elder brother, a farmer, offering a gift to God from his produce. Abel, a shepherd, follows by doing the same from his flock. God attends to Abel's offering but ignores Cain's. Augustine steps in where the Bible is silent, to explain why God did so: "The faith of the New Testament praising God in the harmless service of grace is preferred to the earthly works of the Old Testament. For though the Jews were right in practicing these things, they were guilty of unbelief in not distinguishing the time of the New Testament when Christ came, from the time of the Old Testament."

This passage represents a classic formulation of economic supersession, and so, although economic supersession is taken up more directly in the next chapter, we must unpack the passage briefly here. First, Augustine links Cain's profession, farming, to the "earthly" ritual laws of the Old Testament. Abel, by contrast, as a shepherd, is a figure of Christ. For Augustine, the laws of the Old Testament can be characterized as earthly because they are centered on the body. Indeed, the paradigmatic ritual law in the letters of Paul, circumcision, involves marking the body by excision of the foreskin. Likewise, the sacrificial procedures legislated by the Old Testament concern manipulation of the bodies and blood of animals. As we will see in the next chapter, Augustine assigns allegorical meaning to these earthly laws, as signs pointing to Christ. Thus, these laws were valuable in their time. But because their significance lies in foretelling Christ, they became obsolete with Christ's advent. According to God's plan for the world, God's "economy," the Jews should have abandoned the laws of the Old Testament—should have given up "farming"—once Abel, or Christ, appeared in the world.

Why did the Jews not do so? Augustine finds a clue in the continuation of the story. In response to Cain's anger at the rejection of his gift, God tells Cain—according to Augustine's construal of an obscure verse (Gen. 4:7)—that Cain can find forgiveness for sin through God's grace, but only if he acknowledges his sinfulness, and his inability to achieve righteousness through the earthly works of the law. But this is something that Cain, and thus the

Jews, refuse to do. "Being ignorant of God's righteousness, and wishing to establish a righteousness of their own, proud of the works of the law, instead of being humbled on account of their sins, they have not been content; and in subjection to sin reigning in their mortal body, so as to make them obey it in the lusts thereof, they have stumbled on the stone of stumbling, and have been inflamed with hatred against him whose works they grieved to see accepted by God." The root of the problem is pride. The Jews will not acknowledge their limitedness, and instead seek to be justified through their own deeds. They insist on clinging to the carnal or literal sense of the Old Testament, to the carnal or physical facet of its ritual laws rather than to their allegorical meaning. They therefore react with blindness and hostility toward Abel, or Jesus, who offers them God's grace.

The result is deicide: "Abel, the younger brother, is killed by the elder brother; Christ, the head of the younger people, is killed by the elder people of the Jews. Abel dies in the field; Christ dies on Calvary." God tells Cain that the voice of Abel's blood calls out from the earth. For Augustine, this voice is the Old Testament, which witnesses to Christ, and which finds a responsive audience throughout the earth in the form of the gentiles who say yes to Christ. Their assent condemns the Jews, who killed and continue to reject Christ.

God declares Cain accursed: "And now you are cursed from the ground, which has opened its mouth to receive your brother's blood from your hand. When you till the ground, it will no longer yield to you its strength; you will be a fugitive and a wanderer on the earth" (Gen. 4:11–12). On Augustine's understanding, God thus condemns the Jews to the Sisyphean labor of observance of the ritual law: they will continue to do these earthly works, but fruitlessly, without gain to themselves, because they do not understand that these works find their true meaning in Christ. The veil that conceals the real significance of the Old Testament was torn for those who believe in Christ, but for the Jews the veil endures, preventing them from benefiting from their labor. Augustine finds confirmation of the Jews' "carnal mind" in the fact that Cain responds to the curse by voicing fear for his physical well-being—as a wanderer, he will be vulnerable to violence—rather than by mourning the spiritual loss that comes with being cast out of God's presence.

In response to Cain's expressed concern about his safety, God sets a mark upon him, that anyone might see and recognize that Cain is under God's protection. This mark, for Augustine, is nothing other than the ritual laws.

For "it is a most notable fact, that all the nations subjugated by Rome adopted the heathenish ceremonies of the Roman worship; while the Jewish nation, whether under Pagan or Christian monarchs, has never lost the sign of their law, by which they are distinguished from all other nations and peoples." God insists that the Jews are not to be killed, nor to be compelled to abandon their laws. They should instead be allowed to remain as Cain, vainly and blindly tilling their earthly laws, wandering the world "in terrified subjection to the immensely superior number of Christians," mourning the loss of their kingdom that they once possessed in the land of Israel. One who kills a Jew is subject to a sevenfold penalty (Gen. 4:15), from which Augustine infers that the Jews are supposed to remain in this state to the end of the "seven days of time," i.e., the entire epoch until the second coming of Christ.

What divine purpose is there in preserving the Jews in this condition? Augustine offers: "To the end of the seven days of time, the continued preservation of the Jews will be a proof to believing Christians of the subjection merited by those who, in the pride of their kingdom, put the Lord to death." The persistence of the Jews in their subservient condition is testimony to the truth of Christianity. In the continuation (section 23), Augustine elaborates on this notion of Jewish testimony, and adds that it is not only their subservient condition that proves the truth of Christianity, but also the books of the Old Testament that the Jews preserve in their original language. "For what else is this nation now but a desk for the Christians, bearing the law and the prophets, and testifying to the doctrine of the church, so that we honor in the sacrament what they disclose in the letter?" The testimony of these books is especially compelling because it condemns the Jews themselves, who are blind to it; in legal parlance, the Jews have the persuasive force of hostile witnesses.

It goes without saying that Augustine's allegorical exegesis of the Cain and Abel story, as brilliant as it is, would only have been persuasive to those already committed to the general assumptions that enable it: the opposition between Christianity and Judaism, the Jews' guilt in killing Christ, the salvific inefficacy of the ritual laws of the Old Testament, etc. But by weaving these anti-Jewish assumptions into the fabric of biblical narratives like the story of Cain and Abel, Augustine, along with other theologians engaged in such Christological, allegorical exegesis, gave them new vividness and detail, and produced a set of powerful images through which Christian anti-Judaism could find expression. Christians in subsequent centuries would imagine Jews as Cain:

the original murderers, cursed wanderers. Moreover, importantly, while the image of the Jews as Cain centers on deicide, this charge was bound up with an entire complex of negative traits. The Jews would not have murdered Christ unless they were drawn to carnality, were too proud to confess their sins and accept God's grace, were too blind to see what their own Scriptures said.

In Our Time

The Catechism of the Council of Trent, promulgated in 1566, takes care, in the tradition of prophetic rebuke, to place the guilt for the crucifixion on the heads of Christians themselves: "For, as our sins impelled Christ our Lord to undergo the death of the cross, most certainly those who wallow in sins and iniquity, as far as depends on them crucify to themselves again the Son of God, and put Him to an open shame. In us such guilt may seem even deeper than it was in the Jews, inasmuch as, according to the Apostle [Paul], had they known it, they would never have crucified the Lord of Glory; whereas we both profess to know Him, and yet, denying Him by our works, seem in some sort to lay violent hands on Him."[4] But this passage also takes Jewish guilt for the crucifixion as a given, even though the prooftext that it cites for such guilt, 1 Corinthians 2:8 ("Had they known it, they would never have crucified the Lord of Glory"), in fact speaks not of the Jews, but of "the rulers of this age."

The decisive break in Catholicism from the teaching of punishment supersession came with the Second Vatican Council (1962–1965), and in particular, with the document *Nostra Aetate* (Latin for "in our time"), subtitled the "Declaration on the Relation of the Church with Non-Christian Religions." The fourth paragraph of *Nostra Aetate* declares that the Jewish people are neither collectively guilty of deicide, nor accursed: "True, the Jewish authorities and those who followed their lead pressed for the death of Christ; still, what happened in His passion cannot be charged against all the Jews, without distinction, then alive, nor against the Jews of today. Although the Church is the

4. Part I, chapter 5, question 11. I quote from Theodore Alois Buckley, *The Catechism of the Council of Trent: Translated into English, with Notes* (London: George Routledge and Co., 1852), 55–56.

new people of God, the Jews should not be presented as rejected or accursed by God, as if this followed from the Holy Scriptures."[5]

This assertion, significant as it is, leaves many questions unanswered. As we observed above, the Christian "teaching of contempt" developed a detailed negative profile of Jewish character to explain the Jews' general rejection of Christ, despite the testimony of their own Scriptures. What is the status of this teaching in our time, according to the church, and how should the church think about the real theological challenges that motivated the construction of the Jews' bad character? If God's posture toward the Jewish people is not defined by cursing or rejection, then how should it in fact be understood? Are the Jewish people in "good standing" with God despite their rejection of Christ, and if so, how should the church approach theological developments that have occurred among Jews from antiquity to today, or what we call Judaism?

The very word "Judaism" does not in fact occur in *Nostra Aetate*. Its absence is especially notable in the context of the document as a whole. The subtitle of *Nostra Aetate*, "Declaration on the Relation of the Church with Non-Christian Religions," is accurate in application to the first three paragraphs, which take up, in turn, the category of religion in general, then Hinduism and Buddhism, and then Islam. In each case, the document holds up for praise the "true and holy" teachings of the religion in question. Each religion is named, as an -ism. Paragraph four, however, does not concern "Judaism"; its subject is the church's relation not with the Jewish religion, but with the Jewish people: "Abraham's stock" and Paul's "kinsmen," in the words of the document. *Nostra Aetate* marks out a new path toward reconciliation with the Jewish people, but, unsurprisingly, it does not attempt to address, or even name, the questions that would arise on this path. We will turn to some of these questions in subsequent chapters.

Why did the Catholic Church set itself upon a conciliatory path in *Nostra Aetate*? External factors are important. The most immediate and obvious factor is the Holocaust, whose relationship to the history of Christian anti-Jewish teaching we will explore in chapter 4. Additionally, the Enlightenment put in motion a set of related trends that represent the deep background to *Nostra Ae-*

5. For quotations from *Nostra Aetate* here and throughout the book, see https://www.vatican.va/archive/hist_councils/ii_vatican_council/documents/vat-ii_decl_19651028_nostra-aetate_en.html.

tate. Western culture came to conceptualize the individual human being more distinctly, so that the notion of collective guilt became less tenable. The new science of history undermined the assumption of continuity between the Jews of old and the Jews of today. Another major consequence of the Enlightenment was the rise of secular society, which spurred leaders of different religions to see each other as allies facing a common challenge rather than as competitors.

But it is important to appreciate that the "spirit of the times" (*Zeitgeist*) can only ever leave its mark on theology insofar as it is processed through a theological prism. Change comes when theologians reexamine old texts with the lenses supplied by new circumstances, and reach new interpretive insight. In this respect, too, the Enlightenment and its aftermath spurred theological change, by enabling a historical approach to the canon that recognized the possibility that a text could have meant something quite different, could have served different rhetorical purposes, in its original context than as it was received by later readers in different contexts. We have already made use of this approach in appreciating that the book of Acts and Melito are, to greater or lesser degrees, internal critics punching up, rather than judges from the outside punching down. We will invoke this approach again in chapter 5, in understanding how modern scholarship came to reevaluate Paul's perspective on Jews and Judaism.

Conclusion

Given the role of the Cain and Abel story in the history of Christian anti-Judaism, and the importance of the Holocaust in motivating a shift away from the teaching of contempt, it is fitting to conclude the current chapter with some reflection on the reception of the Cain and Abel story in Jewish post-Holocaust literature. Cain and Abel do not play a large role in the imaginative world of Judaism throughout the ages, though some rabbinic texts take Cain's killing of Abel as a precedent for the suffering endured by Israel in exile at the hands of the nations of the world. But in prose and poetry written after the Holocaust this story looms large, for various reasons. First and foremost, Cain is the first murderer; the story thus represents, as it were, the root of all murders, and a suitably mythic framing for the Holocaust as the ultimate crime. Furthermore, in addition to killing Abel, Cain rejects any obligation to watch over his brother ("Am I my brother's keeper?"). By strangely embodying both the murderer and the bystander, Cain poses in an acute way the question of bystander guilt—the question of the bystander as murderer—that is a preoccupation of reflection on the Holocaust.

Dan Pagis survived the Holocaust as a teenager and emigrated to Palestine immediately after the war. In the new state of Israel, he became a scholar of medieval Hebrew poetry and a great Hebrew poet in his own right. His best-known Holocaust poem—arguably *the* canonical Holocaust poem in Israel today—is "Written in Pencil in the Sealed Railway-Car."[6] Spanning six short lines, the poem presents itself as a message written by Eve, who is with her son Abel in a railway car, destined for a concentration camp. Evidently intending to cast the note from the car, she asks the person who might find it to convey a message to her other son, Cain, but the note cuts off at this point, before the message itself is recorded. The poem conveys the unspeakable horror of the Holocaust through its hermeticism: the text is incomplete; the meaning is obscure; and the railway car is sealed. The effect of hermeticism, of the poem being sealed in upon itself, is conveyed also by the title, though only in the original Hebrew: *katuv be-iparon ba-qaron he-hatum* (woodenly: "written in-pencil in-the-railway-car the-sealed"). The first and last words are joined by their common morphology (as G-stem passive participles) and phonology (sharing the sequence *-atu-*); they also represent semantic pairs, since "written" and "sealed" are always joined together in the liturgy for the Days of Awe (which we will take up later in the book) to describe the divine judgment, which God writes and then seals. As a pair, these words block in, as it were, the two middle words, which likewise form a pair insofar as they share the same initial preposition (*be-/ba-*), the same final syllable (*-ron*), and an unvoiced stop (*p/q*).

In other poetry by Pagis that draws on the biblical story, Abel serves as a figure of death and of evanescence. In the poem "Autobiography," Abel, the narrator of the poem, stands at the head of the armies of the dead. As such, he is ironically more powerful than Cain, the leader of the living, for Abel's side increases inexorably, as "his [Cain's] legions desert him and go over to me." In "Brothers," Pagis describes Abel as "blond and wooly, . . . curly like the smoke of the offering he sent up to the nose of his lord." The analogy of Abel to smoke seems to depend in part on the fact that Abel disappears from the

6. For this poem and others, I rely, with minor divergence, on Stephen Mitchell's translations in the collection of Pagis's poems, *Points of Departure* (Philadelphia: Jewish Publication Society of America, 1981).

scene almost immediately after he is introduced, without saying a word, and that the name "Abel" (*hevel*) in Hebrew means "breath, vapor."

Another poem, "Testimony," does not explicitly refer to Cain and Abel, but it implicitly invokes the story through the same image of human smoke. The poem begins in the middle of a conversation; the speaker—again, as in "Autobiography," speaking from the dead—is evidently responding to someone who questioned the humanity of his killers. "No," he insists, "they definitely were human beings," made in the "image" (*tselem*) of God. In fact, continues the speaker, they were more human than he, for he is only a "shadow" (*tsel*), the work of a different, imageless God. When he was killed, and reduced to smoke, he was restored to his essential, vaporous self, and floated up to his God, "smoke to omnipotent smoke."

This last poem thus takes up the other significant figure in the Cain and Abel story, namely, God. With devastating irony, Pagis, through the voice of the dead Abel, cries out to God not for vengeance, but by way of homecoming. Abel's God was powerless in the Holocaust. He is a God who, as Pagis reminds us in the poem by means of allusion to a famous liturgical composition, *Yigdal* ("great"), which we will encounter in chapter 13, insists that he cannot be embodied in an image. Abel's God lacks substance, lacks solidity. He led Israel as a pillar of smoke in the wilderness. It was thus meet and inevitable, as it were, that his people—Abel, Israel—should become smoke like him.

A church that rejects punishment supersession must of course forswear Augustine's identification of the Jewish people with Cain. But it can hold onto his identification of Jesus with Abel, the necessary victim of and the solution to an inveterate human—not specifically Jewish—inclination to sin. A church committed to Christian-Jewish dialogue might find in Abel not only Augustine's Christ but also Pagis's Jews, as victims of a disaster that, as we will see in chapter 4, cannot be disconnected from the history of Christian anti-Judaism. Such a stereoscopic Abel can figure, in himself, the fraught centrality of Judaism and the Jewish people in Christian theology.

Further Inquiry

There are many books on anti-Jewish Christian teaching throughout the ages, the subject of this and the next chapter. Jules Isaac, noted above, clarified the Christian "teaching of contempt" in his *Jesus and Israel* (New York: Holt, Rhinehart and

Winston, 1971). An ambitious recent work identifying anti-Judaism as a foundational reflex in Western thought is David Nirenberg's *Anti-Judaism: The Western Tradition* (New York: W. W. Norton, 2013). The early history of the charge of deicide is traced in great detail in J. Christopher Edwards, *Crucified: The Christian Invention of the Jewish Executioners of Jesus* (Minneapolis: Fortress Press, 2023). Jeremy Cohen explores the medieval and modern afterlives of some of the texts that we have examined in his books *Living Letters of the Law: Ideas of the Jew in Medieval Christianity* (Berkeley: University of California Press, 1999) and *Christ Killers: The Jews and the Passion from the Bible to the Big Screen* (Oxford: Oxford University Press, 2007). For the political context in which the term "supersessionism" was coined, see Michael Azar, "'Supersessionism': The Political Origin of a Theological Neologism," *SCJR* 16 (2021): 1–25.

●

1. This chapter briefly raises the question of how a religious tradition can address troubling passages in its scriptures. Consider two passages not mentioned above. In Matthew 27:25, the assembled crowd, having called for Barabbas to be released and Jesus to be crucified, shouts: "His blood be on us and on our children!" In John 8:43–44 Jesus tells his Jewish interlocutors: "Why do you not understand what I say? It is because you cannot accept my word. You are from your father the devil, and you choose to do your father's desires." What should a church that rejects anti-Judaism do with such texts? Can they be bracketed out as "outdated," or does the sacred character of Scripture preclude this strategy? We will return to related questions in chapter 5; see the discussion there, and consult parts III and IV of a work that it cites, the Pontifical Biblical Commission's *The Jewish People and Their Sacred Scriptures in the Christian Bible*, published in 2002.

2. One thing to learn from the history of Christian anti-Judaism is how to express disagreement and criticism in a way that does not demonize, and with attentiveness to the ways in which words not intended to demonize might, translated into a different context, offer ammunition to demonizers. How might this lesson from the history of Christian anti-Judaism carry over into areas of intense conflict today, such as the realm of politics?

— *Chapter 3* —

Ritual Law and the Economy of Salvation

JUSTIN THE MARTYR WAS BORN A FEW DECADES before Melito of Sardis. A gentile, native to Nablus (from the Latin name Neapolis, the "new city"), he was drawn first to Platonism, and through it, ultimately, to Christianity, which he found to be the only "safe and profitable philosophy." We learn these things from the beginning of his *Dialogue with Trypho*, Justin's account of a conversation between himself and a non-Christ-worshiping Jew named Trypho.[1] Upon hearing about Justin's spiritual path, Trypho responds, good naturedly but critically, that it would have been better for Justin to remain a Platonist. He contends that Jesus is not the messiah, and that if Justin wishes to go beyond Platonism, he ought to adopt the ritual law: "First be circumcised, then observe what ordinances have been enacted with respect to the Sabbath, and the feasts, and the new moons of God; and, in a word, do all things which have been written in the law: and then perhaps you shall obtain mercy from God."

Thus they enter into a long, earnest conversation about Judaism and the teachings of Christ. Justin begins by clarifying the issue: Does Trypho believe the terrible stories people tell of Christian immorality, or does he hold only this against the Christians, that they do not observe the ritual law? Trypho confirms that the latter is indeed what matters for him.

> This is what we are most at a loss about: that you, professing to be pious, and supposing yourselves better than others, are not in any particular separated from them, and do not alter your mode of living from the nations, in that you

1. I use the Dods and Reith translation from *Ante-Nicene Fathers*, vol. 1: *Apostolic Fathers with Justin Martyr and Irenaeus* (New York: Christian Literature Company, 1885).

> observe no festivals or sabbaths, and do not have the rite of circumcision; and further, resting your hopes on a man that was crucified, you yet expect to obtain some good thing from God, while you do not obey His commandments. Have you not read, that that soul shall be cut off from his people who shall not have been circumcised on the eighth day? [See Gen. 17:14.] And this has been ordained for strangers and for slaves equally. But you, despising this covenant rashly, reject the consequent duties, and attempt to persuade yourselves that you know God, when, however, you perform none of those things which they do who fear God.

Here, with remarkable directness, Justin, through the figure of Trypho, raises a key question for Christ worshipers from Paul forward. The one God formed a covenant with the Israelites and directed them, in this covenantal context, to perform an array of ritual observances: circumcision, sabbath rest, the dietary laws, etc. Surely these rites are good, else God would not have commanded them. Why, then, should Christians not observe them? Before we turn to Justin's own answers to this question, we will return to Augustine's *Contra Faustum.* As we will see, Augustine confronts the same question as Justin, but from the other side of the spectrum (or to put it in the terms laid out in chapter 1: from the other bookend or boundary marker). It is not a Torah-observant Jew who challenges Augustine to join him in adhering to the ritual law, but a gnostic-like Christian, Faustus, who denies a connection between the God of the Christians and the God of Israel. He will say: If you, Augustine, believe, unlike me, that Christ is related to the God of Israel, then why do you not obey this God's laws?

Because the Hebrew Bible presents the Mosaic law, including the ritual law, as the content of God's covenant with Israel, it is around this issue of Christian non-observance of the ritual law, perhaps more than any other, that Christian theologians formulated the claim of economic supersession—that is, that God's covenant with Israel was designed to come to an end with Christ. In this chapter we will examine the approaches of Augustine and Justin to the ritual law and to economic supersession, and consider the roots of their positions in Paul's letters. At the end of the chapter, we will turn to the Catholic Church's teaching today on the Mosaic law. We will complete our discussion of economic supersession in chapter 5.

Augustine v. Faustus

Contra Faustum is Augustine's record of his debate with Faustus, a Manichaean Christian leader. We need not enter here into Manichaeism; for our purposes, it suffices to note that Faustus, like the gnostics described in chapter 1, rejected the authority of the Old Testament and its divinity. For him, Jesus came to defeat Moses. New Testament passages that appear to accept the Jewish Bible as authoritative must either be excised as corrupt, or interpreted so that they do not.

At the beginning of book 19, Faustus confronts a particularly challenging verse, Matthew 5:17, where Jesus declares: "Do not think that I have come to abolish the law or the prophets; I have come not to abolish but to fulfill." How, in light of this verse, can Faustus reject the Old Testament? Doesn't Jesus seem to embrace it? We must distinguish, Faustus says, between different sorts of laws and prophets, and in particular—I simplify somewhat—between the laws and prophets of truth, and the laws and prophets of the Jews. Jesus did not refer in Matthew 5:17 to the Mosaic law, to things like circumcision or the sacrificial rites or the rule of "an eye for an eye." These, in fact, are evil laws that Jesus came to destroy, as is evident from the fact that in the continuation of the Sermon on the Mount in Matthew 5, he rejects the principle of "an eye for an eye" in favor of turning the other cheek. What Jesus fulfills, rather, is the law of truth conveyed by the antediluvian messengers who preceded Moses, figures like Seth and Enoch. These men preached moral laws: against murder, against adultery, etc. And Jesus likewise, in his Sermon on the Mount, upholds these prohibitions and indeed strengthens them.

Having interpreted Matthew 5:17 so that it does not contradict his perspective, Faustus turns the tables on Augustine: How will Augustine make sense of this verse? Yes, Augustine accepts the unity of the Old Testament and the New, so that he can construe Jesus's words in Matthew 5:17 on their plain sense, as referring to the laws of Moses, but then, shouldn't Augustine and his fellow mainstream Christians not observe the laws of Moses? Augustine's chief response is that Jesus "fulfills" the ritual law not by affirming its continued force, but insofar as the ritual law consists of allegorical symbols that find their ultimate meaning in Jesus. Thus, for example, Christians do not circumcise because the removal of the foreskin is an allegory for the "removal of our fleshly nature," which one achieves most perfectly by joining oneself to the death and resurrection of Christ. Again, Christians do not mark the Passover festival by refraining from consumption of leaven, as the Bible commands, because this injunction points toward the notion of "purging out the leaven of the old life" to achieve a new life in Christ.

Augustine finds evidence for his approach to the ritual law in the fact that the New Testament depicts Jesus's Jewish followers continuing to observe rites like circumcision. He reasons that they were permitted to do so "lest by a compulsory abandonment [the ritual law] should seem to be condemned rather than closed." In other words, had Jews raised in the law been compelled immediately to abandon it upon attaching themselves to Jesus, one might have inferred that the law was bad, whereas in fact the law was in itself good, only that it became useless once Jesus arrived. Further evidence for the importance of the law before Christ's advent comes, for Augustine, from the fact that Christians celebrate Jews of the pre-Christian past who observed the law at all costs, like the seven sons who martyred themselves rather than eat the swine's flesh set before them by Antiochus, according to the story in 2 Maccabees 7.

Nor indeed, according to Augustine, should we even think of the ritual law, in the broadest sense, as defunct. For the sacraments of the church can be understood as a "translation" of the ritual law for a different era. Just as the significance of the ritual law lies in prefiguring Christ, in the future tense, so the sacraments point back toward Christ, in the past tense. "For if in language the form of the verb changes in the number of letters and syllables according to the tense, as 'done' signifies the past, and 'to be done' the future, why should not the symbols which declare Christ's death and resurrection to be accomplished, differ from those which predicted their accomplishment, as we see a difference in the form and sound of the words, past and future, 'suffered' and 'to suffer,' 'risen' and 'to rise'?" Finally, Augustine notes that Christians continue literally to observe the elements of the Mosaic law whose significance does not lie in prefiguring Christ, like the injunction not to worship other gods, and the moral injunctions against murder, false witness, and the like. Christ "fulfills" such laws too, but in a different sense: by bestowing on human beings the divine grace without which they cannot properly be obeyed.

Augustine's view of the Mosaic law is thus very positive in its way, certainly by comparison to Faustus's. Indeed, it is in part the challenge from Faustus, who would split the Old Testament from the New, that prods Augustine to formulate such a positive view of the law. At the same time, Augustine's perspective seems clearly to suppose economic supersession: with Christ's coming, God's covenant with Israel, expressed in the law of Moses, no longer has force. Occasionally, Augustine's view of the law even slips into a darker mode familiar from the framework of punishment supersession. Thus, at one point, Augustine reasons about the relationship between the ritual law and the sacraments. If they both "say" Christ, albeit in different "tenses," then why do they feel so different? "Now that the righteousness of faith is revealed, and the children of God are called into liberty, and the yoke of bondage which was required for a carnal and stiffnecked people is taken away, other sacraments are instituted, greater in efficacy, more beneficial in their use, easier in performance, and fewer in number." On this line of thought, though the ritual law represents the beneficent gift of a good God, the form that it takes—carnal, burdensome—reflects the fact that it was meant to redress the distinctive pathologies of the Jewish people.

Justin v. Trypho

Justin's position on the ritual law in his *Dialogue with Trypho*—I focus here on chapters 11–22—is something like a mirror image of Augustine's. He gestures occasionally toward a framework of economic supersession, but in the main, he understands the ritual law as a function of Israel's sinfulness. At the outset of the discussion, he asserts that "the law promulgated on Horeb (Sinai) is now old, and belongs to yourselves alone; but [Christ's law] is for all universally. Now, law placed against law has abrogated that which is before it, and a covenant which comes after in like manner has put an end to the previous one; and an eternal and final law—namely, Christ—has been given to us, and the covenant is trustworthy, after which there shall be no law, no commandment, no ordinance." Overall, this passage seems to propound a logic of replacement, or economic supersession: the old Mosaic law, together with the covenant in which it was embedded, yields to the new, eternal law of Christ. But embedded in the passage is a different logic: the Mosaic law is for Israel alone, while Christ's law is universal. It is in fact this claim that Justin presses in the continuation, in a markedly anti-Jewish direction.

For Justin, the ritual laws were given to Israel "on account of your transgressions and the hardness of your hearts." Israel, more than other peoples, had need of the discipline of the law. Thus, for example, God commanded Israel the dietary laws "in order that you might keep God before your eyes while you ate and drank, seeing that you were prone and very ready to depart from His knowledge," as is evident from the story of the golden calf, which (according to the story told in Exod. 32) the Jews worshiped after feasting. Again, God bade the Jews to worship at a temple and offer sacrifices in order to curb their tendency toward the worship of idols.

Justin has a different though not unrelated explanation for the circumcision commandment: it was a physical sign given to Abraham for the purpose of enabling, far in the future, the singling out of his descendants for punishment because of their killing of the prophets and of Christ, and their persecution of Christians. That punishment has now arrived, in the form of the failure of the Jewish revolts against Rome, and in particular, the Bar Kokhba revolt, which occurred in Justin's own time. "For the circumcision according to the flesh, which is from Abraham, was given for a sign; that you may be separated from other nations, and from us; and that you alone may suffer that which you now justly suffer; and that your land may be desolate, and your cities burned with fire; and that strangers may eat your fruit in your presence, and not one of you may go up to Jerusalem. For you are not recognized among the rest of men by any other mark than your fleshly circumcision."

In accounting for the prohibition against eating leavened bread during the seven-day Passover holiday, Justin adopts a different approach. "This is the symbolic significance of unleavened bread, that you do not commit the old deeds of wicked leaven. . . . After the seven days of eating unleavened bread, God commanded them to mingle new leaven, that is, the performance of other works, and not the imitation of the old and evil works." Here Justin ventures an allegorical understanding of a ritual law, in the manner of Augustine, though Justin's interpretation is not Christological. Justin says that the Jews err in adhering to the literal sense of the law: "But you have understood all things in a carnal sense, and you suppose it to be piety if you do such things, while your souls are filled with deceit, and, in short, with every wickedness." It is not clear whether Justin intends to suggest that God never meant for the law to be observed "carnally," or only that God wished that carnal performance should be accompanied by cultivation of the spiritual sense. In any case, even here, Justin links the ritual law to Israel's sinfulness.

Augustine v. Justin, with Paul

While Faustus stands outside emergent orthodox Christianity for his outright rejection of the God of the Old Testament and of the ritual law that God commands, an affirmation of the ritual law is consistent with a wide range of perspectives on it, and those of both Justin and Augustine fall in this range. Justin's account is considerably more anti-Jewish than Augustine's. For the most part, Justin characterizes the law as a curb against the Jewish people's uniquely voracious appetite for sin, which is manifest in their history of killing those who rebuke them, from the prophets of old to Jesus. Augustine, by contrast, holds up the ritual law as the equivalent, in its time, of the sacraments. Christians properly celebrate the memory of Jews who, before Christ's advent, gave up their lives for the sake of the law. But Augustine agrees with Justin that there is no place for the law with the coming of Christ. Both theologians, likewise, assert or assume economic supersession. Moreover, Augustine's position is by no means free of anti-Jewish animus. Recall his allegorical reading of the story of Cain and Abel. The Jews insist on "farming" the ritual law even after Christ's advent because they are blind to the ritual law's meaning and are inclined, in their pride, to seek their own righteousness rather than humbly to receive God's grace.

The differences between Justin and Augustine can be accounted for, in part, by the different ways in which Paul speaks about the law in his letters. One can draw a straight line backward from Justin's remarks about the law to Paul's Letter to the Galatians. In this letter, arguing against fellow Christ followers who insist that gentiles who attach themselves to Christ must circumcise themselves and observe the ritual law, Paul speaks very negatively about the ritual law. In one chapter alone, Galatians 3, Paul associates the law with the flesh rather than with the spirit; refers to those who rely on the law as being under a curse, a curse from which Christ's death redeems; characterizes the law as a latecomer, powerless to modify a more fundamental covenant that does not depend on the law; and explains that the law was added "because of our sins," to keep guard over us like a disciplining "schoolmaster." Paul neither says nor implies that Israel was uniquely sinful—that it had more need than non-Jews of discipline—nor does he anywhere hint that circumcision is a divine means of singling out the Jewish people for punishment, but Justin could, with reason, construe his approach to the ritual law as continuous with Paul's remarks in Galatians.

By contrast, Augustine's conceptualization of the law owes much to Paul's Letter to the Romans. Consider in particular chapter 7 of this letter. While Paul tells his addressees that they have "died to the law through the body of Christ," he is careful to clarify that he by no means wishes to imply that the law is bad. On the contrary, "the law is holy, and the commandment is holy and just and good." The problem with the law lies, ironically, in the fact that it is too "spiritual": it tells us what is sinful, but it cannot take hold of our carnal persons, sold to sin, and actually stop us from sinning. Augustine's Christological, allegorical approach to the ritual law—the notion, for example, that the meaning of circumcision lies in cutting away our carnality, and that Christ's death and resurrection therefore "fulfill" this law by achieving that which it allegorically figures—is not to be found here in so many words. After all, Paul did not know and was not attempting to account for Matthew 5:17. But Augustine could look back to Paul's positive characterization of the law in Romans, with reason, as a conceptual foundation for his approach.

My aim here is not to offer a coherent account of Paul's perspective on the law; we will turn to Paul's theology more systematically in chapter 5. My point is rather to suggest that both Justin's and Augustine's approaches to the ritual law, and by extension to God's covenant with Israel, represent plausible readings or at least extensions of Paul's writings. To explain why Justin went in one direction, while Augustine took his bearings from other parts of Paul's letters, we should have to engage more comprehensively with their thought and their historical circumstances; I can offer here only the following preliminary suggestions.

We might venture that Justin, in his time, was punching up, and seeking, within the rhetorical framework of his *Dialogue with Trypho*, to set the circle of Christ followers apart from the larger Jewish world in which they still were situated. Augustine, by contrast, wrote after the decisive ascent of Christianity to political power, and in the context of *Contra Faustum* he is resisting those who would altogether dissociate Christianity from Judaism. We might alternatively suggest, in more immediately theological terms, that Justin conceives of the divine economy as a matter of the election of the righteous. Abraham was chosen for his righteousness, as were his signal offspring: Isaac, Jacob, Judah, and others. But on the whole, Abraham's descendants were distinctly wicked, and needed the governance of the toilsome ritual law. The church, consisting still of the righteous, or those made righteous through Christ, has as little need for the ritual laws as did Abraham himself. Augustine, by contrast, is inclined to see sin as an overwhelming problem for all people, so that election can only ever be a matter of divine grace. From this perspective, the notion that the ritual law was meant to check a uniquely wicked people is less compelling.

The Catechism on the Law

In its short treatment of "the Old Law" (sections 1961–64), the Catechism of the Catholic Church, promulgated in 1992, takes its bearings from Romans, which it cites three times.[2] It labors in general to characterize the Mosaic law as a step toward the new teachings of Christianity. The moral injunctions of the Mosaic law, on which this unit focuses, represent "a light offered to the conscience of every man to make God's call and ways known to him and to protect him against evil." Following Paul, the Catechism characterizes the moral law as holy and good, but insufficient, because it only discloses sin, but does not provide the strength to overcome it. The final section of this unit, evidently taking up the language of Matthew 5:17, adopts an Augustinian approach to the ritual law, which "prophesies and presages the work of liberation from sin which will be fulfilled in Christ" by furnishing "images, 'types,' and symbols for expressing the life according to the Spirit."

In the next unit, devoted to "the New Law, or the Law of the Gospel" (sections 1965–74), we learn more, by way of contrast, about the Old Law. Again hearkening back to Matthew 5:17, the Catechism says that the New Law "'fulfills,' refines, surpasses, and leads the Old Law to its perfection." Perhaps most pointedly, "the New Law is called a law of love because it makes us act out of the love infused by the Holy Spirit, rather than from fear, . . . [and] a law of freedom, because it sets us free from the ritual and juridical observances of the Old Law."

Not surprisingly, this last sentence is one that the Jewish tradition, as we shall see, will vigorously contest. It does not conceive of the law as something to be observed only out of fear rather than love, nor does it think of it, on the

2. For quotations from the Catechism here and throughout this book, see https://www.vatican.va/archive/ENG0015/_INDEX.HTM.

whole, as constituted by "ritual and juridical" bonds from which one might hope to be liberated. To be sure, the Catechism does not uphold the aggressively anti-Jewish aspects of Justin's approach to the law; on the whole there is a line of continuity from the Paul of Romans especially, to Augustine, to the Catechism. At the same time, in ways both explicit and implicit, the Catechism expresses a firm commitment to the surpassing of the "Old Law." Christians are set free from substantial elements of it. If the ritual law "prophesies and presages" Christ, then Christ's coming marks an end to its utility. It is fair to say that, at least as far as the ritual law goes, the Catechism commits to a supersessionist position. To characterize the position of the Catechism in this way is not to suggest that the position is bad or wrong, nor even to exclude the possibility that this position is demanded by Christian theology; I use the term "supersessionist" descriptively, not to make a normative judgment.

Conclusion

Perhaps what is most striking about the treatment of the ritual law in the Catechism is its brevity. This question—why do Christians not observe the ritual law?—is *the* starting point for Justin's *Dialogue with Trypho*, and a major preoccupation of Augustine's *Contra Faustum*, and these works are of course only two examples among many. Why does the Catechism have so little to say—and almost nothing directly to say—in answer to this question? In chapter 5, we will return to this puzzle, along with the further pressing and ultimately related question: What are the implications of the church's position on the ritual law for the question of economic supersession? If Christianity proclaims that the Mosaic law, or at least the ritual element thereof, no longer has force with the advent of Christ, does it necessarily follow that God's covenantal relationship with the Jewish people has likewise come to an end? Or is it possible to distinguish somehow between the continuity of the ritual law and the continuity of the covenant between God and Israel, even though the ritual law seems to represent a or indeed the defining expression of that covenant?

Our discussion in chapter 5 will take us to among the most positive expressions toward Judaism in the modern church. It is therefore important, before entering into this discussion, to appreciate the dark consequences of the teaching of contempt detailed in this chapter and the previous one. The next chapter, chapter 4, describes some of these consequences, from the medieval period forward, culminating in the Holocaust.

Further Inquiry

Justin's perspective on the Jews is explored in David Rokeah, *Justin Martyr and the Jews* (Leiden: Brill, 2002), and in Matthijs Den Dulk, *Between Jews and Heretics: Refiguring Justin Martyr's Dialogue with Trypho* (London: Routledge, 2018). On Augustine and the Jews, see Paula Fredriksen, *Augustine and the Jews: A Christian Defense of Jews and Judaism* (New York: Doubleday, 2008), and for the Manichaean context of his *Contra Faustum*, see Jason David BeDuhn, *Augustine's Manichaean Dilemma* (2 vols.; Philadelphia: University of Pennsylvania Press, 2009, 2013). Among other early Christian perspectives on the ritual law that might be put into conversation with Justin's and Augustine's, that of the Epistle of Barnabas is especially noteworthy. See generally David Lincicum et al., eds., *Law and Lawlessness in Early Judaism and Early Christianity* (Tübingen: Mohr Siebeck, 2019), and especially David Lincicum's contribution therein, "Against the Law: The Epistle of Barnabas and Torah Polemic in Early Christianity."

●

1. Consider a ritual law like the commandment to fast on the tenth day of the Hebrew month of Tishre, the Day of Atonement or Yom Kippur. (See Lev. 23:32.) How might Justin explain why Christians need not observe this law? How might Augustine?

2. As manifested both in Augustine's argument and in the passage from the Catechism, traditional Christian reasoning about the laws of the Old Testament often presumes a categorical distinction between the ritual law and the moral law. Distinctions of this sort also surface, in their own way and to different ends, in Jewish reasoning about the law. But how stable is the distinction between the ritual law and the moral law? In what ways do they overlap, and given the overlap, is it nevertheless helpful to distinguish them? You might consider the Decalogue as a test case for the application of these categories. Return to this question after reading chapter 7.

— Chapter 4 —

Anti-Judaism and Violence

IN THIS CHAPTER, WE SURVEY SOME OF THE EXPRESSIONS of discrimination and violence endured by Jewish communities of medieval and early modern Christendom and the ways in which, in the modern period, such anti-Judaism informed or transmuted into antisemitism. We will weigh, in particular, the role of Christian anti-Judaism in enabling Nazi persecution of Jews in the Holocaust. The historical scholarship devoted to these phenomena, stretching across centuries and continents, is vast. The modest ambition of this chapter is only to trace key developments, with a particular focus on Western Europe. The survey below draws especially on syntheses by Marc Saperstein and Jane Gerber.[1]

Christian praxis is often marked by dialogue, interaction, and tension between, on the one hand, the dogmatic teaching of the church and, on the other hand, the beliefs and motivations of the Christian faithful in their particular circumstances. This generalization holds true, as generalizations always do, with exceptions and qualifications, regarding the issue of Jewish life in Christian Europe. With the known exception of Visigothic Spain between roughly the fifth and eighth centuries CE, where the practice of Judaism was outlawed, the consensus posture of western Christian authorities toward the Jews followed the Augustinian line: Jews should live in subservience to the church triumphant, but they should be allowed to live, and to live as Jews. They should not be killed or compelled to convert, though their conversion should be welcomed and indeed encouraged. Treatment of Jews might diverge

1. See Marc Saperstein, *Moments of Crisis in Jewish-Christian Relations* (Philadelphia: SCM Press, 1989); Jane S. Gerber, *The Jews of Spain: A History of the Sephardic Experience* (New York: Simon & Schuster, 1992).

from this line in two directions. A local Christian ruler might, for example, grant Jews privileges or protections that seemed to undermine the projection of Jewish subservience, and he might be challenged on these grounds by church spokesmen. In the opposite direction, religious or lay Christians inspired by religious zeal or by more venal considerations might inflict violence or extreme conversionary pressure on local Jews, to which secular authorities or religious leaders might respond with rebuke or by coming actively to the aid of the victims.

The purpose of the survey below is not, in the first instance, to arouse shame or guilt, or to stake a spot in a victimhood competition. Its purpose is rather to clarify the "real-world" consequences of the Christian teaching of contempt toward Jews and Judaism. Even if theological questions must ultimately be articulated and addressed in theological terms, it is important not only from a historical perspective but also from a theological perspective to appreciate the long history of anti-Jewish discrimination and violence as the backdrop against which new directions in Christian theological thinking about Jews and Judaism, and Jewish theological thinking about Christianity, have occurred.

Persecution in the Premodern Period

Some light on the circumstances of Jews in Christian Europe near the beginning of the Middle Ages is shed by a missive from Pope Gregory I to Januarius, Bishop of Cagliari, in Sardinia, in 599.[2] Gregory reports that Jews from Cagliari came to him to complain that a certain Peter, having been "led from their superstition [that is, Judaism] to the veneration of the Christian faith with God's will," decided, on the day following his Easter baptism, to occupy the synagogue and to station there a cross, an image of Mary, and his white baptismal cloak. The Pope expresses his satisfaction at the fact that the bishop had warned Peter against carrying out this plan, and urges him now to undo Peter's work by removing the image and the cross with "due veneration," and restoring the synagogue to the Jews. "For inasmuch as the legal rule does not suffer the Jews to erect new synagogues, it does permit them to have the

2. See Amnon Linder, *Jews in the Legal Sources of the Early Middle Ages*, 439.

old ones without disturbance." He adds that Peter and his allies should not be allowed to defend themselves as having acted "in their zeal for the faith," to compel conversion, because conversion should occur through persuasion. Gregory also expresses his concern that Peter's disorderliness will undermine the city's unity at a time when it faces external enemies.

Pope Gregory I here endorses a regime of tolerant subordination, while pushing back against a more aggressive act undertaken by certain local Christians. This aggression was inspired by a moment of heightened religious zeal: a convert's Easter baptism. Similarly, and in a much broader way, the relatively benign condition of Jewish life under western Christendom took a decisive turn for the worse at a moment when religious zeal became systemic and sustained, during the Crusades, begun in 1096. The Crusades, a vast and complex initiative to recapture the Holy Land from Muslim conquerors, represent, in Jewish memory, the first great outburst of anti-Jewish violence in Christendom. According to the Mainz Anonymous chronicle, a Jewish record of the event, certain Crusader armies reasoned: "We take our lives in our hands in order to kill and to subjugate all those kingdoms that do not believe in the Crucified. How much more so [should we kill and subjugate] the Jews, who killed and crucified him."[3]

According to the chronicle, death came first to the community of Speyer, where eleven Jews were killed at the hands of Crusader armies, aided by local burghers, before the bishop managed to secure the community's safety. In Worms, the chronicle reports, local burghers took a Christian corpse and accused the Jews of murdering the man, boiling him in water, and pouring the water in the wells to poison Christians. Enraged locals from Worms and surrounding villages, along with Crusaders on the move, attacked the Jewish community, killing and forcibly baptizing Jews, and overwhelming the local bishop's chambers where some had taken refuge. In language taken directly from the story of Abraham's would-be sacrifice of Isaac in Genesis 22, the chronicle—corroborated here as elsewhere by external evidence—tells of Jews who killed their children rather than allow them to be seized and baptized. The violence continued elsewhere in this and subsequent Crusades.

3. I quote from Robert Chazan's edition, published in Lawrence Fine, ed., *Judaism in Practice* (Princeton: Princeton University Press, 2001), 441–52.

We witness in subsequent centuries a turn toward radical demonization of Jews. They became, in the imagination of many Christians, figures not merely of carnality and blindness but of homicidal bloodthirstiness. The most striking expression of this turn is the blood libel, first attested in England in 1144. Jews were accused of killing Christians, often specifically children, in order to reenact the crucifixion of Christ or because they had need of Christian blood for ritual purposes. Around the middle of the thirteenth century, a different demonizing libel arose in the wake of the Fourth Lateran Council of 1215, which laid particular stress on the doctrine of transubstantiation, that is, the real transformation of the consecrated eucharistic wine and bread into the blood and body of Christ. The notion became widespread that Jews sought to desecrate the eucharistic bread, also called the host. If the host was the real body of Christ, then it stood to reason that Jews would undertake to obtain it from Christian accomplices so that they might impale or burn it and thus kill Christ again. These libels circulated throughout Europe, sometimes leading to violence and always fostering hate. A collection of "Jewish Cruelties against the Most Holy Sacrament and Christian Children" published in Polish by Szymon Hubicki in 1602, would become especially influential, informing among others the Nazi propagandist Julius Streicher, who devoted an issue of *Der Stürmer* in 1934 to "Jewish ritual murders from the times of Christ to 1932."

Though Jewish life in Ashkenaz remained, in its way, economically viable and intellectually fertile across the high Middle Ages, it grew ever more precarious in the face of such libels and their attendant violence, alongside other forms of economic and social discrimination. Expulsions over the course of the late thirteenth century to the end of the fourteenth century brought an end to organized Jewish life in medieval England and France. Expulsions also occurred in various German states at this time and later, but Jewish communities remained in the area and became targets of vituperation and violence from both sides in the emerging conflict between Protestants and Catholics. Strikingly, both Protestants and Catholics could accuse the other side of Judaizing. Catholics are really Jews, said Protestants: just look at their legalism, their rituals, their human traditions that obscure biblical truth. No, countered Catholics, the real Jews are the Protestants: see their preference for the Old Testament, even in the original Hebrew, and their iconoclasm. Amid these fluid significations of the category "Jew," the stable assumption, with real-world consequences, was that a Jew is one of the worst things one can be.

While 1492 is famous in the West as the year in which Columbus sailed the ocean blue, in Jewish history it marks the tragic end of the largest medieval Jewish community in Western Europe, in the very kingdom under whose flag Columbus sailed, Spain. The Iberian Peninsula had been for centuries prior the site of a sort of crusade, the *Reconquista*, an undertaking to wrest control of these lands away from the Muslim kingdoms that had ruled over them since the eighth century. As the Reconquista advanced southward, the Jewish communities that fell under the dominion of Christian kings were subjected to violence and conversionary pressure. Thus, for example, in the first half of the thirteenth century, King James I of Aragon compelled Jews to attend conversionary sermons delivered by bishops and by Dominican and Franciscan monks. In 1391, pogroms beginning in Seville led to massive numbers of deaths and forced conversions. Between February of 1413 and November of 1414, a compelled public disputation in Tortosa before Pope Benedict XIII led to further mass conversions.

Conversion did not necessarily solve the problem of persecution. Although some offspring of *conversos* (converts from Judaism), including Teresa of Ávila (b. 1515) and John of the Cross (b. 1542), would achieve great distinction in the church, many doubted the sincerity of conversos, and accused them of being crypto-Jews (*marranos*), holding on to Jewish customs in secret. The economic and political success of families that, only a few years prior, had been despised Jews, also aroused envy. In 1449, a pogrom against conversos was followed by a "purity of blood" ordinance declaring that "so-called *conversos*, offspring of perverse Jewish ancestors, must be held by law to be infamous and ignominious, unfit and unworthy to hold any public office or benefice within the city of Toledo."[4] Although Pope Nicholas V overruled the law, in line with the traditional position of the Catholic Church recognizing converts from Judaism as Christian in all respects, it went into force all the same in 1451. "Purity of blood" laws remained an important fact of Spanish life into the eighteenth century and represent an anticipation of modern, race-based antisemitism.

The Inquisition, an institution in the Catholic Church charged with investigating and punishing heresy among Christians, was introduced into Spain in 1478. In 1481 it organized a public burning (an *auto da fé*, or "act of faith") of conversos. Convinced that the continued ties of family and friend-

4. Gerber, *Jews of Spain*, 127.

ship between conversos and the surviving Jewish communities were harming the conversos' faith, the Inquisition turned its energies to expulsion, and in 1482 succeeded in coordinating with certain cities in expelling their Jews. The Reconquista was gradually reaching its end at this time, as the Kingdom of Granada, the last Muslim kingdom in Spain, began to totter; it would fall in January of 1492. The desire grew for a final solution, concurrent with the completion of the Reconquista, to the problem of the conversos and Jews in Spain. The Inquisition prosecuted a particularly spectacular blood-libel case in 1490/91: a converso in the town of La Guardia was charged with crucifying a Christian child on the eve of Passover. This case was likely designed to prepare the ground for a comprehensive expulsion decree.

The decree came in 1492. According to a later report from a sixteenth-century Inquisitor, Jewish leaders offered the king a large gift to induce him to rescind or delay the expulsion, but Grand Inquisitor Torquemada, in dramatic fashion, came before King Ferdinand and persuaded him that he would be a Judas for accepting it. Showing him the crucifix around his neck, Torquemada said: "See here the crucifix of our Savior, whom the wretched Judas sold for thirty pieces of silver to his enemies and betrayed to their persecutors. If you applaud this action, sell him for a higher price. I, for my part, resign from all power. I will not take any blame; you will be responsible to God for this business deal."[5] Many Spanish Jews fled Spain for Portugal, but Portugal forcibly converted all its Jews in 1497.

The end of organized Jewish life in the Iberian Peninsula did not end the threat to conversos. Portugal established its own Inquisition, and as Spain and Portugal founded colonies in the New World, their Inquisitions became active there too, ever vigilant in the search for crypto-Jews. Among the most prominent victims of the Spanish Inquisition in the New World was Luis de Caravajal the Younger, the nephew of the governor of Mexico. He, together with many family members, was burned at the stake in 1596. He was indeed a crypto-Jew, who wrote an autobiography under a pseudonym, along with, among other things, a traditional list of the principles of the Jewish faith and a prayer manual. Princeton University hosts a digitized version of his collected writing.[6] There (on page 171) one will find, remarkably and poignantly, a list of the names of the

5. Gerber, *Jews of Spain*, 137.

6. See https://catalog.princeton.edu/catalog/99100134253506421.

Hebrew months, transliterated into Roman letters, each correlated with the corresponding month in the Gregorian calendar, as well as a list of the names and dates of the Jewish holidays, including even minor fast days, and the Hebrew words for the numbers one through ten. These things were recorded by a man whose family had not lived openly as Jewish for at least a century.

From Anti-Judaism to Antisemitism to the Holocaust

It is often noted—and I, too, noted it in passing above—that traditional Christian anti-Judaism differs categorically from modern antisemitism in that the former is religious, while the latter is ethnic or racial: a Jew ceases to become a target of anti-Judaism when he converts to Christianity, because Christian anti-Judaism centers on the practice of Judaism, but a Jew never ceases being a target of antisemitism, because antisemitism centers on birth or biology or innate character. The claim for a distinction between Christian anti-Judaism and modern antisemitism is fundamentally true, and important, but it should be qualified. As we have seen, the attempts of early Christian thinkers like Justin, Melito, and Augustine to grapple with Christianity's relationship with Jews and Judaism—to explain why most Jews reject Christ; why Christians do not observe the ritual law, etc.—yielded a deeply negative conceptualization of Jewish character: Jews are inveterate sinners, proud, carnal, and blind. Thus, traditional Christian anti-Judaism, too, makes claims about Jews as such. The Spanish "purity of blood" laws were the rare form of persecution that did not recognize baptism as a definitive break from the convert's Jewish origins, but they were continuous with a tradition that indeed constructed an innate, vicious Jewish character.

The geographic division in the medieval period between Christendom and the world of Islam, and the fact that Christian authorities generally tolerated the existence of Jews but not of pagans, meant that Jews in Europe became, both on the ground and rhetorically, the paradigmatic Other. As Christian Europe entered modernity, the Jews, as the available scapegoat, often came to absorb the blame for the displacements and disruptions that came in modernity's wake. A very precise expression of this tendency may be found in one of the most infamous works of modern antisemitism, the *Protocols of the Elders of Zion*. The *Protocols*, which was published in Russian in 1903 and soon afterward circulated in many lands and languages, is a fabrication that purports to describe the minutes of a meeting of Jewish leaders (the "Elders of Zion"). In this meeting they discuss how they have managed, through cunning and careful planning, to put the world into the hands of the Jews.[7]

> Our call of "Liberty, equality, and fraternity" brought whole legions to our ranks from all four corners of the world through our unconscious agents, and these legions carried our banners with ecstacy (*sic*). In the meantime these words were eating, like so many worms, into the well-being of the Christians and were destroying their peace, steadfastness and unity, thus ruining the foundations of the States. As we shall see later on, it was this action which brought about our triumph. It gave us the possibility among other things of playing the ace of trumps—namely, the abolition of privileges; in other words, the existence of the Gentile aristocracy, which was the only protection nations and countries had against ourselves. On the ruins of natural and hereditary aristocracy we built an aristocracy of our own on a plutocratic basis. We established this new aristocracy on wealth, of which we had control, and on science promoted by our scholars. Our triumph was rendered easier by the fact that we, through our connections with people who were indispensable to us, always worked upon the most susceptible part of the human mind, namely, by playing on our victims' weakness for profits, on their greed, on their insatiability, and on the material requirements of man. . . .
>
> Do not imagine that our assertions are empty words. Note here the success of Darwin, Marx and Nietzsche prearranged by us. The demoralising effect of the tendencies of these sciences on the Gentile mind should certainly be obvious to us.

The plot alleged by the *Protocols* is truly breathtaking: the Jews are the unseen puppet masters behind the French Revolution, the theory of evolution, Communism, and nihilism. The basic claim of the passage is that the breakdown of traditional society in Christian Europe was the work of the Jews. The Jews orchestrated the French Revolution, with its banner of "liberty, equality, and fraternity," because it served them as a weapon against the gentile aristocracy

7. I quote from the first English edition, *The Jewish Peril: Protocols of the Learned Elders of Zion* (London: Eyre & Spottiswoode, 1920), 7–8, 9–10.

that was the bulwark of the traditional social structure. Having broken the latter, the Jews could construct a new society structured by distinctions of wealth, in which the Jews would reign supreme. They were aided in this plan not only by the alluring lie of equality, but also by other modern intellectual innovations that undermined foundational Christian principles: Nietzsche's contention that Christian morality has a genealogy (i.e., is an invention); Darwin's claim that the natural world we see around us is the immediate result of evolution rather than divine providence; and Marx's insistence that religion is a means of dulling the minds of the masses and hiding from them the fact that their alleged betters are appropriating and alienating them from the work of their hands.

The association of Jews with money in this passage is a legacy, in part, of the economic circumstances of Jews in medieval Christendom, which we were not able to trace in the above hurried survey. In any case, the basic posture of the *Protocols* toward the Jews as dangerous outsiders should be familiar enough. Here we see how the traditional image of the Jew as the scheming Christ-killer, as the implacable enemy of Christianity, morphed into the antisemitic image of the Jew as the enemy of traditional society. This image, and the *Protocols* itself, exert their influence even today. For example, the book is cited as a reliable window into the plans of the "Zionists" in the 1988 charter of Hamas (article 32).

When we turn from modern antisemitism in general to the Holocaust in particular, and especially Nazism, the genealogical relationship to Christian anti-Judaism becomes more complicated, because Nazi Germany was in many ways a very inhospitable and indeed a dangerous place for traditional Christianity. The Barmen Theological Declaration of 1934, which the great Protestant theologian Karl Barth helped to frame, and which rejected Nazi totalitarianism as incompatible with Christian political theology, is one of many expressions of this fact, as is Barth's compelled departure from Germany in 1935. The United States Conference of Catholic Bishops, in its 2001 *Catholic Teaching on the Shoah*, goes so far as to claim that, "to create its Third Reich, conceived as a millennium of Aryan domination over the entire earth, the Nazi regime, in its ideology, quite rightly saw that it would have to destroy all memory of divine revelation by destroying first the Jews and then the church. Only by eliminating the moral inhibitions of Judaism and Christianity from the European conscience would Nazism be able to recreate humanity in its own warped racist image and likeness."[8] This formulation surely goes too far, both because it elides the dramatic differences between Nazi attitudes toward the Jews and the church, and because it does not acknowledge that organized church life persisted in areas under Nazi control, under leaders who not only preached obedience to the governing power but in some cases taught a gospel that purported to be largely compatible with Nazi ideology. Nevertheless, it is clear enough that the immediate sources of the Nazis' racial, pseudo-scientific Jew-hatred were different from and in fundamental ways contrary to traditional Christian teaching about Jews and Judaism. At the same time, however, continuities, first and foremost in the identification of the Jew as the ultimate Other, are just as obvious. Ultimately, the Christian teaching of contempt must be understood as a necessary though by no means a sufficient condition for the emergence of Nazi antisemitism.

In thinking through the relationship between Christian anti-Judaism and the Holocaust, we must consider not only the Nazis who perpetrated the Holocaust but also the collaborators and bystanders who helped to enable it, both within Germany and far beyond it, most of whom either were themselves Christian or were shaped by a Christian world. It is important to underscore, in this connection, that having discerned a basic continuity, with differences, between modern antisemitism and premodern Christian anti-Judaism, we should not suppose that Christian anti-Judaism dissipated in modernity and was *replaced* by antisemitism. While the advent of modernity moderated some forms of Christian anti-Judaism in some places, the teaching of contempt continued robustly up to and through the Holocaust, and we cannot escape the conclusion that the Christian teaching of contempt directly and indirectly impacted the action and inaction of Christian collaborators and bystanders. The *Catholic Teaching on the Shoah* document does not go far enough when it ventures that "the polemical teachings of the Church Fathers against Judaism that began in the second century . . . and the severe persecutions of Jews that so marred the second millennium were so pervasive over time that the consciences of twentieth-century Christians were 'lulled,'" but surely it is correct as far as it goes.

The above summary statements are not intended as judgments against particular people or institutions. Such judgments can and should sometimes

8. https://www.usccb.org/resources/catholic-teaching-shoah-implementing-holy-see-s-we-remember-2001.

be made, but each case must be considered on its own, in light of its specific circumstances, with due acknowledgment of the risks entailed by a possible act of resistance and the question of the prospect of effectiveness. A comprehensive accounting must also, of course, take cognizance of the heroism of those who did act. The great deeds of André Trocmé, the Protestant pastor of the southern French town of Le Chambon-sur-Lignon, and of his wife Magda, are well-known, and deserve retelling, as do many other portraits of courage, but I will take up here a story of particular relevance for Jewish memory of the Holocaust. The Vilna Ghetto was one of the first sites of organized Jewish resistance to the Nazis. One of the resistance leaders there, Abba Kovner, offered inspiration for this and other ghettos when he issued a pamphlet in the winter of 1941/42 urging Jews not to go "as sheep to the slaughter," but to fight. Armed Jewish resistance against the Nazis came to play an enormously important role in the collective memory of the Holocaust in the first decades of the state of Israel, which saw in it, amid the devastation, a glimmer of the new Israeli Jew, willing and ready to defend himself. Israel in fact fixed its Holocaust Remembrance Day to the date on which the largest of the uprisings broke out, in the Warsaw Ghetto. It is therefore especially striking that an instrumental role in the Vilna Ghetto uprising was played by a nun.

Anna Borkowska was mother superior to a small group of Dominican nuns in a convent close to the Vilna Ghetto. As Avrom (Abraham) Sutzkever, the great Yiddish poet and a Holocaust survivor, tells it in his 1946 memoir, Borkowska opened the convent to Kovner and other resistance leaders, dressing the men in nun's habits when searches occurred. "It was in this very convent that our comrades came up with the idea of organizing armed resistance in the ghetto."[9] It also fell to Borkowska to become an arms supplier, when she provided Kovner with specially assembled grenades—the first grenades obtained by the resistance—and instructed him in their use. She told Kovner, on Sutzkever's report: "I want to join you in the ghetto. I want to fight and die alongside you. Your battle is sacred. You are noble warriors. And even though you are a Marxist and not religious, you have a God, and your God is great. You are closer to Him than I am at this moment. May God be with you!"

9. Abraham Sutzkever, *From the Vilna Ghetto to Nuremberg: Memoir and Testimony*, ed. and trans. Justin D. Cammy (Montreal and Kingston: McGill-Queen's University Press, 2021), 144.

Conclusion

Within the Catholic Church, as among Christians more broadly, the crucible of Nazism helped to crystallize among a growing number of theologians a nascent sense of identification with the Jewish people. Henri de Lubac, a French Jesuit priest who bristled against the institutional church's deep engagement with the Vichy regime, insisted in a 1941 essay that circulated clandestinely in wartime France that the Jewish foundation of Christianity "places, between Israel and us Christians, a first bond of solidarity."[10] De Lubac would go on to play an important role in Vatican II, the ecumenical Catholic Church council that, through *Nostra Aetate*, declared its opposition to antisemitism, and rejected the notion that the Jewish people are collectively responsible for the killing of Christ. In the same essay from 1941 de Lubac nevertheless continued to espouse economic supersession, and *Nostra Aetate*'s teaching on Jews and Judaism is ambiguous on this issue. However, as we will see in the next chapter, voices in the church today have come unequivocally to reject not only punishment supersession, but economic supersession.

Further Inquiry

A helpful overview of the Jewish experience in the Middle Ages, with comparison of Christendom and the Muslim world, is Mark R. Cohen, *Under Crescent & Cross: The Jews in the Middle Ages* (Princeton: Princeton University Press, 2008). For the perspective of Pope Gregory I in the context of a broad survey of the ways in which medieval Christendom formulated and put in practice a notion of Jewish service on behalf of Christianity, see Anna Sapir Abulafia, *Christian-Jewish Relations 1000–1300: Jews in the Service of Medieval Christendom* (New York: Routledge, 2025). Magda Teter surveys the histories of the blood libel and the charge of host desecration in *Blood Libel: On the Trail of an Antisemitic Myth* (Cambridge: Harvard University Press, 2019) (where the above observation about Julius Streicher occurs, at 200), and *Sinners on Trial: Jews and Sacrilege after the Reformation* (Cambridge: Harvard University Press, 2011). Teter's most recent

10. The translation is from Sarah Shortall, *Soldiers of God in a Secular World: Catholic Theology and Twentieth-Century French Politics* (Cambridge: Harvard University Press, 2021), 132.

book, *Christian Supremacy: Reckoning with the Roots of Antisemitism and Racism* (Princeton: Princeton University Press, 2023), argues for continuities between the ideologies of Christian anti-Judaism and Christian racism. Careful studies of the church under Nazism confirm but also complicate the notion of Christianity as a target of Nazism. See, for example, Kevin Spicer's *Resisting the Third Reich: The Catholic Clergy in Hitler's Berlin* (De Kalb: Northern Illinois University Press, 2004), and *Hitler's Priests: Catholic Clergy and National Socialism* (Ithaca: Cornell University Press, 2008); Susannah Heschel, *The Aryan Jesus: Christian Theologians and the Bible in Nazi Germany* (Princeton: Princeton University Press, 2008); Robert P. Ericksen, *Complicity in the Holocaust: Churches and Universities in Nazi Germany* (Cambridge: Cambridge University Press, 2012). For a collection of Jewish and Christian reflections on the Holocaust, see Michael L. Morgan, *A Holocaust Reader: Responses to the Nazi Extermination* (Oxford: Oxford University Press, 2001). A recent, wide-ranging collection of papers on antisemitism can be found in Scott Ury and Guy Miron, *Antisemitism and the Politics of History* (Waltham, MA: Brandeis University Press, 2024).

●

1. In Chaucer's *Canterbury Tales*, the prioress tells a blood-libel story. A seven-year-old boy, a widow's son, took great pains to learn a hymn in praise of Mary, "Alma Redemptoris Mater." Hearing him singing the hymn as he walked in his innocence through the Jews' street, the Jews, urged on by "the serpent Sathanas, that hath in Jewes herte his waspes nest," became enraged, and plotted to kill him. This they did, and cast his body in a sewer pit. Whereon the prioress addresses the Jews: "Oh cursed folk of new Herods, / What may your evil intent avail you? / Murder will come out, certainly, it will not fail, / And especially where the honor of God shall spread; / The blood cries out on your cursed deed."[11] Chaucer appears to evoke the story of Cain and Abel, but links it to another biblical story, from the New Testament. Which one? Consult, too, the very beginning of the prologue to the tale (ll. 453–59), and read these lines against Psalm 8; how does the allusion

11. I quote from Harvard's Geoffrey Chaucer website (https://chaucer.fas.harvard.edu/pages/prioress-prologue-and-tale), ll. 574–78. In the original, likewise from the website: "O cursed folk of Herodes al newe,/ What may youre yvel entente yow availle?/ Mordre wol out, certeyn, it wol nat faille,/ And namely ther th'onour of God shal sprede,/ The blood out cryeth on your cursed dede."

implicitly construct the Jews? Reflect on the way in which a certain postulate, in this case, the bloodthirsty, Christ-hating Jew, once integrated into the interpretive tradition, can propagate throughout the Bible.

2. In addition to and intersecting with its implications for the church's anti-Jewish teachings, the Holocaust challenged the church to consider its relationship to society. Should the church serve as an ark, a space to shelter from a sinful world, or must it rather seek to make the world better through active engagement with it? The Holocaust seems clearly to teach the importance of the latter, and yet it also teaches how wrong the church can go when it entangles itself in politics. Consider, for example, the "Aryan paragraph" through which the German Protestant Church excluded Jewish Christians from the clergy. While many church leaders, including, perhaps most famously, Dietrich Bonhoeffer, opposed the paragraph, another theologian of great repute, Adolf Schlatter, did not oppose it. "In this hour," he said, "it is more important to maintain community with our German comrades than with the Jewish Christians."[12] What, then, is the lesson? Might one say that the church should engage with the world, but with wariness about aligning itself with regnant political ideologies? That it must, in short, indeed engage in politics, but only on its own terms? We will return to this topic briefly in chapter 17 in connection with liberation theology.

12. See James E. McNutt, "A Very Damning Truth: Walter Grundmann, Adolf Schlatter, and Susannah Heschel's *Aryan Jesus*," *Harvard Theological Review* 105 (2012): 288–89.

— Chapter 5 —

Paul and the Irrevocable Gifts

THE LATECOMER APOSTLE PAUL FAMOUSLY SAID: "I have become all things to all people, that I might by all means save some" (1 Cor. 9:22). Paul did indeed save some, indeed many, as he understood the need for and the means of saving; no less did he become all things to all people. Each person and her Paul; the number and variety of attempts to make sense of Paul's theology can hardly be counted. This chapter is devoted to contemporary Christian teaching on the question of economic supersession, but because this question is so closely bound up with the problem of how to understand Paul, the chapter is as much about Paul. We will first work through the new ways in which modern scholarship has approached the interpretation of Paul's writings in their original historical context, and we will examine, in this light, Romans 9–11, the chapters in which Paul most directly grapples with the fact that most Jews do not accept Jesus as the messiah. Then we will observe how, in tandem with the new scholarly approaches to Paul and especially to Romans 9–11, the Catholic Church, alongside other forms of Christianity, has come today to reject economic supersession. Finally, we will consider two sets of questions that emerge in the wake of this new perspective. The first concerns the interpretation of the Bible in the post-supersessionist church, while the second revisits the traditional dogmatic stances of the church on the ritual law and on evangelizing Jews.

Approaches to Paul from Antiquity to Today

Paula Fredriksen helpfully distinguishes among three ways of thinking about Paul's relationship to Judaism.[1] The first, which she dubs "Paul *against*

1. Paula Frederiksen, "Paul and Judaism," in *The Jewish Annotated New Testament*, ed. Amy-Jill Levine and Marc Zvi Brettler (Oxford: Oxford University Press, 2017), 633–37.

Judaism," is assumed in the traditional teaching of economic supersession. On one version of this approach, when Paul, who had persecuted the church, experienced his famous vision of Jesus on the road to Damascus, he converted from Judaism to Christianity, accepting Christ in place of the law. A proponent of this approach might find his transformation expressed in his two given names, Paul and Saul: He began as a Jewish man with a Hebrew name, Saul, but set this identity aside on the road to Damascus, and took on a new identity as a Christian with a new, gentile (Latin) name, Paul. But this approach is deeply false to Paul's own self-understanding. In the first place, no change of name occurred; presumably the apostle, like many Jews of his day, was given two names at birth, a Hebrew one and a vernacular one, and he would have used them either interchangeably or in different social contexts, and in just the same way after his visionary experience as before. More fundamentally, Paul's transformation did not involve leaving Judaism, nor taking on something called Christianity. The Paul who was Christ's apostle continued to identify himself as a Jew on numerous occasions, and he did not know the word "Christianity."

But, as we noted in chapter 3, Paul does seem to reject the law as a means of salvation and labors to establish that gentiles who have been baptized into Christ should not be circumcised. How are we to construe these facts, if not as a mark of abandoning Judaism? Modern scholars have underscored a key fact about Paul's letters, and his own self-understanding: he takes himself to be Christ's apostle to the gentiles specifically, and it is to them that he writes. On the approach that Fredriksen labels "Paul *and* Judaism," Paul should be understood as envisioning two distinct paths toward salvation, one for Jews and another for gentiles. Christ has come for the gentiles, and therefore they should not adopt the law. Jews, however, have no need of Christ, and should continue to observe the ritual law. But this approach likewise fails, because, although Paul does indeed address himself chiefly to gentiles, he very clearly insists, as we shall see, that Jews, too, cannot be saved except through Christ.

As different as these two approaches are, they share the assumption that Paul's theology centers on the distinction between Jews, on the one hand, and gentile Christ worshipers (or for short, Christians), on the other. On the approach of "Paul *against* Judaism," the Jews adhere to Judaism, and are damned, while Christians are saved. The approach of "Paul *and* Judaism" maintains that both groups are saved, but through fundamentally different methods: the Jews through the ritual law and Christians through Christ. A substantial contingent of modern Pauline scholars, who adopt a third approach, "Paul *within* Judaism," take this assumption to be fundamentally mistaken, an error arising from a version of what psychoanalysts call the "narcissism of small differences." The narcissism of small differences is the tendency to make much of the minor points of deviation between two closely related groups, precisely because they are so hard to distinguish. As a result of the effort invested in distinguishing the two groups, one ends up thinking of these groups as worlds apart, and one misses the fact that they are in fact much closer to each other than either of them is to other groups. Because Paul's extant letters devote so much space to clarifying how gentile Christ worshipers should and should not act like the Jewish people, the adherents of the first two approaches end up supposing that the dividing line that matters most for Paul is that between gentile Christ worshipers and the Jews.

On the approach of "Paul *within* Judaism," we cannot understand Paul unless we take a step backward and appreciate that, for Paul and his peers, the differences between gentile Christ worshipers and the Jews were dwarfed by a contrast that would have been far more immediately prominent in the Roman context, between those who worship the God of Israel exclusively, and the overwhelmingly larger number of pagans who worship many gods. For Fredriksen and many other modern scholars, the church, for Paul, consists in its ideal form of the Jewish people, who worship the God of Israel, together with the gentiles who have joined them in such worship. The contrast that defines Paul's thought is between the church, so defined, and pagan polytheists. All those within the church, Jewish and gentile, attain to salvation through Christ, who defeats the conditions of sinfulness and death that human beings are heir to as Adam's offspring, and draws the blessings of Abraham upon the gentiles by making them Abraham's children in the spirit. Christ does not erase the distinction between the Jews and the gentiles in the church, though he does narrow it. Jews who reject Christ find themselves more or less outside the church, alongside pagan gentiles who do not know Christ and worship other gods, but such Jews still have one foot inside the church because they do, after all, worship the God of Israel exclusively.

Reading Romans 9–11

Let us try to make sense of Paul's words in Romans 9–11 through the lens of the "Paul within Judaism" approach. Paul in these chapters puts his argument through many turns, and we will misunderstand him if we do not hear him through to the end. He begins by identifying with the Jewish people, and expressing sympathetic anguish at their failure, in the main, to recognize Christ. "I could wish that I myself were accursed and cut off from Christ for the sake of my own brothers and sisters, my own flesh and blood. They are Israelites, and to them belong the adoption, the glory, the covenants, the giving of the law, the worship, and the promises; to them belong the patriarchs, and from them, according to the flesh, comes the Christ, who is over all, God blessed forever" (9:3–5).

But then Paul seems immediately to dissociate himself from the Jewish people. God's promises to the Jews, he says, should not be understood to have failed, because in fact "not all those descended from Israel are Israelites. . . . It is not the children of the flesh who are the children of God, but the children of the promise are counted as descendants" (9:6–8). Paul connects the Jewish people's failure to their insistence on holding fast to the law: "Gentiles, who did not strive for righteousness, have attained it, that is, righteousness through faith; but Israel, who did strive for the law of righteousness, did not attain that law. Why not? Because they did not strive for it on the basis of faith but as if it were based on works" (9:30–32). More strikingly still, Paul seems to insist that, with Christ's coming, nothing survives of God's treasured relationship with the Jews; rather, "there is no distinction between Jew and Greek; the same Lord is Lord of all and is generous to all who call on him" (10:12).

Paul will not let the matter end at that, however. For Paul, the Jewish people in fact represent a distinct and indeed foundational category in the economy of salvation. If one thinks of the economy of salvation on the model of the cultivation of an olive tree, says Paul, then the Jews represent the natural branches. The gentiles are branches of wild olive trees, but through baptism into Christ, they have been grafted into the cultivated olive tree. Jews who reject Christ have been broken off from that cultivated tree, but they can be grafted back in again, and more easily, in light of their pedigree, than the gentiles in the church. "For," Paul tells the gentiles in the church, "if you have been cut from what is by nature a wild olive tree and grafted, contrary to nature, into a cultivated olive tree, how much more will these natural branches be grafted back into their own olive tree" (11:24). God has hardened Israel's heart, says Paul, but with the intention of forgiving them, for God says that "this is my covenant with them" (11:27). Ultimately, the Jewish people are "beloved for the sake of their ancestors; for the gifts and the calling of God are irrevocable" (11:28–29).

One might wonder, reading Paul's stirring words in Romans 11, how a tradition of Christian anti-Judaism of the sort reflected in the words of Justin, Melito, and Augustine could ever have gotten off the ground. How could various Christian theologians across the ages have preached punishment supersession against a people "beloved" of God, or economic supersession in the face of Paul's insistence that God's gifts are not subject to revocation?

But it isn't really so hard to imagine. In a church that had become entirely gentile, it would have been easy to construe Paul's anguished concern for his Jewish brothers and sisters as mere atavistic sympathy, of biographical rather than theological import. And really, what does Paul promise the Jewish people here? What does God's love for Abraham's descendants amount to? What is the content of God's covenantal commitment to them? Nothing more—so one might read Paul—than a promise of forgiveness should the Jews repent and accept Christ, and an assurance that at some point in the future some Jews will indeed repent, and be grafted back by God into the olive tree of salvation. But the Jews of today, who reject Christ, are broken branches that must bear the brunt of God's anger. Or they should be compelled to abandon their disbelief and become Christian. This is an available construal of Romans 11. And for an interpreter inclined to read Paul in light of other, darker statements in the New Testament about (to all appearances) the Jewish people, like Matthew 27:25 ("Then the people as a whole answered, 'His blood be on us and on our children!'") or John 8:44 ("You are from your father the devil, and you choose to do your father's desires"), this cramped account of Romans 11 follows quite straightforwardly.

But Romans 11 can be read very differently. Paul does seem to insist that the Jewish people are beloved, *now*, despite the fact that they have rejected Christ. After all, why should God be willing to forgive them in the future if God did not still love them now? And does not Paul's readiness to identify with his fellow Jews speak as well to God's love for them in the present? Paul often (e.g., 1 Cor. 11:1) admonishes his audience to imitate him. Should not a Christian approach the Jewish people, as Paul does, with a sense of sympathy and affection?

Already in the nineteenth century among some Protestant churches, and in the wake of *Nostra Aetate* for the Catholic Church, this alternative reading of Paul, and with it, a warmer approach to the Jewish people, came to prevail. Among the many expressions of this approach we might note Pope Francis's apostolic exhortation from 2013, *Evangelii Gaudium*, in which he declares (citing Rom. 11:29): "We hold the Jewish people in special regard because their covenant with God has never been revoked, for 'the gifts and the call of God are irrevocable'" (section 247). In the continuation, he characterizes the Jews as "the people of the covenant," and insists that the covenant bears fruit even now. "God continues to work among the people of the Old Covenant and to bring forth treasures of wisdom which flow from their encounter with his word" (section 249). These statements represent an unambiguous rejection of the notion of economic supersession.

Which of these readings of Paul is the better one? The answer to this question depends, of course, on what one means by "better." If by "better" we mean "kinder," then surely the new reading is better. If by "better" we mean "truer to Paul's original intent," then the new reading is also better, though this judgment comes with qualifications, to which we will turn in the next paragraph. Depending on one's theological method, these considerations—kindness and faithfulness to the original intent—can play a lesser or greater role in evaluating a line of interpretation, though neither can be determinative in itself, and perhaps not even in combination.

Why do I say that the claim that the new reading is more faithful to Paul's original intent must be qualified? The qualification lies in the yawning chasm between Paul's world and ours, and between his church and the church of today, in general but also in two particularly salient respects. First, in Paul's time, even though most Jews were not Christ followers, most Christ followers were Jews. For Paul, following Christ was an undertaking that marked one as Jewish (or Jew-adjacent); he could not conceive of a world in which Christ following specifically marked one as *not* Jewish. Second, Paul believed that the end of the world—the end of history as we know it—was nigh. In an early letter (1 Thess. 4:16–17) he even ventured that the resurrection of the dead would come in his own lifetime. "The Lord himself will come down from heaven, with a loud command, with the voice of the archangel and with the trumpet call of God, and the dead in Christ will rise first. After that, we who are still alive and are left will be caught up together with them in the clouds to meet the Lord in the air; and so we will be with the Lord forever." If the eschaton did not press on Paul quite as urgently by the time he wrote his letter to the church in Rome, he surely still did not imagine that the breaking off of the olive tree's natural branches—the Jews' general rejection of Christ—was a circumstance that might persist for generations and indeed millennia. He took it to be but a transitory state, after the fashion of the psalmist: "For his anger is but for a moment; his favor is for a lifetime" (Ps. 30:5). Paul did not have to grapple with the question of how, if at all, God's love for Abraham's children according to the flesh might find expression across centuries, as the Jewish people, living apart from the church, wended their own theological way. We simply cannot say with certainty whether a modern Paul would construe God's irrevocable covenant as Augustine did, to signify no more than a future in which the Jews would accept Christ and be accepted back into God's grace, or as the Catholic Church and many other Christians do today, to signify a loving, still fruitful relationship, in spite of Israel's rejection of Christ.

The Open Question of Reading Scripture

The full-throated rejection of economic supersession, the warm embrace of Jews and Judaism that we find in *Evangelii Gaudium* and in many other statements issued by the Catholic Church and other Christian denominations, raises substantial theological questions. The first set of questions that I wish to take up, but only briefly, concerns the Bible: How should the church read the Bible today? Which prevalent interpretive reflexes must it sideline or even condemn as inimical to its new understanding of the Jewish people and the church's relationship to it? To what methodological approaches should it assign new emphasis as corollaries of this new understanding? In what ways should the church approach verses in the New Testament that seem or in any case can readily be construed to support punishment or economic supersession, or to demonize Jews?

I will focus here on the relationship between the Old Testament and the New. The calibration of this relationship can go "wrong" in two opposing directions, among others, with negative consequences for Christian theology as such, and in particular for Christianity's self-positioning with respect to Jews and Judaism. On the one hand, it is possible to assimilate the Old Testament too much to the New Testament, to suppose that the significance of the Old Testament lies in the ways in which it points forward to Jesus, and that it exhausts its significance through such pointing. This tendency creates two interrelated problems. First, it overlooks the great themes of the Old Testament—the creation of the world, divine providence, election, covenant, and so forth—that constitute the shared patrimony of Jews and Christians, and that testify to their common bond. Second, it implicitly revives a foundational principle of traditional anti-Judaism, a point trenchantly made in the Pontifical Biblical Commission's magisterial treatment of the topic at hand.

> It would be wrong to consider the prophecies of the Old Testament as some kind of photographic anticipations of future events. All the texts, including those which later were read as messianic prophecies, already had an immediate import and meaning for their contemporaries before attaining a fuller meaning for future hearers. The messiahship of Jesus has a meaning that is new and original. . . . [E]xcessive insistence, characteristic of a certain apologetic, on the probative value attributable to the fulfilment of prophecy must be discarded. This insistence has contributed to harsh judgements by Christians of Jews and their reading of the Old Testament: the more reference to Christ is found in Old Testament texts, the more the incredulity of the Jews is considered inexcusable and obstinate.[2]

To conceive of the Old Testament as a set of signs loudly signifying Christ is to suggest that the Jews' rejection of Jesus can only be explained as a manifestation of willful blindness. Christianity indeed insists that Christ represents the fulfillment of the Old Testament, but the concept of fulfillment must be understood in a nuanced and non-reductive way.

On the other hand, it is possible to go wrong by reading the New Testa-

2. *The Jewish People and Their Sacred Scriptures in the Christian Bible* (Vatican: Libreria Editrice Vaticana, 2002), section 21. The document is also available online: https://www.vatican.va/roman_curia/congregations/cfaith/pcb_documents/rc_con_cfaith_doc_20020212_popolo-ebraico_en.html.

ment as standing against the Old. Of course, the church must suppose that Christ's coming achieves something vital and new, and it is reasonable and inevitable that this novum be clarified by comparison with God's relationship with the world prior to Christ's coming, as articulated in the Old Testament. But the ever-looming threat, which persists for the post-supersessionist church, is what Catholic theologian Philip Cunningham calls the "oppositional imagination," the instinct to set the Jews and their Bible in opposition to the church and the New Testament, to suppose that "it is in the fundamental nature of Judaism and Christianity to be opposed to one another." Among the many instantiations of this instinct that Cunningham collects, we may note the following example, from a recent Catholic textbook: "Jesus driving out the money-changers . . . spoke to his challenging the old and corrupt sacrificial system, abolishing all sacrifice but the one he was about to make."[3]

As this example indicates, and as Cunningham and others underscore, the correction of these two opposing but ultimately similar tendencies, as well as other interpretive habits with similar consequences, cannot be an academic matter only. Christian educators in schools and churches can reasonably devote only a small portion of their time to direct treatment of the topic of Christianity's relationship to Judaism, but Scripture rightly pervades curricula, the liturgy, and homilies, so that anti-Jewish messages that implicitly arise from insufficiently careful readings of Scripture have the power to undermine and overwhelm discrete explicit expressions of pro-Jewish dogmatic commitments.

The Open Questions of Ritual Law and Mission

Let us turn now, in greater detail, to two interrelated questions that follow from Christian affirmation of the continuity of a loving covenantal relationship between God and Israel. The first one follows directly from our discussion in chapter 3: From a conceptual perspective, what does it mean for God's covenant to persist with Israel in a substantial, productive way when the ritual law, which is so central to that covenant as described in the Five Books of

3. Philip A. Cunningham, "Catholic-Jewish Relations in the USA Today: Past Progress, Present Problems, Promising Paths," *Ecumenical Trends* 53, no. 1 (January/February 2024): 13.

Moses, no longer has force? Or to frame the same question in more practical terms: Could it be that a church that rejects economic supersession should reconsider its traditional commitment to the desuetude of the ritual law?

Reflection on this question must return to Paul as a starting point. The church as envisioned by Paul consists, as we have noted above, of the Jewish people and the engrafted gentiles. Paul argues passionately that these engrafted gentiles should not be circumcised, nor, by extension, should they take on the ritual law in general. To do so would be to misunderstand Christ's significance, and perhaps, relatedly, to underestimate the gap between Jews and gentiles that Christ manages to bridge. What about the Jewish Christ followers in Paul's church? Did Paul envision them continuing to observe the ritual law or not? This question is surprisingly difficult to answer; if Paul was exercised by the status of the ritual law for Jewish Christ followers, the question hardly arises as such in his extant letters. I am inclined to think that he was rather indifferent on the matter. He probably assumed that Jewish Christ followers would continue in their Jewish way of life until the end time, not because it was necessary for their salvation—for salvation, Christ was necessary and sufficient—but simply because the inertia of this way of life would carry them along up until the very imminent end time.

Ultimately, the difficulty of interpreting Paul in his original context, and the gap between Paul's world and our own, means that historical reconstruction of Paul's positions on the ritual law can only serve as a starting point for theological reflection, rather than the last word. The canonical status of Paul's letters does appear to commit Christianity to a rejection of the salvific efficacy of the ritual law. But the rejection of economic supersession does open up limited possibilities for new thinking about the ritual law, in at least two ways.

First, it becomes easier to imagine Christians adopting some Jewish rituals as instantiations of biblical wisdom. Within a framework of economic supersession it is reasonable to treat the ritual law, with Augustine, as a set of symbols pointing to and thus fulfilled in Christ. But today the church might take a less overtly Christological approach to, for example, the dietary rules and the sabbath, and think of them simply as worthy practices giving expression to the notion of a divinely ordered creation. (We will explore the dietary rules and the sabbath in detail in chapters 7 and 11.) Just as Christians read the Old Testament as a source for creation theology, so they might consider refraining from shellfish, or resting for part of Saturday, to remind themselves of God's capacity as creator. Such practices could not be deemed generally obligatory for Christians; they acquire their obligatory status in the Bible from the role that they play in God's covenant with Israel, in which gentiles, Paul teaches, do not directly participate. But Christians could take guidance from them. Some Christians already do so, in limited ways: Seventh Day Adventists, for example, famously rest on the Jewish sabbath, and less famously, encourage adherence to the dietary rules of Leviticus.

The Jewish theologian Michael Wyschogrod takes this prospect of reevaluation of the ritual law in a post-supersessionist church one step further.[4] In an open letter to a Jewish friend who has converted to Catholicism, and who conceives of his conversion, in post-supersessionist fashion, not as an abandonment of his Jewish faith but as the fulfillment of it, Wyschogrod ventures that, as a Jewish convert to Catholicism, his friend should continue to observe the ritual law. Perhaps, indeed, the church should obligate him to do so. As noted above, Paul might supply some support for the notion that Jewish Christ followers are covenantally bound to observe the law, but the evidence from Paul is difficult to construe. Wyschogrod, however, advances a different argument for his suggestion, an argument that combines theology with sociology. He reasons as follows. The Catholic Church today no longer postulates or hopes for the disappearance of the Jewish people. On the contrary, it thinks of the church as ideally composed of Jews—Jews who continue to conceive of themselves as Jews—and of gentiles. But a Jewish convert to Catholicism who ceases to observe the ritual law, who behaves just like other, gentile Christians, will indeed become indistinguishable from the latter; for all practical purposes, for all that one can discern from the outside, he will cease to be Jewish. The post-supersessionist church should therefore call upon Jewish converts to Christianity to observe Jewish law. We might add: by the same logic, Jewish converts to Christianity should perhaps marry other Jewish converts, so as to ensure the perpetuation of the Jewish people within the church across generations.

The status of the Jewish convert in a post-supersessionist church takes us from the question of law to that of mission. Evangelizing—bringing the good news of Jesus Christ to those outside the Church—is a great Christian duty: "Go therefore," says the resurrected Jesus, "and make disciples of all nations,

4. Michael Wyschogrod, "Letter to a Friend," *Modern Theology* 11 (1995): 165–71.

baptizing them in the name of the Father and of the Son and of the Holy Spirit, and teaching them to obey everything that I have commanded you" (Matt. 28:19–20). Should Christians seek also to evangelize among Jews, as among other non-Christians? It might seem obvious that they should. It is true that Pope Francis can say, in *Evangelii Gaudium*, that "as Christians, we cannot consider Judaism as a foreign religion; nor do we include the Jews among those called to turn from idols and to serve the true God." But it is not enough, for Christianity, that Jews serve the true God, when they reject Christ. Christianity teaches that Christ saves all, and even if salvation is nevertheless possible for non-Christians, it is still better for everyone, Jews included, to worship Christ, the source of their salvation. We might take it as a given, then, that Christians should evangelize to Jews as much as to anyone else who does not worship Christ.

But this view has been contested in some circles. In 2015, a Vatican-sponsored institution, the Commission for Religious Relations with the Jews, commemorated the fiftieth anniversary of *Nostra Aetate* by issuing a document entitled "'The Gifts and the Calling of God are Irrevocable' (Rom 11:29)." The commission recognizes "the universal salvific significance of Jesus Christ and consequently the universal mission of the Church," but it insists on "a principled rejection of an institutional Jewish mission." Instead of a mission, with its institutional trappings, Christians should instead, in a more informal way, "bear witness" before Jews to their faith in Christ.

What is the logic of the committee's position? The document mentions "the great tragedy of the Shoah" as a reason for sensitivity, but its reluctance to missionize seems more than just an expression of good taste. Although the commission does not articulate its reasoning plainly, it seems that its starting point is the following theological insight: "It is and remains a qualitative definition of the Church of the New Covenant that it consists of Jews and Gentiles, even if the quantitative proportions of Jewish and Gentile Christians may initially give a different impression." Like Wyschogrod, the commission seems to recognize that a mission to convert the Jews cannot achieve what the post-supersessionist church hopes to achieve, namely, a church composed of gentiles and of Jews who identify as Jews. Even today, hardly less than in centuries past, for a Jew to convert to Christianity means in general for him to cease to be Jewish, if not in his own self-understanding, then in the eyes of others and, on a generational scale, in practice. From the perspective of a post-supersessionist church, theological principle no longer demands such a conclusion, but social reality—among Jews, and in the main, among Christians too—still does, for the most part. Given this social reality, a mission to the Jews becomes self-defeating for the church, because winning a Jew to Christianity means losing him to the Jewish people.

The question of the law and the question of mission thus coalesce around the issue of conversion from Judaism to Christianity. One might think of a post-supersessionist church, a church guided by the vision of a community of Jews and gentiles in Christ, as faced with two choices vis-à-vis these questions. The church could make it possible for Jews to live as Jews within the church, by establishing the expectation that Jewish Christians will constitute a community set apart, to a degree, from gentile Christians, probably by observance of the ritual law. Or it could refrain from missionizing Jews altogether, and leave it to God, in God's time, to manage the desired reconciliation of Jews and gentiles in Christ. The Catholic Church seems currently to embrace the latter approach. Arguably, however, the Catechism's relative brevity about the ritual law, a fact noted at the end of chapter 3, is the mark of an incipient gesture toward the former approach too. If the Catholic Church is not ready to adopt a new doctrinal approach to the ritual law, it will for the moment say little about the traditional Augustinian approach.

Beginning in the nineteenth century, Jews who espouse Jesus as the messiah sometimes have not become fully absorbed into existing churches, but have instead formed their own communities in which they combine elements of traditional Jewish observance with Jesus-worship. The rubric "Hebrew Christian" was common in the past for such Jews; today they typically identify instead as Jewish Christians or Messianic Jews. Messianic Jews constitute, in principle, precisely the sort of Jesus-worshiping Jewish community that the post-supersessionist church might embrace. But Messianic Judaism emerged within and in general still remains bound to evangelical Protestantism, so the Catholic Church has had little to do with it, while within Protestant Christianity itself it remains a marginal phenomenon. From the other side, Jewish communities of all sorts tend to treat Messianic Jews as pariahs. Hybrids are always fearsome things, but the opposition to them among Jews stems especially from their embrace of symbols and beliefs strongly linked to the historical persecution of Jews, and from concern over Messianic Jews' missionary intentions.

Conclusion

The rejection of both punishment and economic supersession among many modern Christian communities represents something of a leap of faith. One might compare it, in one respect, to a marriage. A marriage entails a commitment to stand with one's spouse even in the face of changes, challenges, and considerations not foreseen. While a contract aims to specify all eventualities, a commitment is constituted by the fact that one does not know what, precisely, one has committed to; commitments are by definition open-ended. Likewise, the post-supersessionist church's embrace of Jews and Judaism marks the foundation of a relationship whose contours cannot at present be specified in all respects. The question of Scripture and the question of ritual law and mission are two among many facing the post-supersessionist church. Later in the book we will take up another one: how to view the notion of a Jewish state in the land of Israel. The analogy to marriage also raises the question of how Jews have responded and should respond to the overtures of the post-supersessionist church. This question, too, we will take up later in the book.

A final question that will serve as the entry point into the next part of the book is: If the Jewish people persist in right (if also imperfect) relationship with God, in one sense or another, can Christians find God's revealed word in post-biblical Jewish theology? They can of course find wisdom there, as in any intellectual tradition, but might its teachings be construed as issuing more directly from God? Pope Francis in *Evangelii Gaudium* seems to take a step in this direction. Recall his words, quoted above: "God continues to work among the people of the Old Covenant and to bring forth treasures of wisdom which flow from their encounter with his word." He continues: "For this reason, the Church also is enriched when she receives the values of Judaism. . . . There exists . . . a rich complementarity which allows us to read the texts of the Hebrew Scriptures together and to help one another to mine the riches of God's word." Without resolving the question of the precise status of post-biblical Jewish theology for a post-supersessionist church, let us examine now how Jews have mined the riches of God's word.

Further Inquiry

For a recent attempt at a holistic account of Paul that engages with much contemporary scholarship on the subject, see Matthew Thiessen, *A Jewish Paul: The Messiah's Herald to the Gentiles* (Grand Rapids: Baker Academic, 2023). Detailed treatments of the turn in Catholic teaching on Judaism may be found in John Connelly, *From Enemy to Brother: The Revolution in Catholic Teaching on the Jews, 1933–1965* (Cambridge: Harvard University Press, 2012); Gavin d'Costa, *Catholic Doctrines on the Jewish People after Vatican II* (Oxford: Oxford University Press, 2019); Karma Ben-Johanan, *Jacob's Younger Brother: Christian-Jewish Relations after Vatican II* (Cambridge: Harvard University Press, 2022). In addition to God's covenant with the Jewish people, the ritual law, and mission, D'Costa's book considers how the Catholic Church ought to approach the state of Israel, a topic we will turn to in chapter 17. Ben-Johanan's book also engages with modern developments in Jewish approaches to Christianity, a subject taken up in chapter 9. For an attempt to grapple with the question of supersessionism from the perspective of Messianic Jewish theology, see Mark S. Kinzer, *Postmissionary Messianic Judaism: Redefining Christian Engagement with the Jewish People* (Grand Rapids: Brazos, 2005).

●

1. For one of the Sundays in Ordinary Time, the Catholic lectionary pairs an Old Testament reading about the laws of leprosy (Lev. 13:1–2, 44–46) with the story of Jesus healing the leper (Mark 1:40–45). Read through these texts. What might someone comparing these two passages infer about the relationship between the Old Testament and the New? For analysis of the lectionary in general from this perspective, see Michael Peppard, "Do We Share a Book? The Sunday Lectionary and Jewish-Christian Relations," *Studies in Christian-Jewish Relations* 1 (2005–2006): 89–102. Peppard discusses this particular case on page 99.

2. On the question of reading the Bible in a post-supersessionist framework, the analysis above is mainly concerned to identify potential pitfalls. But the church's turn also creates new interpretive opportunities. Consider, for example, the figure of Mary, mother of Jesus. She does not, of course, appear in the Old Testament, but in what ways does the Old Testament set the terms for the theological roles

that she plays? In what ways might the Old Testament help us understand her? In fact, the Christian tradition is rich with reflections on the connections between the Old Testament and the New, even in resolutely anti-Jewish texts, and these reflections can be rescued as sources of insight and as bridges to Judaism by a post-supersessionist church. Consider Chaucer's "Prioress' Tale," introduced in the "Further Inquiry" section at the end of the preceding chapter (and see there for bibliographic information). Before telling her tale, the prioress calls on Mary to aid her, in these words: "Oh mother Maiden, Oh generous maiden and Mother! / Oh bush unburned, burning in Moses' sight, / That ravished down from the Deity, / Through thy humility, the Ghost that alighted in thee, / By whose power, when he illuminated thy heart, / The Father's Wisdom was conceived, / Help me to tell it in thy reverence!"[5] To what biblical passage does the prioress allude? How does the prioress's interpretation of the passage put Mary in relation to Israel? For more on this topic, see Gary A. Anderson, "Mary in the Old Testament," *Pro Ecclesia* 16 (2007): 33–55, and for more of Anderson's approach to the question of Christian interpretation of the Old Testament, see his book, *Christian Doctrine and the Old Testament: Theology in the Service of Biblical Exegesis* (Grand Rapids: Baker Academic, 2017).

5. Lines 467–73. In the original: "O mooder Mayde, O mayde Mooder free! / O bussh unbrent, brennynge in Moyses sighte, / That ravyshedest doun fro the Deitee, / Thurgh thyn humblesse, the Goost that in th' alighte, / Of whos vertu, whan he thyn herte lighte, / Conceyved was the Fadres sapience, / Help me to telle it in thy reverence!"

— Chapter 6 —

Torah and Study

TORAH IS THE AIR THAT JUDAISM BREATHES, the water in which it swims. So Rabbi Akiva, the greatest of the early rabbis of the second century CE, described it when asked why he was teaching Torah to large crowds of people even though the Romans, who ruled in the land of Israel at the time, had forbidden the study of Torah. (The story—of dubious historicity, but meaningful nonetheless—is told in the Babylonian Talmud, Berakhot 61b.) I will tell you what it is like, he said. It is like a fox, who, proceeding along the riverbank and seeing fish fleeing fishermen's nets, suggests to them that they might be safer if they joined him on dry ground. They reply that, as dangerous as it is in the sea, they would face more peril still on land, outside their natural element (and in the company of the fox). Likewise me, reasoned Akiva: If my life is at risk now, when I am occupied in Torah, which is "your life and the length of your days" (Deut. 30:20), how much more so if I should abandon it. (Akiva was soon captured by the Romans, and died a martyr's death; we will return to the end of this story in chapter 13.)

Rabbi Akiva's parable is one of innumerable expressions in the rabbinic tradition of the notion that there is no Jewish life without Torah. What is Torah? The literal meaning of the word, which occurs numerous times in the Hebrew Bible, is "instruction"; the word is also often translated as "law." Recall from chapter 1 that rabbinic Judaism has a dual canon: the "written law," namely, the Hebrew Bible, and the "oral law," which coalesced in the corpus of works produced by the rabbis in late antiquity. In the narrowest usage, "the Torah" is the Pentateuch, the five books attributed to Moses and associated with Sinai. More broadly, "Torah" (typically thus, without the definite article) encompasses the entirety of the written law and the oral law. And while the rabbinic canon from late antiquity is the foundation of the oral law, the oral law does not end with the ancient rabbis. Their project of exposition of and elaboration on the written law extends forward to today in a continuous tradition in which the Jewish people as a whole participate. Innumerable commentaries, codifications, handbooks, legal responsa, homiletical works, and so forth have been composed over the centuries, and continue to be published in great numbers today. All these books, too, are Torah, and a typical Orthodox home today might have shelves of them.

Just as Torah extends forward until today, so it extends backward to the beginning of creation. A passage in the book of Proverbs portrays wisdom as a personified cosmic principle that declares that it (or she) was with God "at the first, before the beginning of the earth" (Prov. 8:23). The rabbis, heir to a tradition that extends at least to the book of Ben Sira in the second century BCE (see Sir. 24:23), identify this primordial Wisdom, which accompanied God at creation, with Torah. On this view, the words with which God brought the world into being in Genesis 1 are Torah, and the conversation of Torah students today belongs to the very same continuous, world-making and world-sustaining discourse. When early Christian texts like the prologue to the Gospel of John identify Wisdom, at God's side from the beginning, with Christ, they are working a turn on the same tradition.

Torah is something that one learns and teaches. As the translations "instruction" and "law" imply, this study is oriented toward action, toward performance of God's word in the world. But the orientation of Torah study toward practice does not render Torah study of mere instrumental value. On the contrary, the Jewish tradition tends strongly to idealize Torah study in itself, for itself, as the ultimate religious act. The following rabbinic text (Mishnah Pe'ah 1:1), integrated into the daily blessing over Torah study, is one of many expressions of this ideal: "These are things concerning which one consumes the interest in this world, while the principal remains for him in the world to come: honoring one's father and mother, acts of kindness, and bringing peace between a person and his fellow. But study of Torah is equal to them all." The passage conceptualizes the reward for doing these deeds in terms of investment principal and interest. A person who, for example, honors his parents, receives from God a certain quantum of reward, and this reward awaits him in the world to come, but he still has benefit from the reward in this world because God pays "interest" on it all the time he is alive, until he passes on to the world to come to claim the principal. All of the listed items have this special character, but Torah study, according to the passage, is exalted over the others.

This chapter will introduce the concept of Torah in Judaism generally, with a particular focus on Torah study. We will begin by working through David Hartman's "covenantal anthropology of Judaism," which finds in Torah study the fullest expression of a foundational principle of Jewish theology. We will then survey the basic features of the oral law, and, by way of example, work in detail through one specific passage from the Babylonian Talmud, the central work of the oral law.

Hartman's Covenantal Anthropology

David Hartman, an influential American-Israeli rabbi, philosopher, and institution-builder, was a student of Rabbi Joseph Dov Soloveitchik (1903–1993), the leader of American modern Orthodox Judaism in the twentieth century. Soloveitchik's thought is famous for its interest in the phenomenology of human experience and its emphasis on human beings' creative capacity. It is therefore not surprising that where one might expect a "theology" of Judaism, David Hartman's account of Judaism in his book, *A Living Covenant*, instead presents an "anthropology," that is, a theology that centers on and highlights the agency of human beings.[1]

For Hartman, the creation story establishes freedom as the characteristic feature of God. There is nothing prior to God that might constrain God; God wills and acts. For human beings to have been created in the image of God is for them to have been gifted by God with like freedom, even if this freedom cannot be the same as God's, precisely because it is a gift, a result of God's willed self-contraction. Human beings' freedom becomes manifest first, and most basically, in the choice that Adam and Eve must make whether to obey or disobey God's command. But such freedom is very limited, akin to that of a child vis-à-vis its parent. Hartman traces from this point, through the Bible and into the rabbinic period, a process of maturation, where the child grows older and more free. In relationship with God, human beings transform into

1. David Hartman, *A Living Covenant: The Innovative Spirit in Traditional Judaism* (Woodstock, VT: Jewish Lights, 1998).

something more like an adult child who has left the parental home, or even like a spouse.

The crucial turning point does not come with Noah, whose righteousness is realized chiefly in the Adamic form of obedience to God, but rather with Abraham. When God tells Abraham that God intends to destroy Sodom (Gen. 18), Abraham challenges the fairness of this decision. The contrast with Noah, who, informed of God's plan to annihilate all terrestrial life, accepts it as a given, highlights, for Hartman, Abraham's greater maturity in relationship to God. This greater maturity underlies, likewise, a momentous innovation: God enters into a covenant of mutual responsibility with Abraham, which obligates both God and Abraham, in the manner of a marriage. (God's earlier covenant with Noah, in Gen. 9, was not in fact with Noah alone, but with all life, and set obligations only on God.) The covenant at Sinai, between God and Abraham's descendants, represents a fuller flowering of this spousal relationship.

Rabbinic Judaism marks a further, critical stage in this development. "Whereas the Bible liberates the moral will, the Talmud liberates the intellect.... God's self-limiting love for human beings is expressed in His entrusting the elaboration and expansion of the Torah to rabbinic scholars." The oral law is dedicated to the interpretation of the written law through the application of human reasoning. By empowering human beings to interpret, and thus in effect to determine the content of, the law, God enables the fullest realization of mature, adult freedom.

Hartman highlights stories in the Babylonian Talmud that indicate profound rabbinic self-awareness of and celebration of the freedom that the Talmud's interpretive program enables. The most famous of these concerns the ritual status of a certain sort of oven assembled from parts, called the oven of Akhnai (Bava Metzi'a 59a–b). The majority of the sages rule that such an oven is subject to defilement like any other vessel, while Rabbi Eliezer deems it not subject to defilement. After failing to win the sages over to his side through reasoned argumentation, Eliezer turns to less conventional means of persuasion. He calls upon the nearby carob tree to prove him right, which it does, by uprooting itself. The sages are unimpressed: "One cannot bring evidence from a carob tree." Eliezer turns to a stream, and then to the walls of the academy in which they sit, with similar miraculous results, to which the sages retort in the same way. Eliezer then appeals to heaven, and indeed, a voice from heaven declares that his position is correct. Rabbi Joshua, the sages' representative, has a ready reply: "It is not in heaven," he says, quoting Deuteronomy 30:6, which in the story is taken to mean: "the Torah was already given at Sinai; we pay no heed to voices from heaven." The era of prophecy is over. Human beings have (in Hartman's terms) grown up. They have left the home and must make their own choices about how to live. Of course, this freedom is not freedom *from* God, but freedom *with* God. The rabbis who trust to their own reasoning about the law have not turned their back on God any more than an adult child abandons her parents when she makes a life independent from them. And of course, the rabbis do not construct their adult lives from the ground up. They do so through interpretation of and elaboration on divine revelation.

The great foil for Hartman's covenantal anthropology is mysticism. The mystic seeks to be dissolved into God. The mystic conceives of an underlying reality in which everything is God, in which God's self-constriction is shown to have been only apparent, and the human personality a mere figment of the mundane imagination. This mystical impulse, which we will take up in brief in chapters 14 and 15, has its own roots in traditional Judaism, and it should be clear that Hartman's position is only one of many Jewish theological voices. The fact that the story that Hartman tells is also an Enlightenment story, and a post-war twentieth-century American story, celebrating the principles of human reason, progress, and freedom, also cautions against construing Hartman as the unmediated voice of rabbinic normativity.

Nevertheless, and recognizing that I am formed by many of the same modern currents that shape Hartman's thought, I think it is fair to say that his covenantal anthropology does in fact capture a vitally important aspect of rabbinic thought, and thus of Jewish theology. This aspect of Jewish theology offers a fruitful occasion for comparison with Christian theology. And here, as we undertake our first such comparison, we will do well to clarify the limitations of the comparative enterprise as we will engage in it in this book. In light of space limitations that preclude attentiveness to the range of voices and nuances within each tradition, our comparisons should be understood as starting points for further reflection rather than summary conclusions.

The covenantal anthropology that Hartman identifies in rabbinic Judaism, especially in its elevation of Torah study, conceptualized as a project of the human intellect, presupposes a rather optimistic conception of human nature: human beings possess, as a general matter, the capacity to do well, to make good choices, to flourish as responsible, free decisionmakers. As creatures of God, they owe this capacity to God, but it belongs to their nature as human beings. Christianity tends to adopt a darker conception of human nature, though the shade varies according to denomination and theologian. In Catholicism, the doctrine of original sin supposes that human beings' capacity to choose rightly was fundamentally though not fatally impaired when Adam disobeyed God and ate from the tree of knowledge. The church comes to this conception of human nature through reflection on Christ; as the Catechism of the Catholic Church (section 407) puts it, the doctrine of original sin is "closely connected with that of redemption by Christ." It is precisely because human beings are "deprived of original holiness and justice" (section 404), and ruled by the devil, that Christ must come to save them. The view that human beings need saving from sin occurs even among Christian groups that do not adhere to the Catholic doctrine of original sin; it represents a legacy of the apocalyptic strain within the particular Jewish circles in the late Second Temple period from which Christianity emerged. In the apocalyptic worldview of these circles, Satan has ruled in the world from almost the very beginning, corrupting human beings, but the kingdom of God is now at hand. Soon the reign of the devil will come to an end in an "apocalyptic" battle between good and evil.

Apocalyptic elements are much more muted in the Judaism of the rabbis, who do not in general think of Adam's sin as having decisive implications for human beings' capacity to choose well. Adam's descendants confront the choice of heeding or disobeying God's word with the same inherent and untrammeled freedom as Adam himself possessed; they do not need to be saved by an outside force. The Catechism (section 406) contrasts the Catholic view of human nature with that articulated by Pelagius, who "held that man could, by the natural power of free will and without the necessary help of God's grace, lead a morally good life; he thus reduced the influence of Adam's fault to bad example." Pelagius's position, as summarized here, is more or less that of mainstream Judaism. This does not mean, of course, that human beings cannot sin; on the contrary, the rabbis and their heirs maintain a healthy respect for the potency of the "evil inclination." Nor does it mean the rejection of God's grace; God's grace underlies the gift of free will, and also finds expression in God's willingness to forgive human beings when they do sin.

The Nature and Content of the Oral Law

We have described the oral law in general terms, but given its decisive importance for Jewish theology, it behooves us to enter into it in more detail. Broadly, the foundational texts of the oral law, composed by the rabbis in the first few centuries of the Common Era, might be compared to the New Testament in Christianity, as both the rabbis' teachings and the New Testament represent supplements to and authoritative interpretations of what Judaism calls the Tanakh or the written law, and what Christianity calls the Old Testament. From a doctrinal perspective, however, the distinction between the written law and the oral law in Judaism tends to be received as a difference in kind, corresponding in some way or another to a difference in authority, with the written law, as a product of prophecy or divine inspiration, superior to the oral law. By contrast, the distinction between the Old Testament and the New Testament in Christianity marks instead, in the main, only a difference in time, between what was revealed first and what was revealed later, so that the New Testament is the same sort of thing as the Old Testament—God's revealed word—and carries the same sort of authority.

From this starting point, the better comparison, at least for certain forms of Christianity like Catholicism, is between rabbinic literature and patristic literature, the works of the early church fathers. These two corpora were composed in a non-prophetic mode, in roughly the same time and places, by figures who were, to a limited degree, aware of and even spoke to each other. But the rabbis arguably carry more authority in rabbinic Judaism than the church fathers in Catholicism, in that the rabbis' interpretation of biblical law cannot in general be controverted within traditional Judaism. In any case, the concept of tradition in Catholicism, as something distinct from Scripture, as the living faith of the church that works out the meaning of God's word across time, is especially close to the Jewish notion of oral law.

The foundational work of the oral law is the Mishnah, which reached its final form around the year 200 CE, in Roman Palestine. The Mishnah is dedicated to legal topics, to the clarification of what Jews must do, must not do, and may do. It divides into six "orders," each of which is further divided into tractates. The six orders concern, respectively, the laws of agriculture (e.g., the obligation to leave a corner of one's field unharvested, for the poor); the laws of the festivals; laws concerning women (e.g., levirate marriage, divorce); civil and criminal law; laws regarding sacrifices; and finally, ritual purity laws.

The subsequent centuries witnessed the compilation of two massive commentaries on the Mishnah, two Talmuds, one from each of the two main centers of rabbinic Judaism at the time. The Palestinian Talmud was completed around the end of the fourth century. The Babylonian Talmud, the product of the Jewish community living under Persian rule in modern-day Iraq, reached something like its final form roughly two centuries later. The rabbinic center in Babylonia achieved special prominence with the rise of Islam, and its Talmud became the core and pinnacle of Jewish education from the medieval period to today. One could fairly call the Babylonian Talmud the most important book in the history of Judaism, not as holy as the Bible but in certain respects more canonical. Below we will examine a passage from the Babylonian Talmud and describe how it has been studied in the past and today. Alongside the Mishnah and the two Talmuds, which are organized by legal topic, the rabbis also produced commentaries on all the five books of Moses, as well as on other parts of the Bible that were read in the synagogue on festival days.

As a whole, the rabbinic corpus is traditionally divided into two sorts of material: *halakhah* ("walking," though the etymological story is more complex) and *aggadah* ("telling"). Halakhah indicates, broadly, the law. Halakhah encompasses both "ritual laws," like the prohibition against doing work on the sabbath, and "moral laws," like the prohibition against theft. Both categories carry the same legal force and are elaborated using the same methods. The rabbis approach the halakhah as exegetes, identifying and explicating the various obligations, prohibitions, and rule-governed processes in the Bible. But they also come to the halakhah as jurists, seeking to produce a rational, comprehensive legal system. We will see how exegesis and legal reasoning combine in halakhic discourse in the extended case study below. Almost all the content of the Mishnah, and most of the content of the Talmuds, is halakhic. Some of the rabbis' biblical commentaries also have a halakhic focus.

Aggadah is everything that is not halakhah. It can include exegesis of biblical stories that do not have legal content, or even reflections on legal material that occur in a homiletical vein rather than for the purpose of clarifying the content of the law. Traditional theological topics—the nature of God, creation, providence, miracles, God's covenantal relationship with Israel, the afterlife, the messiah, and so forth—typically fall under the rubric of aggadah. The line between halakhah and aggadah is sometimes blurry, especially in connection with stories about rabbis, a genre that abounds in the Mishnah and the Talmuds. Despite this fuzziness, and even though the contrast between halakhah and aggadah finds explicit formulation only in later stages of the emergent rabbinic movement, it is present *in nuce* from the very beginning. Broadly, the core expertise of rabbis is and always was halakhic. The rabbis emerged from circles in the Second Temple period that held themselves out as ritual experts, and developments in their methods of reasoning suggest awareness of contemporaneous Roman jurists who were working out the principles of the empire's system of civil law.

The distinction between halakhah and aggadah thus encodes a hierarchy. Halakhah is more important within rabbinic Judaism than aggadah. The study of halakhah is more prestigious, more rigorous, more systematic, more high-stakes, than aggadah. We will enter further into this contrast in chapter 13; for now, we may note that the valorization of halakhah in the Jewish tradition suggests that the traditional Christian characterization of Judaism as legalistic has in it an important measure of truth. What this characterization, insofar as it is pejorative, misses, is that for Judaism, halakhah is shot through with theological meaning. The valorization of halakhah is premised on the notion that halakhah means walking with God, along paths that God, first and foremost through the Bible, has laid out. The halakhic system describes the world as it ought to be, what one might call the kingdom of God. One who studies it not only learns about and becomes configured to this kingdom, but gains the opportunity to configure it in turn through his or her own trained creative capacities.

A partial analogy to halakhah in Catholicism and certain other branches of Christianity is canon law, the internal legal system governing church matters. Like halakhah, it is genealogically connected to Roman law. Canon law is a specialized field with which the ordinary Christian rarely if ever directly engages. Many Catholic universities have departments of theology, with majors and minors and even required courses at the undergraduate level, but vanishingly few teach canon law, and then, only at the graduate level, typically only to students with professional aspirations in this field. Imagine if the situation were reversed. Imagine if the intellectual energy of the Catholic university were centered on canon law, and most or all undergraduates took courses in a department dedicated to it, not because they intended to become canon lawyers but because it was understood that knowledge of God is present in a special way in canon law as the framework within which the church operates in the world. The place of halakhah in Jewish intellectual life, in formal schooling and beyond, is something like this.

A Case Study from the Babylonian Talmud

In the traditional Jewish curriculum, a student begins at the elementary level with the Bible. He progresses afterward to the Mishnah, and then to the Babylonian Talmud, also known as the *Bavli* (Hebrew for "Babylonian") or simply the Talmud. One never gets past the Bavli; one only ever delves deeper into it. The sheer size of the Bavli is one reason that it looms so large in the Jewish curriculum. In the standard pagination—the invention of early printers, now employed throughout the Jewish world—the Bavli runs on so long that if one were to study a single page (both sides) per day, it would take roughly seven and a half years to complete. Beyond its size, what characterizes the Bavli is its complexity. The Bavli is written in a combination of Hebrew and Aramaic (a cousin of Hebrew), in a terse style replete with technical terms. It is not meant to be read like a novel, but rather to be pored over slowly. The notion of slow, careful progress might evoke the experience of a poem, but while poetry is characteristically read in a meditative manner, by oneself, the tradition calls for the Talmud to be studied ideally in pairs (though one can study it alone too). A pair of readers, called a *havruta* ("comradery" in Aramaic), might spend an hour reasoning through, probing, consulting the traditional commentaries on a short passage of only a few lines.

In the past, advanced education in the Bavli was confined to small cohorts of advanced students, all male. Today, thanks in part to changing gender norms and in part to the availability of translations and study aids, Talmud study is much more widespread, and, outside of ultra-Orthodox circles, girls and women also often enjoy the opportunity to engage in it. In a typical contemporary Orthodox day school (*yeshiva*, "session," pl. *yeshivot*), Talmud study begins in elementary school and continues throughout high school. In some ultra-Orthodox contexts, boys might spend half or more of their school day during high school studying Talmud. Between high school and college, modern Orthodox students in America often spend a gap year studying at a yeshiva in Israel, where they might devote eight or more hours per day to Talmud study. In limited ways in modern Orthodox circles and much more extensively in ultra-Orthodox circles, communities sponsor institutions called *kollelim* (sg. *kollel*) that enable young men to continue full-time intensive Talmud study for a few years after marriage.

For rabbi and layperson alike, Torah study is in principle a lifelong undertaking; it is not something from which one can or would wish to graduate. As an adult, a person might dedicate time in the evening after work, or part of the sabbath day, to study of the Bible with traditional commentaries, or the Mishnah or the Talmud, or a recent work on, say, Jewish medical ethics or the dietary laws. Such study can occur alone, or in a havruta, or in one of many classes typically offered within Jewish communities.

A popular form of regular adult Torah study today is *daf yomi* ("daily page"). The brainchild of ultra-Orthodox Jews of the 1920s, daf yomi is a means of literally putting all Jews worldwide on the same page in a project of collective study of the Babylonian Talmud. Each calendar day is dedicated to a particular page of the Talmud, so that it is completed every seven and a half years, at which point the cycle begins again. Thus, for example, on Sunday, September 3, 2023, the daf was the nineteenth page of Qiddushin, a tractate dedicated chiefly to the laws of marriage. We are in the midst of the fourteenth daf yomi cycle, which will end in June of 2027. At least a few hundred thousand Jews participated in the last study cycle, which came to a conclusion in January of 2020, marked by large celebratory gatherings and extensive media coverage. In an uncannily fruitful intersection of ancient tradition with modern habits of online communication and self-improvement routines, daf yomi has spawned hundreds of daily synagogue classes, even books and podcasts, devoted to the daf. A recent award-winning memoir by the author Ilana Kurshan is structured by her progress through daf yomi, and this cycle's daf is the subject of a popular TikTok series, *Daf Reactions*, with all the characteristic features of the genre, by artist and social media personality Miriam Anzovin.

Let us have a look inside the Babylonian Talmud. We will work through parts of a *sugya*—the Aramaic term for a sustained Talmudic discourse—stretching from the end of page 61 of tractate Yebamot to the beginning of page 62; all told the material constitutes the equivalent of roughly half a daily page. Tractate Yebamot in the Bavli is of course a commentary on tractate Yebamot in the Mishnah, which is dedicated to the passage in Deuteronomy 25:5–10 that describes the obligation of a man to marry the widow of his brother who dies childless, so that a child can be born who will carry on the deceased brother's name. In the course of its survey of these laws, the Mishnah enters into an ancillary question concerning bearing children. Here is the Mishnah text, quoted in Bavli Yebamot 61. (The English translation is my own. The interested reader can track down the Hebrew text with a different translation at www.sefaria.org. All of the classical rabbinic texts quoted in this book can be found on the same site.)

> A person may not abstain from being fruitful and multiplying until he has children. The house of Shammai says: two males. The house of Hillel says: male and female, as it says, "male and female he created them" (Gen. 5:2).

The Mishnah begins with an apparent allusion to Genesis 1:28, where God blesses the first human beings, telling them to "be fruitful and multiply, and fill the earth." As jurists, as lawyers, the rabbis, confronted by this verse, were faced with a choice: Should procreation be viewed merely as a religious value, a good thing, or should it be construed as a legal (or law-like) obligation? If it was to be construed as a legal obligation, then the Bible's vague exhortation had to be transformed into a real law, specifying in detail who is obligated, and how they satisfy their obligation. The rabbis chose this track, and the Mishnah, accordingly, takes up the scope of the obligation.

It is characteristic of halakhic discussion to feature debate. By taking up multiple facets of a question, debate brings its complexity to the fore. (Compare to Thomas Aquinas's dialectical method in his *Summa*.) Here, as often in the Mishnah, the debating parties are the "houses" (study circles) of Shammai and Hillel, which date to the end of the Second Temple period. The house of Shammai rules that a person satisfies the procreation obligation with two sons, while the house of Hillel instead names one son and one daughter as the standard. The house of Hillel supports its position by citing a prooftext: in Genesis 5:2, alluding to the creation story in Genesis 1, the Bible tells us that God created humankind male and female. The house of Hillel evidently reasons that when human beings work to "create" the next generation, they should each act like God, contributing a male and a female.

The Mishnah text immediately invites a question. The house of Hillel offers a prooftext for its position, but the house of Shammai does not. How, then, does the house of Shammai support its own position? The Talmud will get to this question, but it begins its commentary on the Mishnah with an observation about the first line.

> But if he does have children, he may abstain from being fruitful and multiplying, but not, evidently, from having a wife. This supports what Rav Nahman said in the name of Samuel: Even if a person has many children, he is forbidden to remain without a wife, as it says, "It is not good for the human to be alone" (Gen. 2:18).

Because the Mishnah says that "a person may not abstain from being fruitful and multiplying until he has children," the Talmud infers that the only legal implication of having the required number of children is freedom from the obligation to procreate. But this means that even after a person has produced the required number of children, he remains bound by a different obligation: he may abstain from sex, yes, but he may not separate from his wife. (The Talmud assumes, in accordance with the period's patriarchal norms, that the default legal subject is a man. The patriarchal character of the Talmud is evident throughout this passage, in the fact that all the rabbis are men, for example, and most strikingly in the position of the house of Shammai, that only male births legally count as procreation.) And this stands to reason, continues the Talmud, because Genesis 2:18 (God's justification for creating the woman: "it is not good for the human to be alone") indicates that the spousal companionship of marriage is a separate and essential good, distinct from the good of children.

Eliding a further turn in this inquiry, we move to the next passage in the Bavli, which addresses the aforementioned gap in the Mishnah.

> "The house of Shammai says: two males." What is the reasoning of the house of Shammai? They learn from Moses, as it is written: "The sons of Moses were Gershom and Eliezer" (1 Chronicles 23:15). And the house of Hillel? They learn from the creation of the world.
>
> And let the house of Shammai learn from the creation of the world! One does not infer the possible from the impossible.

> And let the house of Hillel also learn from Moses! They would say to you: Moses did so on his own, as it was taught, "Three things Moses did on his own, and God agreed to them: He abstained from his wife, he broke the tablets, and he added a day (of preparation), prior to the Sinai covenant."

The Talmud first supplies a reason for the house of Shammai's position. They derive the minimum measure of two males from Moses, for Moses had two sons, and afterward (on the rabbinic interpretation of verses in Exodus and Numbers, assumed here) abstained from intercourse with his wife. And so, there is support both for the view of the house of Shammai (from Moses) and for that of the house of Hillel (from God).

The Talmud then takes the debate one step further in the above passage: How would each house respond to the evidence of the other? The Talmud supposes that the house of Shammai would reject the evidence from God because "one does not infer the possible from the impossible." The medieval commentator Rashi, whose Hebrew commentary is printed alongside the Bavli text in every modern printing, parses this opaque statement as follows: what God did in creating the world cannot serve as an exemplary precedent, because it was not possible for God to have done otherwise than create a man and a woman, given that God's intent was for them to reproduce. We thus have no evidence that, as a general matter, there is a particular impetus to bear a male and a female.

And what of the house of Hillel? How would it respond to the house of Shammai's evidence from Moses? They would say, so the Bavli suggests, that Moses cannot serve as a model for human beings in general because we know that there were several bold things that he did without God's permission, and even if God afterward assented to them, they were hardly normative for the average Jew. One of these was in fact his decision to abstain from sex with his wife, which he undertook not (the house of Hillel would contend) because he had satisfied the obligation to procreate but despite the fact that he had not; he was compelled to do so once he realized that, as the sort of prophet to whom God could appear at any moment, he ought to maintain the strictest standard of ritual purity, a standard incompatible with sexual intercourse.

The continuation of the Talmud cites other traditions, diverging from the Mishnah's report, concerning the position of the house of Shammai—according to one alternative, the house of Shammai rules that one must have two sons and two daughters; according to yet another, one need have one child only, whether it be a son or a daughter—and explores possible reasons for those positions. It then enters into a new question concerning the obligation to procreate.

> It was said: If he had children when he was a pagan, then converted, Rabbi Yohanan says: He has fulfilled "being fruitful and multiplying." Resh Lakish says: He has not fulfilled "being fruitful and multiplying." Rabbi Yohanan says that he has fulfilled "being fruitful and multiplying," because he has them. Resh Lakish says that he has not fulfilled "being fruitful and multiplying," because a convert is like a newborn baby.
>
> And they follow their reasoning, for it was said: If he has children when he was a pagan, then converted, Rabbi Yohanan says: There is no firstborn for purposes of inheritance, because he already had "the first of his strength" (Deut. 21:17). Resh Lakish says: There is a firstborn for purposes of inheritance, because a convert is like a newborn baby.

Here, having clarified the debate about how many children one must have in order to fulfill the procreation obligation, the Bavli asks: What if a person had the requisite number of children while a gentile, and then afterward converts to Judaism? Do these children enable the convert to satisfy his obligation to procreate, even though his legal status is now categorically different? Here again there is debate, this time among rabbis of the early third century CE. Rabbi Yohanan says yes, since, after all, he has had these children. Resh Lakish disagrees. Conversion, according to Resh Lakish, is not just any change of status. It is a rebirth, even to the degree that the children from prior to his conversion are not, for the purposes of the law of procreation, deemed his own.

The Talmud then observes that the positions that Rabbi Yohanan and Resh Lakish take in this debate are consistent with those that they take on another, related matter. According to Deuteronomy 21:17, a firstborn son—"the first of [the father's] strength"—is entitled to double his share in his parents' inheritance. But what if a convert had a son before his conversion? The question (though this is hardly obvious at first glance) is not whether the son born prior to the conversion is entitled to a double portion. In fact, this son does not inherit at all, because, with the father's conversion, he no longer counts as his son for the purpose of inheritance law, though the father could certainly transfer part of his estate to him in his lifetime under the rubric of a gift. The question is rather: If the convert marries and has a "firstborn" son with his Jewish wife (either a new wife, or his previous wife who converted with him), does this son have firstborn status under Jewish law, so that he inherits double? As in the case of the law of procreation, Rabbi Yohanan rules that the law of inheritance takes cognizance of the child born prior to conversion. Inheritance law recognizes the biological fact that this man fathered a child before he converted, and therefore the child born after conversion is not "the first of his strength" and does not have the status of a firstborn. Resh Lakish, consistent with his position in the procreation debate, disagrees. For Resh Lakish, conversion is so radical a transformation, at least from a legal perspective, that it entirely erases the convert's past. With his conversion, he is born again, and the son that he fathers after conversion is "the first of his strength," and a legal firstborn.

In the continuation, which I will not quote, the Talmud takes a next step. It assumes that rabbinic tradition as a whole is maximally economical, and therefore, the fact that the tradition preserves two different debates between Rabbi Yohanan and Resh Lakish that boil down to the same issue (i.e., are biological facts legally recognized following conversion) becomes a problem. Why not only record the debate in connection with one of the laws only (say, the procreation obligation), and we could ourselves infer their positions on the other law (inheritance)? It must be that there is a reason that each of their positions is more compelling in one of the two legal areas, so that, even if we knew Rabbi Yohanan's position in one of the two cases, we might have supposed he would agree with Resh Lakish in the other case, and vice-versa for Resh Lakish. The Talmud then proceeds, of course, to identify such reasons.

Conclusion

What do we learn about the Bavli, and about Torah study in general, from this passage? Torah study emerges, in the first instance, as a deeply analytical undertaking, involving reasoning, inference, comparison, and contrast. The passage is indeed legalistic; a law student, and even more, a student of ancient courtroom rhetoric, would find the flavor of much of the argumentation familiar. Another, related feature of the passage is that, beginning with the

Mishnah and continuing into the Bavli commentary, it introduces debate after debate with no attempt at resolution. On the contrary, the Bavli labors to present arguments for both sides, to ensure the viability of each position. It seeks, in short, to preserve debate. This aim is indeed characteristic of the Bavli as a whole, and marks Torah study not as a handmaiden to performance of the Torah, but as an end in itself. Later codifiers of the halakhah would have to subject the Mishnah and the Bavli to somewhat artificial decision principles in order to make them serviceable as the foundation of a coherent code of conduct. (One such principle, articulated already in the Talmud itself, is that the law generally follows the more humanistic view of the house of Hillel over the more stringent view of the house of Shammai. A reader troubled by the male bias in the house of Shammai's position on procreation can perhaps find some comfort in this.)

But Torah study is not simply an intellectual exercise. Or rather, although there is a danger of it becoming a mere intellectual exercise, a danger that Jewish tradition acknowledges in many ways across the centuries, Torah study is also a theological undertaking. The theological character of Torah study can be appreciated on at least two levels. First, at the general level, Torah study constitutes the most immediate and consuming form of engagement in Judaism with the word of God. The tradition holds it up as a religious command and a religious value, indeed, arguably the foremost religious value, and this fact demands theological interpretation. Hartman's covenantal anthropology represents one such interpretation, and having worked through the Bavli passage, we can see why he conceptualizes Torah study as the ultimate expression of Judaism's commitment to the notion that God gives human beings the freedom and responsibility to realize God's word in the world through their own interpretive capacities. Second, at the level of detail, the Bavli passage engages throughout with issues of immediate theological interest: the purposes of marriage; the relationship between procreation and creation; the status of biblical heroes like Moses as exemplars; the nature of conversion. Theological reflection can occur "directly" in Judaism, through engagement with aggadic texts, but its stakes are highest insofar as it occurs in the shadow and through the prism of the law.

Further Inquiry

In connection with Hartman's celebration of human autonomy in relation to God, see the study of the motif of protest against God in Judaism, with extensive comparison to Christian perspectives, in Dov Weiss, *Pious Irreverence: Confronting God in Rabbinic Judaism* (Philadelphia: University of Pennsylvania Press, 2016). Moshe Halbertal offers a subtle introduction to the concept of canonicity in Judaism in his book, *People of the Book: Canon, Meaning, and Authority* (Cambridge: Harvard University Press, 1997). On the Bavli, see Barry Scott Wimpfheimer, *The Talmud: A Biography* (Princeton: Princeton University Press, 2018). Ilana Kurshan's daf yomi memoir, referenced above, is *If All the Seas Were Ink: A Memoir* (New York: St. Martin's Press, 2017). Recent treatments of the rabbinic concept of law are Christine Hayes, *What's Divine about Divine Law? Early Perspectives* (Princeton: Princeton University Press, 2015) (from the perspective of a scholar of rabbinic literature in its Greco-Roman context, including Paul), and Chaim N. Saiman, *Halakhah: The Rabbinic Idea of Law* (Princeton: Princeton University Press, 2018) (from the perspective of a legal scholar and a close follower of contemporary Orthodox life).

●

1. We noted at the beginning of the chapter that as Judaism identifies Torah with primordial Wisdom or the Word of God, so Christianity identifies Christ with it. We might go further and say that, just as the Word became flesh in Jesus, as the Gospel of John puts it (John 1:14), so Torah took on concrete form as "the Torah" in the narrow sense, the five books of Moses that trace to Sinai. In chapter 8 we will take up the question of incarnation in relation to the people Israel, but here is a possible Jewish theology of incarnation, of a sort, in relation to Torah. Is this characterization helpful? What similarities to Christianity does it illuminate? What differences does it obscure? Consider in this connection a report from an English Protestant about his visit to a Venice synagogue in 1581: "I went into their Sinagogue upon a Satturday, which is their Sabbath day, and I founde them in their service or prayers, very devoute. They receive the five bookes of Moses and honour them by carrying them about their Church, as Papistes doe their crosse." (The quotation is from Yaacov Deutsch, "Christian Presence in Jewish Ritual," in *Ritual Dynamics in Jewish and Christian Contexts: Between Bible and Liturgy*, ed.

Claudia D. Bergmann and Benedikt Kranemann [Leiden: Brill, 2019], 152.) On the early history of the processing of the Torah scroll in the synagogue, see Ruth Langer, "From Study of Scripture to a Reenactment of Sinai," *Worship* 72 (1998): 43–67.

2. Bava Qamma is a Talmud tractate devoted to tort law, that is, the laws of damages. This subject might seem a matter for lawyers only; in our educational system, one must in general go to law school to study tort law. But perhaps the study of tort law could be a praxis that teaches sensitivity to and consideration of others? Something like this notion seems to underlie the following passage, from Bavli Bava Qamma 30a. The Mishnah rules that if someone, having found a thorn or a piece of glass, thrusts it into his hedge, and then it causes damage to a person passing by in the public domain, he is legally liable for the damage. The Talmud, commenting on the Mishnah, cites a tradition that the pious people of old would take care to conceal thorns and glass within their own fields, even digging down to a depth of three handbreadths so that (here I diverge from the Bavli passage to incorporate the Palestinian Talmud parallel) the plow would not raise up these objects. Rabbi Judah then comments: "One who wishes to be pious should fulfill the words of [the tractate on] damages."

3. In parts of the world of advanced Torah study, the notion that a student of Torah ought to be, in the Yiddish parlance, a *mensch*, a decent person, motivates the dedicating of part of the school day to the study of *musar*, a body of texts and practices directed at the improvement of character. Consider the following passage from a memoir by Israel Meir Lau (b. 1937), famous as a child survivor of the concentration camp Buchenwald and later as the Ashkenazi Chief Rabbi of Israel. He writes of his studies as a teenager with Rabbi Eliezer Lapian, a master of musar. Rabbi Eli, as he calls him, was also a great Talmudist, who, old and almost blind, taught Talmud and commentaries to the young Lau entirely from memory. But he also insisted that his students "make a point of performing at least three altruistic acts of *chessed* (loving-kindness) daily. . . . I [Lau] could not fall asleep until I had performed my three charitable deeds for that day. . . . Another rule that Rabbi Eli established was that at least once a week, usually on Shabbat, we would abstain from talking about other people. For one day, we erased from our vocabulary such seemingly innocuous phrases such as 'he said' and 'he did' in order to excise from our speech all praise, slander, and gossip, even though it might not be hurtful or defaming." (The quotations are from Israel Meir Lau, *Out of the Depths: The Story*

of a Child of Buchenwald Who Returned Home at Last [New York: Sterling, 2011], 156–57.) One might say that these ethical praxes have a legalistic character that enables them to integrate well into the world of halakhah. How so? And what does this passage tell us about the relationship between student and master in the yeshiva world?

4. Hartman construes the boldness of the oven of Akhnai story in anthropological terms, as a lesson about the human condition: God's vision for human beings is that they achieve and exercise the adult capacity to reason independently about the meaning of God's word. But it could also be construed as an expression of God's intimate relationship with Israel. On this perspective, to the degree that the rabbis embrace their interpretive freedom, they do so as Israel, God's beloved children, whose boldness, even impertinence, God laughingly indulges. (Read the continuation of the story in the Bavli for support for this approach.) Which of the two approaches do you find more theologically appealing? Are they mutually compatible? In tension with each other? You might wish to return to this question after we take up the topic of God's relationship with Israel in chapters 8 and 9.

— Chapter 7 —

Torah as Practiced

THE RHYTHM AND STRUCTURE OF TRADITIONAL JEWISH life is determined by the commandments (*mitzvot*, sg. *mitzvah*). A passage from the Babylonian Talmud (Makkot 23b) claims that there are 613 commandments, that is, 613 rules enjoined upon Israel in the Pentateuch. The Bavli does not specify what they are, nor does it arrive at this number by counting verses. Rather, 613 is a typological number, as the sum of 365 and 248. There are, on this view, 365 prohibitions ("do not!" commandments), corresponding to the 365 days of the year, and 248 obligations ("do!" commandments), corresponding to the 248 parts of the body (according to contemporaneous anatomical knowledge). The point is that the commandments are all-encompassing for the Jewish people: there is no day of the year that is free of them, and there is no part of the body that the mitzvot do not enlist into the service of God.

Medieval jurists would go on to produce lists specifying what they took to be the 613 commandments, from the great and famous, such as the prohibition against doing work on the sabbath, or against murder, to the small and obscure, such as the obligation to anoint a priest for the task of addressing the army before battle, or to help a neighbor adjust the load of his overburdened donkey. With the destruction of the temple and of an independent Jewish state at the hands of the Romans in 70 CE, commandments like the one concerning the priest of war, bearing on the operation of the state and of the temple, fell into desuetude, but hundreds of commandments remain applicable today.

When the Torah speaks of the commandments in a general sense, it typically links them to reward and punishment. Thus, for example, in Deuteronomy 11:26–28, Moses tells Israel that he is "setting before you today a blessing and a curse: the blessing, if you obey the commandments of the Lord your

God that I am commanding you today; and the curse, if you do not obey the commandments of the Lord your God but turn from the way that I am commanding you today, to follow other gods that you have not known." In light of the concern in the Torah, and following it in rabbinic Judaism, about the consequences of observing and violating the commandments, we will begin this chapter, dedicated to the commandments, with the question of reward and punishment. We will begin, in particular, with the question of the afterlife as a site for reward and punishment, and turn from there to some general reflections on the reasons motivating observance of the commandments. Then we will examine two sets of commandments of particular importance for traditional Jewish life today and throughout the ages: the laws of menstrual purity and the dietary laws.

Reward, Punishment, and the Afterlife

In an episode of the sitcom *The Big Bang Theory* (season 5, episode 21), Sheldon, having just insulted Howard's intelligence, learns that Howard will be assisting Stephen Hawking on his visit to the university. Sheldon asks for an invitation to meet him, and Howard naturally says no: "Sheldon, you're a condescending jerk. Why on earth would I want to do something nice for you?" Sheldon responds: "Um, to go to Jewish heaven?" Howard counters: "Jews don't have heaven." Sheldon offers: "Then to avoid Jewish hell?" Howard then delivers the punchline: "Have you met my mother? I live in Jewish hell."

It is not true, from the perspective of traditional Jewish theology, that "Jews don't have heaven." Rabbinic literature is dense with references to heaven (or the garden of Eden) and hell (or Gehenna). Recall the quotation from Mishnah Pe'ah 1:1 in chapter 6, on the deeds that earn a person reward both in this world and in the world to come. Another example (Genesis Rabbah 84:3) occurs in a comment on the verse that opens the story of Joseph: "Jacob settled in the land where his father had sojourned, in the land of Canaan" (Gen. 37:1). The rabbinic reader is sensitive to the occurrence in this verse of two different verbs for dwelling. The first one, "settling" (*yashav*), is assigned to Jacob, while the second one, "sojourning" (*gar*), is attributed to Isaac. The latter verb indicates transience and instability, while the former connotes permanence and real ownership. The contrast suggests, for the rabbinic reader, an implicit critique of Jacob. Jacob, they suppose, having endured many hardships in his youth, imagined that he might now, in his old age, enjoy a sort of tranquility that his forefathers had not. To which Satan objected before God: "Is it not enough that [tranquility] is set for [the righteous] in the future to come (i.e., the next world), that they seek to dwell in tranquility even in this world?" As a result, Jacob was forced to endure the sorrows of the Joseph story.

Such examples could be multiplied a thousandfold. Whence, then, the popular notion that Jews don't believe in heaven and hell? Likely it results, in part, from the prevalence of secularism among contemporary Jews; perhaps it is also the vestige of an anti-Jewish animus construing Jews as godless. But I will make the argument that this notion, though false, does track the fact that the afterlife does not loom as large in Jewish theology as in Christian theology. The afterlife is there in Judaism, but for two reasons, it is less important for Judaism than for Christianity.

The first reason concerns the question of the difficulty of attaining to eternal reward, or of entering the garden of Eden. One possible approach to the relationship between this world and the next is to think of this world as a tightrope suspended over a chasm, where one false step to the right or to the left means falling into the abyss of Gehenna; only those who strictly toe the line can make it through to a blessed afterlife. There is a basis for this approach in a passage in the book of Numbers that spells out the sacrifices that are to be offered if one sins unintentionally, and concludes with the fate of one who sins "high-handedly," or intentionally: that sinner "shall be cut off from among the people" (Num. 15:30), perhaps a reference to death by the hand of heaven. The plain sense of this passage seems to be that a single sin, committed intentionally, will undo any good that one might have done, and bring with it the severest consequences.

This perspective—we can call it the tightrope model of the afterlife—may indeed have been the one that informed Paul, who appears to take the view (e.g., in Rom. 4:13–15; 7:21–25; Gal. 3:10) that while the law is good in itself, it is impossible to observe. He seems to come to this conclusion not out of the belief that one can *never* choose rightly, but out of the belief that one cannot *always* choose rightly. The inclination to sin is too strong, the opportunities too pervasive, and even one transgression means perdition. The tightrope model becomes even more a source of despair when combined with the apocalyptic conception of human beings as enslaved to sin. But of course, for a Christian, there is hope in Jesus.

Rabbinic Judaism rejects the tightrope model. It interprets Numbers 15:30, against its plain sense, as a reference to the worship of other gods: only this especially severe transgression results in being "cut off" in the manner described in the verse. In general, however, the rabbis conceive of this world in relation to the next on the model of a balance. God weighs the good deeds that a person has done against the bad, and if the former exceed the latter, then she is judged for good. Not only that; God is willing, out of kindness and sympathy for God's own creatures, and especially for God's people Israel, to forgive transgressions, or to put a thumb on the scale in support of acquittal. And even in the first place, as we noted in the previous chapter, human beings are basically capable of choosing well. Because sin is not an existential threat but a manageable problem—because, all things being equal, a human being is more likely to choose well, to heed rather than violate the law—the Mishnah (Makkot 3:16) can explain the great number of commandments in the Torah as following from God's desire to offer Israel the opportunity to acquire merit and be acquitted in God's judgment. In sum, then, the first reason that the afterlife occupies a relatively marginal place in Jewish theology is that it is not a source of anxiety. One need not be particularly righteous in order to attain a portion in the world to come; one attains it as a matter of course.

The second reason for the marginality of the afterlife is that, while fulfillment or violation of the commandments does have implications for one's status in the afterlife, reward and punishment in the afterlife are not the main reasons for observing the commandments. In this respect rabbinic Judaism follows the lead of the Hebrew Bible. Outside of frozen and relatively rare formulas concerning descending to Sheol and being "gathered to one's fathers," the Hebrew Bible does not refer to the afterlife until the very late book of Daniel. The blessing and the curse in the passage from Deuteronomy 11 quoted in the introduction to this chapter concern good and bad fortune in this world: rain or drought (11:13–17), victory or defeat in battle (11:22–25). The beatific vision of Judaism, emerging from the Hebrew Bible, is not the communion of the disembodied soul with God in heaven, but the sort of overflowing abundance described, for example, in Psalm 128:2–6.

> You shall eat the fruit of the labor of your hands; you shall be happy, and it shall go well with you. Your wife will be like a fruitful vine within your house; your children will be like olive shoots around your table. Thus shall the man be blessed who fears the Lord. The Lord bless you from Zion. May you see the prosperity of Jerusalem all the days of your life. May you see your children's children. Peace be upon Israel!

Of course, Jewish theology inherits the quandary posed by the book of Job, that righteous people often appear to suffer, and it holds out the afterlife as a means of squaring accounts. But Judaism nevertheless centers this world, and the prospect of a fulfilled life in it.

Even more to the point, the commandments are not meant, in the first instance, to be observed for the sake of reward at all, whether in the next world or this, but rather for their own sake. There are different ways one might parse this ideal. One might conceive of the commandments mainly as expressions of the divine will, in which case observing them for their own sake means relishing the notion of doing God's will, of being a servant of God. Or one might instead take one's bearings from Deuteronomy 4:6: "You must observe [God's statutes] and perform them, for this will show your wisdom and discernment to the peoples, who, when they hear all these statutes, will say, 'Surely this great nation is a wise and discerning people!'" On this approach, to observe the commandments for their own sake is to appreciate them as God's loving guidance, as from parent to child, for how best to live in the world.

The notion that adherence to the commandments is an inherent good, greater indeed than the reward (worldly or otherworldly) that one earns for such adherence, leads to the conclusion that the living, who have the opportunity to perform the commandments, are more fortunate than the dead, even the righteous dead, who no longer enjoy this opportunity. This notion finds expression in a prohibition in the Talmud (Berakhot 18b) against carrying a Torah scroll—a scroll on which the Pentateuch is written—through a cemetery. One might suppose that the concern is for the ritual purity of the Torah scroll, but in fact the basis for the prohibition is entirely different. By carrying a Torah scroll through the cemetery, one mocks the dead, who are no longer able to observe the laws written therein. This perspective might be said to construe the relationship between this world and the next on the model of the sports stadium. This world is the playing field, while the next world is the stands. Life is easier in the stands. The attendee watches from above, enjoying the spectacle at his leisure. But it is better—more exciting, more meaningful—to be on the playing field. The meaning of the attendee's experience in the stands is derivative of the experience of the players on the field.

In what sense, then, might it be true that "Jews don't have heaven"? Not in the literal sense. Traditional Jewish theology asserts both a heaven and a hell, and devotes considerable attention to them. But heaven and hell do not figure as consuming preoccupations, first because attaining to heaven is within the capacity of the average person, so that this task does not become a source of anxiety, and second because obedience to the law is an end in itself, and that end can be realized only in this world. Together, these considerations lend Judaism a more this-worldly character relative to Christianity.

Having contextualized the question of reward and punishment at the hand of God, let us take up briefly the question of punishment at the hand of human beings. What does Judaism envision as the community's response to someone who violates the law? The Bible describes a range of consequences, up to and including capital punishment. Someone who intentionally violates the sabbath, for example, is supposed to be stoned at the direction of a judicial body (Num. 15:32–36). Without entering in detail into the complex question of how passages of this sort were received in the rabbinic tradition, and, in the main, transformed into dead letters in Jewish communities over the centuries, I note that, for all intents and purposes, there are no immediate practical consequences today for violation of the law in Judaism. If, for example, a person eats pork, by accident or intentionally, the response is a matter of conscience. Ideally, he will repent, and there are prescribed rituals for repentance, especially in the penitential season preceding the New Year judgement, but he undertakes this process at his own initiative and counsel.

Reasons to Observe the Commandments

We have described some general factors motivating adherence to the mitzvot of the Torah: the extrinsic consideration of reward and punishment, both in this world and the next; the notion of obedience or service to God; and the conceptualization of the commandments as embodiments of wisdom, a path to living well in this world. The corollary of this last framework is a project of identifying the particular wisdom inherent in each commandment. But the Jewish tradition is wary of this undertaking—the search for "the reasons for the commandments" (*ta'ame ha-mitzvot*)—on principled and practical grounds. At the level of principle, the undertaking has in it the air of hubris: Will human beings deign to enter into the mind of God? Perhaps more importantly, the notion that a commandment achieves or enables some wise end tends to undermine the force of the commandment as a command; it tends to imply that the commandment ought to be obeyed not because God commands it but because it has some instrumental value. This tendency translates, in practical terms, into the concern that, having identified an apparent reason underlying a commandment, a person might come to lay aside the commanded deed and seek to achieve its purported aim through another means that seems more immediately intelligible.

At first glance, the notion of uneasiness with searching out the reasons for the commandments seems incompatible with the core aims of the Talmud. The Bavli excerpt that we examined in the last chapter appears to be thoroughly engaged in this search. It identifies reasons for supporting each position concerning the scope of the procreation commandment and reflects on these reasons. But Talmudic dialectic of this sort does not threaten to undermine the law because the Bavli's very framework is legal; reasoning occurs in the service of explicating and specifying the law. The search for reasons becomes a source of anxiety in the Jewish tradition chiefly when it occurs outside a legal framework, in a philosophical mode oriented toward essence and ultimate meaning. We will return to this issue glancingly when we take up medieval Jewish philosophy in chapter 13.

From a sociological perspective, the commandments become compelling insofar as they construct the people of Israel as a community, in two important senses. First, Jews are joined together by the common performance of a set of behaviors that distinguish them from other groups. In this sense, the commandments make Israel into an imagined community: I, as a practicing Jew, am bound to other practicing Jews whom I have never met, from the past and in the present. Second, and more concretely, many of these commandments can only be performed, or performed meaningfully or enjoyably, within the context of an actual Jewish community. As we will see in the continuation of this chapter, the laws of menstrual purity presuppose the existence of a ritual bath, constructed by the community, while the dietary laws make it almost impossible to eat at the home of anyone who does not observe them. Likewise, the laws of prayer, the holidays, and above all the sabbath demand, in very concrete ways, the immediate presence of other Jews, as we will note in coming chapters.

Of course, sociology cannot be detached from theology when one of the central theological categories in Judaism is the Jewish people, a social unit. We will take up the Jewish people as a concept in Jewish theology in the next chapter. Before doing so, we will survey two sets of commandments, both for their intrinsic importance in Jewish life and as case studies in the nature of the commandments and the question of meaning that they pose.

The Laws of Menstrual Purity

Menstruation occurs at the intersection of many central concerns of the Hebrew Bible, including sexuality, gender relations, reproduction, and blood as the physical manifestation of life. The laws of the Pentateuch specify two implications of menstruation. First (Lev. 15:19–24), a woman is deemed ritually defiled for seven days from the beginning of her period; the menstruant woman (in Hebrew, *niddah*) also transmits ritual defilement to people and objects whom she touches. Ritual defilement has no practical relevance today, or for the past two millennia from the destruction of the temple, because ritual defilement is more or less only of concern insofar as it enters into contact with the temple or with things associated with it. But the Pentateuch names a second implication of menstruation (Lev. 18:19; 20:18): sex during a woman's menstrual period is stringently prohibited. The reason given for the prohibition in Leviticus 20:18—that sex during a woman's period exposes "the font of her blood"—is obscure, but evidently reflects the view that menstrual blood emerges from a source that ought to be contained and concealed.

The intercourse prohibition gives rise in rabbinic literature to a body of laws—the laws of niddah, or the menstrual purity laws—that takes its bearing from the Bible, but develops according to rabbinic interpretive assumptions and customary practices. In brief, according to the consensus tradition, a couple must refrain from sex and, by extension, from other intimate acts, when the woman's period begins. She allows four or five days (depending on the halakhic community) for her menstrual bleeding to stop, then counts another seven "clean" (i.e., non-bleeding) days, then immerses in the evening in a body of water (in Hebrew, *mikveh*, also spelled *mikvah*), at which point the couple may resume having sex.

The notion of immersion in water as a means of ritual purification is rooted in the Hebrew Bible; Christian baptism derives from the same source. Although certain natural bodies of water can serve as a mikveh, considerations of geography, privacy and convenience militate against this option. Instead, immersion typically occurs in a built structure that collects rainwater. Here, then, is one important way in which halakhah literally structures community: a nonnegotiable requirement for a traditional Jewish community of any size is a mikveh building, containing the ritual bath itself and rooms for preparation for immersion. Likewise, it is very difficult for a traditional, young Jewish family to live in a place that is not within easy driving distance—or even walking distance, given that driving is not permitted on the sabbath and festivals—from a mikveh.

The laws of menstrual purity can be immensely complex. Questions arise around such issues as distinguishing menstrual blood from other sorts of bleeding; determining when a woman's period has ended so that she may begin to count the seven clean days; implementing leniencies that may be necessary in a situation in which a woman's menstrual cycle is such that the standard application of niddah law would interfere with conception; and innumerable other issues. Ordinarily, Jewish tradition encourages householders confronted with halakhic questions to consult with their local rabbi. But Jewish tradition also supports a modesty regime that discourages free conversation between men and women, especially around matters connected with sexuality. How, then, is a woman supposed to consult with a rabbi about a question relating to menstrual purity? One imperfect solution to this challenge is to have the husband serve as a go-between, but modern Orthodox Judaism has in recent years introduced a novel solution. While modern Orthodoxy does not in general embrace the notion of a woman rabbi, it has come to support the notion of training women to serve as "halakhic advisers" (*yo'atsot halakhah*) in the area of menstrual purity, so that women can consult with them on questions in this area.

In a recent anthology of reflections on the mikveh, a woman named Frieda Sossonko recounts a powerful story from her past.[1] During World War II,

1. See Rivka Slonim, ed., *Total Immersion: A Mikvah Anthology* (New York: Urim Publications, 2006), 302–6.

she, with many other Jews, fled Ukraine for Central Asia, and she ended up remaining in Tashkent for many years, even as the post-war Communist regime shuttered Jewish institutions like the mikveh. Observant Jewish women surreptitiously began instead to use a deep well as a mikveh. Sossonko tells how she came to the well for the first time and began to descend the two rope ladders that had been lashed together to enable the descent. "I felt fire. I had never experienced such cold. I tried this way and that way and saw that I couldn't take this water. So I decided to go without immersing myself, thinking I would wait"—in the meantime, of course, abstaining from sex with her husband—"until, with *Hashem*'s help, we could build a mikvah." (The word *Hashem*, Hebrew for "the name," is a standard way of referring to God in Judaism. Rather than actually pronouncing God's holy name, one piously speaks of it indirectly.)

But at that moment, two other women approached to use the well, and Sossonko felt that she could not give up, or else these women would likewise postpone immersion, and they might not be as careful as she in abstaining from intercourse in the interim. Sossonko therefore determined that she would steel herself to enter the water by conjuring a terrible memory. A decade earlier, her husband had been imprisoned by the Communist authorities, and while he was away, both of her young daughters passed away, on a single day. Sossonko had ever since tried resolutely never to think about that day. But now, she intentionally called it to mind. "I sank deeper and deeper into the memory of what had happened that day." Thus immersed in her past tragedy, she became numb to everything else, and was able to enter the water without feeling the cold at all.

Sossonko does not tell us why the menstrual purity laws were so important to her that she was willing, for their sake, to take on, in a psychological way, the burden of Abraham, and lose her daughters again. Presumably this set of laws, like the other commandments of the Torah, was for Sossonko a given: the binding word of God, as understood by the rabbis. This givenness is enough to support both routine observance and Sossonko's heroic sacrifice in the face of persecution. But Jews in various contexts, past and present, have also sought to identify the logic underlying the commandments, including, of course, the menstrual purity laws. The traditional underpinning of this search, as noted above, is the assumption that God's law is the epitome of wisdom. The search can occur in an open-ended philosophical mode. Or it can occur in an apologetic mode, motivated by some apparent problem with a law, a concern that the law is unreasonable or immoral or outdated. In a modern context, the undertaking can take on a constructive character, out of a desire to find personal meaning in a practice to which one is already committed.

Assorted biblical passages use the term "niddah" to convey the notion of rejection or even degradation. It stands to reason, in light of this usage and other considerations, that the original rationale for the menstrual purity laws lay in the (male) perception of menstrual blood as revolting or even dangerous.[2] From this perspective, the laws of menstrual purity seem offensive to our modern commitment to gender equity, and at odds with our recognition that the feeling of disgust should be interrogated, because it sometimes represents a culturally determined manifestation of deeply rooted prejudice. The challenge to the niddah laws from changing gender norms is reinforced by technological and social changes. For example, can a ritual regime that crystallized at a time when women spent many or most of their fertile years pregnant, when menstruation could thus be construed as a sign of failure to conceive, even a sort of death *in potentia*, make sense for a modern world in which pregnancy is the exception in the life of a woman of childbearing age?

As the historical gap between the biblical world and our own threatens to render the menstrual purity laws unintelligible, philosophers, apologists, and individual practitioners enter to assign it new meaning. Some medieval interpreters already suggested that the intercourse prohibition is grounded in the fact that sex during this point in a woman's menstrual cycle will not typically result in conception. Others offered that the regime of menstrual purity endows women with a blood-centered obligation that is the equivalent of circumcision blood for Jewish men. (This approach both justifies the menstrual purity laws and explains why Judaism obligates only men and not women to be circumcised.) Over the last decades, perhaps the most prevalent rationale given for the menstrual purity laws, one with roots in the Talmud (Bavli Niddah 31b), is that they help to foster a healthy marital relationship. Spouses learn new ways to communicate with and show appreciation for each

2. Ethan Tucker's helpful review essay surveys the evidence for this view in the Bible and among later interpreters; see "*Niddah*, Part 1: Fundamentals, Motivations, Critiques," available at https://www.hadar.org/torah-tefillah/resources/niddah-fundamentals-motivations-critiques-part-1. I also draw on Tucker's survey for some of the analysis in the continuation.

other when they cannot be physically intimate, and the enforced abstinence kindles desire. Some may also find in the menstrual purity laws a sort of countercultural affirmation of gender difference.

To what extent are those who proffer such rationales conscious of their distance from the original, biblical rationales? Surely there is no single answer to this question, but we may say the following in principle about the dynamic at work in the emergence of new meaning around the commandments. On the one hand, the commitment to observing the commandments is primary; this commitment is the starting point for reflection on them. On the other hand, the search for meaning in the commandments, the attempt to make sense of them, is not, ideally, a mere epiphenomenon. It is not just a sort of psychological coping, a mechanism for coming to terms with one's choice. Rather, the search for meaning construes the commandments as nexuses for thinking through the question of how to be Jewish in the world, faithful to the tradition and to one's general worldview. This dynamic, of a commitment that is understood not to bring an end to human reasoning but to provide a foundation for it, should be familiar to anyone acquainted with the conceptualization of Christian theology, after Anselm, as *fides quaerens intellectum*, or "faith seeking understanding."

The Dietary Laws

The dietary laws, like the menstrual purity laws, help to structure traditional Jewish community. Here I will only summarize the basic features of the dietary laws and reflect briefly on the question of meaning in relation to them. The key term in connection with the dietary laws is "kosher." This word, received into English from Yiddish, traces ultimately to the Hebrew word *kasher*, meaning "valid." Kosher food is food that may be eaten. Prohibited food is *treyf*, likewise a Yiddish word from Hebrew *taref*, meaning "torn." Just as an animal that was torn apart as prey may not be eaten, because it was not killed via slaughter, so, by extension, any food that may not be eaten is called treyf, or non-kosher. The body of dietary laws is called *kashrut* ("validity").

Among the creatures of the land, the sky, and the water, the Torah (Lev. 11 and Deut. 14) distinguishes between those that may be eaten and those that may not. The Torah does not offer reasons for these distinctions, but one can speculate with some confidence. For land animals, the criteria for kosher status are split hooves and rumination. These criteria seem designed to pick out herbivorous herd animals (cattle, sheep, deer, etc.) and to exclude pigs and predators. Likewise, the list of non-kosher birds appears to center on predators. In the case of fish, the reasoning is different. For a water creature to be kosher, it must have fins and scales, presumably because these are properties of the paradigmatic fish. Something that lives in the water but lacks these properties—a lobster, for example, or a shrimp—is apparently taboo because it is out of place. If the criteria for land and sky creatures seem to encode a moral injunction (i.e., the creatures to which you attach yourself should be pacific, not martial), then the criteria for sea creatures seem to encode a principle of natural order (i.e., associate yourself with things that conform to nature).

Building on developments in biblical interpretation in the Second Temple period, the rabbis put forward additional constraints on meat consumption. Even kosher land and air animals may not be eaten unless they have been slaughtered according to very specific standards. (There is no slaughtering requirement for sea animals.) As a result, the beef and chicken generally available in a supermarket are not kosher, because the animals from which they derive were killed according to modern methods that do not conform to the rules for kosher slaughter. The farthest-reaching rabbinic innovation in the area of kashrut is a prohibition on the mixing of meat and milk. The Bible (Exod. 23:19 and elsewhere) prohibits cooking a kid in its mother's milk. This injunction condemns the cruelty and indifference inherent in such an act, but the rabbis generalize the prohibition so that it applies to any sort of mixing between meat and milk. One may not eat a meat product and a dairy product together, nor may one even eat a dairy product for some time (in some traditions, even many hours) after one has eaten a meat product, out of concern that some meat might remain stuck in one's teeth. Even more, the rabbis presume that when food is cooked in a pot, the pot absorbs the "taste" of the food, which is then introduced into any food that is later cooked in the same pot. Thus, if one cooks meat in a pot, and then uses the same pot afterward to cook a food with milk or cheese, the cooked food is not kosher, because it is a mixture of dairy and meat. A kosher kitchen must therefore, as a general rule, have two sets of pots and utensils, one for dairy and one for meat. In fact, it typically has a third set of pots and cooking utensils, for preparing foods that are neither dairy nor meat, like pasta, so that they can be eaten with either dairy or meat.

The tendency and in part the purpose of these and other dietary restrictions is to encourage traditionally observant Jews to eat and by extension live among themselves, and to discourage commensality with others. It is almost impossible for an orthodox Jew to eat a meal cooked in the home of a non-observant Jew or a non-Jew. For a restaurant to be kosher, it must generally pay a local rabbinic organization (the *vaad*, or "association") to have the organization send a supervisor (*mashgiah*) to monitor compliance with the dietary laws. Thus, if an orthodox Jew wishes to have a regular dining-out option, she must live in a Jewish community large enough to support one or more kosher restaurants.

By far the most complicated area of kashrut today is processed foods. Modern food science poses innumerable new questions and creates daunting challenges concerning supervision. For example, does gelatin derived from a non-kosher animal make the food product into which it is integrated treyf, or perhaps gelatin does not count as a food because it is not edible by itself, and therefore it cannot affect the kosher status of the food that incorporates it? More generally, how can a traditionally observant Jew know that a supermarket item with tens of ingredients, some of them unpronounceable, produced in a faraway factory on assembly lines that may contain trace food elements not listed among the ingredients, is kosher? The solution that the Orthodox Jewish American world developed, with enormous success, is the formation of regional and national organizations (e.g., the Orthodox Union and the OK) with specialized knowledge of kashrut and of modern food science. These organizations field kashrut questions and work with food conglomerates to supervise their products. A product for which a kashrut organization vouches bears the seal of that organization on its packaging, which signals to the Jewish consumer in the supermarket that it is kosher.

How do Jews today find meaning in the observance of the dietary laws? No doubt, the typical observant Jew does not dwell much on this question on a day-to-day basis; these laws are simply a given, so much so that the thought of eating a patently treyf food like a cheeseburger might be nauseating. But we may venture that the above prohibitions, coupled with other laws related to food, especially the obligation to pronounce a specific blessing before and after eating, which we will take up in chapter 10, can combine to instill a consciousness about food, an awareness that human beings are bound up through food to the natural world and to its creator. For Jews attuned to modern expressions of food consciousness, whether from wellness, environmental, or other perspectives, the dietary laws furnish a framework for coordinating these perspectives to God, and thus imbuing them with special significance. In a different direction, the practice of certifying restaurants as kosher has led an Orthodox Jewish social justice organization, Uri L'Tzedek, to develop a mechanism for certifying restaurants as compliant with halakhic rules and values concerning treatment of employees.

Conclusion

This chapter has described the mitzvot or commandments as the framework for Jewish life in the world. Many of the commandments directly enjoin moral behavior, but many, like the laws of niddah and kashrut, have a ritual expression, and we have devoted attention to the ways in which such commandments carry meaning. Of course, ritual practices can become rote. Even more problematic than the evacuation of meaning is the tendency of ritual to act as a black hole, drawing to it the attention and devotion of adherents at the expense of non-ritualized elements of the tradition, especially ethics. I conclude the chapter with some reflections on this tendency.

The prophets of old condemned the perversion of ritual. Amos, for example, in a fierce and rousing attack on festival sacrifices and their attendant music, says: "I hate, I despise your festivals, and I take no delight in your solemn assemblies. . . . Take away from me the noise of your songs; I will not listen to the melody of your harps. But let justice roll down like waters, and righteousness like an ever-flowing stream" (Amos 5:21–24). Again, here is Isaiah, mocking penitential rituals that obscure injustice: "Is it to bow down the head like a bulrush and to lie in sackcloth and ashes? Will you call this a fast, a day acceptable to the Lord? Is not this the fast that I choose: to loose the bonds of injustice, to undo the straps of the yoke, to let the oppressed go free, and to break every yoke?" (Isa. 58:5–6).

Rabbinic Judaism acknowledges and internalizes these critiques. For each festival and sabbath day, the lectionary specifies a reading from the Pentateuch and a related reading from the Prophets. For the Day of Atonement, Yom Kippur, the holiest day of the Jewish calendar, which is given over entirely to fasting and synagogue prayer, the Pentateuchal reading is naturally Leviticus 16, which describes in detail the temple rites prescribed for this day.

But the passage from the Prophets that the lectionary pairs with this Pentateuchal reading is none other than Isaiah 58, centered on the passage quoted above. Along the same lines, in the tractate devoted to the Day of Atonement (Tosefta Yoma 1:12), the following story appears. It refers to the practice of apportioning honors among priests serving in the temple by means of a race up the altar ramp.

> Once two priests were running neck and neck up the ramp, and one inched ahead of the other within four cubits. The other took a knife and stabbed it in the frontrunner's heart. . . . The father of the child came and said: . . . My son was convulsing, and so the knife is not defiled. (I.e., the knife was withdrawn from the body before death occurred, and so it did not contract death defilement.) This teaches that the defilement of a knife was a weightier matter to them than the spilling of blood.

This story, set on the eve of the destruction of the temple, depicts a society in which the temple's holiness has become perverted, a place in which a priest might stab his fellow so as to win a role in the sacrificial service, and the father of the deceased might be less exercised by the murder than by the question of the knife's ritual status. Of course, this story occurs alongside the tractate's detailed engagement with the sacrificial rites for the Day of Atonement, just like the reading from Isaiah 58 complements rather than undoes the reading from Leviticus 16. The critique of ritual does not envision the rejection of ritual, but its proper contextualization.

Further Inquiry

Movies and television series have a unique capacity to portray lives shaped, to one degree or another, by the commandments. See, in particular, two Israeli series set in different Jerusalem neighborhoods: *Srugim* (3 seasons, 2008–2012), which portrays the dating lives and daily dramas of a group of modern Orthodox or religious Zionist twenty-somethings, and *Shtisel* (3 seasons, 2013–2021), centered on a family that is fully a part of but also runs up against the constraints of their ultra-Orthodox community. On the rabbis' descriptions of hell, see Dov Weiss, "Gehinnom's Punishments in Classical Rabbinic Literature," in Eitan P. Fishbane and Elisha Russ-Fishbane, eds., *Jewish Culture and Creativity: Essays in Honor of Professor Michael Fishbane on the Occasion of his Eightieth Birthday* (Brookline, MA: Academic Studies Press, 2023), 77–90. Isaac Heinemann, *The Reasons for the Commandments in Jewish Thought: From the Bible to the Renaissance* (Boston: Academic Studies Press, 2009 [1953]), is a classic treatment of the eponymous topic, and see now, for the modern period and from a different methodological perspective, Yonatan Y. Brafman, *Critique of Halakhic Reason: Divine Commandments and Social Normativity* (Oxford: Oxford University Press, 2024). A detailed historical examination of the Bavli texts that are the foundation of laws of niddah may be found in Shai Secunda, *The Talmud's Red Fence: Menstrual Purity and Difference in Babylonian Judaism and its Sasanian Context* (Oxford: Oxford University Press, 2020). For a comparative study of ways in which dietary laws in the Abrahamic religions serve to enforce interreligious borders, see David M. Freidenreich, *Foreigners and Their Food: Constructing Otherness in Jewish, Christian, and Islamic Law* (Berkeley: University of California Press, 2014), and for an ethnographic study centered on contemporary Los Angeles, see Jody Myers, *Eating at God's Table: How Foodways Create and Sustain Orthodox Jewish Communities* (Detroit: Wayne State University Press, 2023). On the history and institutional structure of kashrut supervision in America, see Roger Horowitz, *Kosher USA: How Coke Became Kosher and Other Tales of Modern Food* (New York: Columbia University Press, 2018), and Timothy D. Lytton, *Kosher: Private Regulation in the Age of Industrial Food* (Cambridge: Harvard University Press, 2013). Arnold Eisen, the former Chancellor of the Jewish Theological Seminary, the flagship seminary of American Conservative Judaism, offers a vision for a revitalized liberal American Jewish community centered on Torah and the commandments in his *Taking Hold of Torah: Jewish Commitment and Community in America* (Bloomington: Indiana University Press, 1997).

●

1. Support for the poor counts among the commandments, indeed among the most important of them, though charity is a topic that blurs the line between halakhic requirement—a commandment in the narrow sense—and moral duty. On charity in the Bible and among its Jewish and Christian interpreters, see Gary A. Anderson, *Charity: The Place of the Poor in the Biblical Tradition* (New Haven: Yale University Press, 2013). Is it a contradiction in terms to think of charity as a

legal requirement? Or is there some moral advantage to thinking of charity as a legal requirement? Consider, in relation to this question, that one of the topics that the rabbinic tradition takes up in thinking about charity as an obligation is whether the poor, too, should have to give charity.

2. One of the commandments important enough to have been included in the Decalogue is honoring one's parents. As we saw briefly in this chapter and will see in greater detail in the next, the rabbis are extremely close readers of the Bible, always looking to find meaning in the smallest detail. When they explore the Bible's teaching on this topic, they notice a discrepancy between the Decalogue verse, "Honor your father and your mother" (Exod. 20:12), and a later verse, "You shall each revere your mother and father, and you shall keep my sabbaths: I am the Lord your God" (Lev. 19:3). The first verse lists the father before the mother, while in the second verse, the mother appears before the father. If you couldn't dismiss this discrepancy as mere rhetorical variation, but had to find meaning in it, how would you do so? For the Bavli's answer see Qiddushin 30b–31a. The rabbis also notice an oddity about the second verse in itself: Why does the verse juxtapose reverencing one's parents to the apparently unrelated topic of observance of the Sabbath? Try to think of an explanation (keeping in mind, perhaps, that in the Decalogue itself, the commandment to honor parents follows the sabbath commandment), then look up the Bavli's explanation in Bava Metzi'a 32a.

3. The traditional Jewish liturgy includes the following prayer of thanksgiving in the daily evening service: "With everlasting love You have loved Your people, the house of Israel. You have taught us Torah and commandments, decrees and laws of justice." (In the Koren prayer book introduced in chapter 10, these words may be found on page 244.) On the basis of this chapter and the previous one, how would you account for this claim? How does the fact that God taught Israel the Torah and the commandments express God's love for Israel?

— *Chapter 8* —

Children of God, Children of Abraham

THE TORAH, AS AN OBJECT OF STUDY AND AS the sum of the commandments, is one of three pillars of rabbinic Jewish theology; the others are God and the people Israel. Of the many ways one might describe the relationship among these pillars, the most straightforward is that the Torah, given at Sinai, represents the terms through which the relationship between Israel and God finds expression in the world; it articulates the content of their shared covenantal life. In this chapter, we take up the bond between Israel and God in itself, which came into existence prior to and underlies the Sinai covenant. The first half of the chapter reflects on the notion of Israel as God's people, and especially the conceptualization of this status under the rubric of sonship. The second half of the chapter explores the role of the patriarchs and matriarchs—Israel's ancestors—in mediating the relationship between God and Israel. Here, the people Israel is figured less as God's children than as the children of God's beloved servants of yore, especially Abraham.

We will have occasion in this chapter to delve into classical rabbinic works devoted to biblical interpretation, and it will be helpful to say more about this corpus now. Rabbinic biblical interpretation is called *midrash*, literally "searching out." Midrash can be halakhic—that is, having as its aim the clarification of things obligatory, permitted, and prohibited—or it can be aggadic; the latter will be our focus in this chapter. Midrash probes the biblical text very closely, and yet it is categorically different from any modern sort of commentary. To introduce the methods of midrash, as well as some of the motifs we will take up in this chapter, let us examine two passages from Genesis Rabbah 55–56. (Genesis Rabbah is a rabbinic commentary on Genesis edited in the land of Israel in roughly the early fifth century CE.)

Genesis Rabbah 55–56 interprets the story told in Genesis 22, where God tests Abraham by commanding him to take his son Isaac and offer him up as a sacrifice to God. Abraham dutifully takes his son on a three-day journey to Mount Moriah, where he binds Isaac and raises his knife to slaughter him. But then an angel calls to him and stays his hand. Because of Abraham's willingness to heed God's command, says the angel in God's voice, "I will indeed bless you, and I will make your offspring as numerous as the stars of heaven and as the sand that is on the seashore. And your offspring shall possess the gate of their enemies" (Gen. 22:17). In Judaism this story is called the Binding (*aqedah*) of Isaac, or the Akedah, and, as we will see, it occupies a very important theological role.

The first passage (Genesis Rabbah 55:1), which opens the unit, is a comment on Genesis 22:1.

> "After these things, God tested [*nissah*] Abraham." (Genesis 22:1) It is written: "You have given a banner [*nes*] for waving to them who fear you, because of rightness" (Psalm 60:6). This means, trial upon trial, greatness upon greatness, so as to try them in the world, so as to make them great in the world, like the mast [*nes*] of a ship. And why all this? "Because of rightness," that is, so that the measure of judgement should be found to be in the right. For if someone should say: [God] makes wealthy him whom he wishes; he makes poor him whom he wishes; he makes king him whom he wishes; he made Abraham rich as he wished; he made Abraham king as he wished, then you can respond to him and say to him: Could you do what Abraham did?

The passage begins by linking the word *nissah* ("tested") in Genesis 22:1 to the word *nes* ("banner") in Psalm 60:6. By means of this wordplay, the commentator is able to suggest that Genesis 22:1 means to say not so much that God tested Abraham—after all, surely God knew how Abraham would respond, so that a test would have been otiose—but that, through the Akedah, God gave Abraham a banner, a sign. The aim of this sign is specified by the end of Psalm 60:6: "because of rightness." That is to say: God's purpose in Genesis 22 was to demonstrate Abraham's fear of God to others, so that if someone should contend that God is unjust, that God's choice of Abraham and his descendants was just a matter of playing favorites, there will be a response that proves God's rightness: Could you do what Abraham did?

The theological claim in this passage could have been formulated directly as a remark on Genesis 22:1: God's purpose in testing Abraham was to make Abraham's heroic piety visible, and thus justify the election of Abraham. But the instinct of midrash is to elucidate one verse through another, in this case Psalm 60:6. Midrash assumes the unity of Scripture, not in the sense that all Scripture says one thing, but in the sense that Scripture is like a vast collection of locks and keys, with each verse capable of unlocking new meaning in another verse. From a substantive perspective, the passage reveals anxiety about the notion of God's election of Abraham and his descendants; the homilist acknowledges that one might, at least at first glance, reasonably accuse God of unfairness. We will expand below on the notion of Israel's election, and take up in the next chapter the correlate question of God's relationship to non-Jews.

For our second exemplary passage from the Genesis Rabbah unit, we pick up the narrative at its climax. Abraham's knife is poised over Isaac's bound body, but the angel interrupts him: "Do not lay your hand upon the boy, and do not do anything to him" (Gen. 22:12). The midrash (Genesis Rabbah 56:7) comments:

> "And he said: Do not lay your hand upon the boy." And the knife, where was it? Tears had fallen upon it from the ministering angels, and it dissolved. [Abraham] said to him: Let me strangle him. [The angel] said to him: "Do not lay your hand upon the boy." [Abraham] said to him: Let me take from him a drop of blood. [The angel] said to him: "Do not do anything to him."

The commentary begins with a question rooted in an almost comical literalism: if the angel tells Abraham not to lay his *hand* on Isaac, then it must be that the knife that was in his hand had somehow already disappeared. What happened to it? The answer: the angels who minister to God in heaven, seeing Abraham prepared to slaughter his son, had been crying, and their fiery tears fell upon the knife and dissolved it. And yet, evidently, Abraham was determined to carry on with the sacrifice; after all, God had so commanded. He must have been attempting to slaughter Isaac by strangling him with his bare hands, hence the angel's intervention: "Do not lay your hand upon the boy." The verse reports that the angel also said: "Do not do anything to him." Of course, according to the plain sense, these words simply lend emphasis and urgency to the angel's injunction. But for the rabbinic reader, Scripture is maximally economical, or omnisignificant: every holy word is pregnant with meaning. It must be, then, that something happened after "do not lay your hand upon the boy" that compelled the angel to add, "Do not do anything to him." The midrash surmises that Abraham, having been instructed not to kill Isaac by any means, sought at least to draw a drop of blood from Isaac, to make a token sacrifice, so that God's command not return utterly empty. It was to this proposal that the angel replied: "Do not do anything to him."

From a methodological perspective, we see in this passage that the way of midrash in explicating a biblical story is to employ hyperliteralism and the assumption of omnisignificance to retell the story, to expand it, to embellish it, often in a sort of playful way, but for a serious purpose, so that the story can speak to the theological concerns and even the aesthetic expectations of a new audience. Substantively, the passage, in making the angels, moved to tears, the audience of the Akedah, exemplifies a tendency to which we will return below, to conceive of the Akedah in mythic, world-historical terms, in a manner not altogether unlike the crucifixion of Christ for Christianity.

Children of God

In Exodus 4:22 God states: "Israel is my firstborn son." The affirmation of Israel as God's firstborn implies that other peoples are likewise God's children, but Israel's status is distinctive among them. We find elsewhere in the Bible (e.g., Exod. 22:29; Num. 3:12; 1 Sam. 1) evidence that a firstborn child is supposed to be given over to God, to serve in a priest-like role, or specifically as an aide to the priests. From this perspective, for Israel to be God's firstborn is for Israel to be reserved for God's service, with the privileges and obligations attendant on such service. And indeed, at the Sinai covenant God calls upon Israel to "be for me a kingdom of priests and a holy nation" (Exod. 19:6). Likewise, God enjoins the Israelites to build a house for God in their midst: "And they shall make me a sanctuary, so that I may dwell among them" (Exod. 25:8). Israel lives on God's land—the land surrounding the temple—on the strength of their role as God's servants. "For they are my servants, whom I brought out of the land of Egypt" (Lev. 25:42).

To link Israel's firstborn status to its priestly or servant role is to draw out the implication of this status for Israel's role as mediator between God and the world. There is clearly a basis for this outward-directed perspective in the Bible, and as we will see in the next chapter, modern Jewish thought amplifies it in various ways. But the more fundamental expression of Israel's status as God's firstborn son lies in the very relationship between God and Israel: God has a passionate love for Israel. This inward-directed notion finds pervasive expression in the Bible, and even more so among the rabbis. The firstborn son is especially beloved, so that the prophet Zechariah, for example, can use "the bitter mourning over a firstborn" (Zech. 12:10) as a figure for intense sadness. Israel is the child in whom God especially delights. God may discipline Israel, but even then, as their parent, God is moved by love. "Truly, Ephraim is a dear son to me, a child that is dandled. Whenever I have turned against him, my thoughts would dwell on him still. That is why my heart yearns for him; I will receive him back in love, declares the Lord" (Jer. 31:20). Or again, in a verse that figures God's love in maternal terms: "Can a woman forget her baby, or disown the child of her womb? Though she might forget, I never could forget you" (Isa. 49:15).

Is God incarnate in Israel, according to Judaism? Does God dwell in a special way in the bodies of God's firstborn son, in the way that, according to Christianity, God becomes flesh in Jesus the Son of God? Michael Wyschogrod, whom we already encountered in chapter 5 suggesting that Jewish converts to a post-supersessionist church ought, from the perspective of Christian theology, to continue to observe Jewish law, devotes an article to this question of incarnation.[1] Wyschogrod ventures that post-supersessionist Christians, and Jews responding to them, might find a theological meeting ground of sorts around incarnation. Looking retrospectively at Israel, Christians might see Christ's incarnation prefigured in the Jewish people as children of God. And Jews might be able to recognize Jesus as the particular Jew through whom the gentiles came to recognize the truth of God's real presence in all Jews. "The church found God in this Jewish flesh. Perhaps this was possible because God is in all Jewish flesh, because it is the flesh of the covenant, the flesh of a people to whom God has

1. Michael Wyschogrod, "A Jewish Perspective on Incarnation," *Modern Theology* 12 (1996): 195–209.

attached himself, by whose name he is known in the world as the God of Israel." This bold formulation diverges not only from the traditional Christian conception of Christ, who is much more than simply one Jew among others, but also from the traditional Jewish conception of God's indwelling in Israel, which, as Wyschogrod himself acknowledges, does not in fact concern Jewish flesh. Jewish tradition does not generally speak of Jewish bodies themselves as divine; God dwells among collective Israel, rather than in the flesh of Jewish individuals. Wyschogrod's suggestion makes rather too much of Israel, from a Jewish perspective, and undoubtedly too little of Christ, from a Christian perspective.

But it is possible to identify an intersection between rabbinic theologies of election and the Christian notion of incarnation from a different vantage point. God in the Bible is anthropomorphic—humanlike—from the very beginning. In the first few chapters of Genesis, God examines, makes judgments, works, rests, fashions an image of Godself (namely, human beings), and regrets previously made decisions. But rabbinic literature, in elaborating on God's relationship with Israel, offers up a still more radically humanlike portrayal of God. The God of the rabbis, out of love for Israel, overlooks God's lordly status—undertakes, to use the Christian term, "kenosis," or self-emptying—so that God can pray alongside Israel, can accept from Israel instruction and rebuke, can even sympathetically suffer with Israel, though not to the point of death, nor indeed even close to it. In other words, while God does not dwell in Jewish flesh, God becomes more humanlike through God's relationship with the Jewish people.

Let us take up three examples of this tendency. The first is a passage from the Babylonian Talmud (Berakhot 7a).

> Said Rabbi Yohanan in the name of Rabbi Yose: Whence that the Holy One, blessed be He, prays? For it says, "I will bring them to my holy mountain, and make them joyful in the house of prayer of mine" (Isaiah 56:7). "The house of prayer of them" is not stated, but rather, "the house of prayer of mine"; thus the Holy One, blessed be He, prays. And what does he pray? Said Rabbi Zutra son of Tobia in the name of Rav: "May it be My will before Me that My mercy press down My anger, that My mercy overwhelm My attributes, so that I act toward My children with mercy, and enter for their sake within the line of the law."

In Isaiah 56:7, God refers to the temple as "the house of prayer of mine." Clearly, the meaning is: my house, in which (or toward which) people pray. But in Hebrew, the possessive suffix "mine" attaches to the word "prayer," and Rabbi Yohanan finds meaning in this. In fact, the prayer belongs to God; God, too, prays. And God's prayer is the same as Israel's prayer. Just as Israel prays that God judge God's children, Israel, with mercy, and that God not exact from them the punishment that the law would allow, so God prays that God be so disposed. What does it mean for God to pray that God should act a certain way? The prayer seems to divide God from and indeed subordinate God to God's will, and to fissure God's personality into different attributes. If this portrait of God is even coherent, it seems at best unseemly. Nevertheless, Rabbi Yohanan is willing to insist that, attendant on God's relationship with Israel, God prays. (We will return in chapter 14 to the topic of God's attributes.)

The second passage is from Leviticus Rabbah, a commentary on Leviticus edited around the fifth century CE. A passage in one of the homilies therein (Leviticus Rabbah 23:9) takes up the incident at Sinai in which Moses, Aaron, and the seventy elders see God, "and under his feet there was like sapphire brickwork, and like the very heaven for clearness" (Exod. 24:10). The verse evidently means to convey that God is situated above a sort of sky-like floor. The midrash fastens on two features of the description. First, the verse uses two distinct similes to describe this floor: "like sapphire brickwork" and "like the very heaven for clearness." For the rabbinic reader, these comparisons cannot be assimilated to each other as rough synonyms; the assumption of omnisignificance demands that the verse be describing two different things. The second noteworthy feature is the bricks: Why should there be bricks in heaven? The midrash proceeds to a solution by linking these bricks with the bricks that the Israelites made during their enslavement in Egypt (Exod. 1:14; 5:6–21). The verse is telling us that when the Israelites were laboring at brickmaking, God, too, was making bricks with them, subjecting Godself to harsh servitude. Hence the sapphire brickwork. And when Israel was redeemed from Egypt, God, too, went free, and set aside the brickwork, so that now God's place was "like the very heaven for clearness." The notion that God accompanies Israel in their exiles, amid their suffering, is a commonplace in rabbinic literature, but it finds expression in this passage in an especially concrete way.

The third and final passage comes from a much later period; it was written during the Holocaust. Among the most powerful theological compositions forged in that conflagration is a collection of homilies called "Holy Fire" or "Sermons from the Years of Rage." These homilies were delivered by a Hasidic rabbi, Kalonymus Kalman Shapira, during his confinement in the Warsaw Ghetto between 1940 and 1942. Though Shapira did not survive the war, he took care to have the manuscript of his homilies concealed, and it was recovered afterward and published. In the homilies Shapira attempts to support traditional observance despite the dire circumstances, and to grapple with the question of theodicy that these circumstances ever more acutely raised.

In one of his last homilies, from the early spring of 1942, Shapira reflects on a passage in the Babylonian Talmud (Hagigah 5b). From Jeremiah 13:17 ("My soul will weep in secret . . . because the Lord's flock has been taken captive"), on the assumption that the speaker is God, the Talmud deduces that God weeps over Israel's exile. A challenge comes from 1 Chronicles 16:27, which asserts that "strength and joy are in [God's] place," implying that God does not weep. The Talmud responds by observing that Jeremiah 13:17 locates the weeping "in secret." There is always joy, then, in God's outer chamber, but God allows Godself to weep in God's inner chamber. From this solution Shapira makes a radical inference: there is an element of divine essence that becomes manifest precisely in God's weeping over Israel, for it is in such weeping that God retreats to God's innermost self. And further, when a Jew weeps in distress, he joins God in God's inner chambers, and attains there to a new and especially intimate revelation. "He weeps and wails together with him, as it were, and even finds the strength to study Torah and serve him."[2]

The God of these three passages—and many others like them could be adduced—is not unlike Christ incarnate. To be sure, rabbinic Judaism never envisions God literally taking on human flesh, or still less, dying. (On the question of whether God has a distinctive divine body, there are different voices in the tradition, ranging from an absolute no to an insistence on divine sexuality; we take up this topic in chapters 13 and 14.) But God does become strikingly human here. If God's creation and direction of the world already implicate God in the human condition, God's covenantal commitment to

2. Daniel Reiser, ed., *Sermons from the Years of Rage: The Sermons of the Piaseczno Rebbe from the Warsaw Ghetto, 1939–1942* (Jerusalem: Herzog Academic College, 2017), 293.

Israel binds God much more closely to it. As the rabbis understand it, the covenant commits God to sympathetically mirroring Israel: praying as they pray, doing slave labor with them, weeping when they weep.

This section has focused on the use of the figure of sonship to describe the covenantal relationship between God and Israel, in part because this figure enables comparison between Israel and Christ. But Judaism employs many other figures for this relationship. Alongside sonship, perhaps the most powerful is erotic love: God and Israel are lovers, ever seeking and taking pleasure in each other's company. We will explore this figure in chapter 15.

Children of Abraham

While Jewish theology puts Israel in direct relation to God as God's children, it also envisions the relationship as mediated through the patriarchs, so that the Jewish people represent, in the first instance, the children not of God but of the patriarchs. After all, though God enters into a covenantal relationship with the people of Israel at Sinai, this covenant follows from God's prior covenantal commitment to Abraham, Isaac, and Jacob. This commitment serves Israel in good stead especially when they transgress. Thus, for example, when God threatens to destroy Israel after the sin of the golden calf, Moses pleads successfully with God (Exod. 32:13): "remember Abraham, Isaac, and Israel, your servants, how you swore to them by your own self, saying to them, 'I will multiply your descendants like the stars of heaven, and all this land that I have promised I will give to your descendants, and they shall inherit it forever.'"

Taking its bearings from such passages, rabbinic Judaism devotes much attention to what it calls the "merit of the patriarchs" (*zekhut avot*), that is, the "credit" that the patriarchs, through their great deeds, have accrued with God, and that can be drawn down by their descendants when they have need of God's mercy. (The rabbis debate whether zekhut avot is a finite or infinite resource, and later commentary distinguishes the *merit* of the patriarchs, which may indeed be a finite resource, from the *covenant* with the patriarchs, which obligates God forever. See Bavli Shabbat 55a and the commentary thereto.) As we will see in chapter 10, the central liturgical text in Judaism, the Amidah, begins with a blessing dedicated to God's relationship to the patriarchs. This blessing characterizes God as one "who remembers the loyalty of the fathers and brings a redeemer for their sons' sons." By far the most important specific deed of the patriarchs that Jewish tradition invokes in this framework is the story of the Akedah. As discussed at the beginning of this chapter, the Akedah is the justification for God's election of Abraham; the challenge, "could you do what Abraham did," is the decisive response to any complainant.

The Akedah plays an especially central role during the Days of Awe, or the High Holidays, the sequence of two festivals that occurs at the beginning of the Hebrew month of Tishre, which coincides roughly with September. The first of these holidays is the New Year (*rosh ha-shanah*, "the head of the year"), and the second (discussed briefly at the end of the previous chapter) is Yom Kippur, or the Day of Atonement. The New Year marks the anniversary of the creation of the world, and the coronation of God as the world's king. Because one of the chief roles of the king is (as in 1 Kings 3, for example) to judge his people, the New Year serves as an annual day of judgment. A person's fate for the coming year is written on the New Year and sealed on the Day of Atonement.

The Bible describes the New Year as a "day for blowing the horn" (Num. 29:1). It does not explain why; perhaps the horn blast is supposed to signal God's coronation. But the rabbis find special meaning in linking this horn to the horn of the ram at the Akedah. According to Genesis 22:13, Abraham saw a ram tangled in the thicket by its horns, and he took the ram and sacrificed it in Isaac's place. It is this ram, for the rabbis, that Jews invoke in blowing a ram's horn on the New Year, in the hope that God will recall the Akedah and look kindly on Abraham's descendants when they pass before God for judgment. For the same reason, the lectionary features Genesis 22 as one of the readings from the Pentateuch for the New Year.

The rabbis magnify the Akedah in other ways. First, although it is clear, on the plain sense of the biblical text, that Abraham passes God's test in virtue of his willingness to offer Isaac to God, even though he did not actually slaughter him, the midrashic imagination insists, in different ways, on carrying the sacrifice through to the end. Thus, for example, a work called Midrash ha-gadol comments: "Although Isaac did not die, Scripture regards him as though he had died, and his ashes lay piled on the altar. That is why it says, 'so Abraham returned to his servants' (Gen. 22:19)."[3] That is to say, since the

3. The translation is taken with modification from Shalom Spiegel's remarkable survey of

verse describes only Abraham, and not Isaac, returning to the servants upon the descent from Mount Moriah, Scripture means to treat Isaac as absent, as having actually been sacrificed, even though he wasn't. (The simple solution to Isaac's omission from Gen. 22:19 lies in the fact that Abraham is the figure through whom the biblical text focalizes the story; Isaac is more or less an object, not a subject. Hence the verse does not bother to mention that Isaac accompanied Abraham down from the mountain.) Other texts go even further, and claim that Isaac was indeed slaughtered, and consumed by the flames, but afterward was resurrected.

A passage in Genesis Rabbah 56:9 finds in the ram of Genesis 22 not only the reason for blowing the horn on the New Year, but an encapsulation of the entire sweep of Jewish history. As the ram was entangled by its horns in the thicket, so Israel is entangled in a succession of exiles: from the Babylonian exile, connected with the destruction of the first temple, to the current, Roman exile, which began with Rome's destruction of the second temple. And the final redemption of Israel from exile will be accompanied by the blowing of a ram's horn. Another midrashic passage (Tanhuma [Warsaw] *va-yera* 18) goes so far as to make the very existence of the world dependent on the Akedah. This passage takes Psalm 8:5 ("What are mortals that you are mindful of them?") as the words of the angels at creation, seeking to dissuade God from creating the world, on the ground that human beings are undeserving of such a gift. God's reply: "in the future you will see a father slaughter his son, and the son slaughtered, for the sanctification of my name."

The foundational significance of the Akedah is also reflected in ancient synagogue art. Archaeologists have discovered a large number of late antique (ca. fifth and sixth centuries CE) synagogues in the Galilee whose floors are covered by mosaics. One pattern among these mosaics (as, for example, in the Beth Alpha synagogue) features two horizontal panel series, one at the front of the synagogue and the other at the back, with a zodiac circle in between them in the middle of the floor. The symbols of the twelve zodiac signs form the outer ring of the circle, while a chariot, linked with the sun, occu-

premodern Jewish commentary on the Akedah, *The Last Trial: On the Legends and Lore of the Command to Abraham to Offer Isaac as a Sacrifice: The Akedah* (Woodstock, VT: Jewish Lights Publishing, 1993), 3–4.

pies the center of the circle. The zodiac circle evidently means to represent the cosmos under the guidance of God. The horizontal panel at the front features imagery of the Jerusalem temple, such as the facade of the temple building or the candelabrum, while the one at the back depicts the story of the Akedah, especially the sacrificial scene. Paired together, the front and back panels implicitly suggest that Abraham's sacrifice in Genesis 22 represents the origin of the service of God in the temple, and thus also, by extension, of the bloodless service of God in the synagogue itself. (Indeed, already in the Bible [2 Chron. 3:1], Mount Moriah is identified with the site of Solomon's temple.) Put in relation to the central panel, the front and back panels convey that the stable operation of the cosmos depends on the principle of divine worship founded by Abraham.

A visitor to the Church of the Holy Sepulchre in Jerusalem who goes to the site within the church that many Christians identify as Golgotha, the place of Christ's crucifixion, will find two large murals alongside each other, one of the Akedah and one of the crucifixion. In the Akedah scene, the child Isaac lies flat on a stone, wearing a white loincloth. In the crucifixion scene, the cross lies flat on the ground, with Christ nailed to it, wearing a white loincloth. This juxtaposition makes Isaac a figure of Christ, who completes, as it were, Isaac's abortive sacrifice. The aforementioned ways in which Judaism elevates the Akedah, especially by assigning it the power to atone for sin and even to rescue the world, sharpens this connection.

And yet we must appreciate the considerable differences between the role of the crucifixion in Christianity and that of the Akedah in Judaism. The chief significance of the Akedah in Judaism lies in the fact that it cements God's covenantal commitment to Abraham and his descendants. Put differently, it fixes the Jewish people as a theological category. If, as Genesis Rabbah and the synagogue floor mosaic pattern suggest, the Akedah redeems the world as a whole, then it does so in the first instance by firmly establishing God's relationship with Israel. But given the fact that this relationship begins earlier, with Abraham's departure from his family, and the fact that the culmination of the relationship, for rabbinic Judaism, happens later, in the giving of the Torah at Sinai, the importance of the Akedah for Judaism cannot be said to approach that of the crucifixion for Christianity.

The comparison of the Akedah to the crucifixion also returns us to the question of human nature, which we introduced in chapter 6. In the Akedah, the father-son relationship occurs on the human plane: it is a human father who gives up his human son. The crucifixion translates this human event to the divine realm. The difference might suggest, along the lines laid out by David Hartman, greater optimism about human agency in Judaism. At the same time, the incarnation of the divine in human flesh in Christianity, a possibility not recognized in Judaism, as noted in chapter 7, represents a foundation in Christianity for the prospect of human beings, through baptism into Christ's crucifixion, becoming god-like.

Conclusion

I conclude this chapter with a passage about Abraham that instantiates a direction in Jewish theology that we will expand on in chapter 14. The passage is from a work written by Rabbi Isaac Hutner (1906–1980), one of the great Orthodox Jewish thinkers of the twentieth century. At the background of Hutner's second discourse in his *quntres ha-hesed* ("A Quire on Kindness") from his magnum opus, *Pahad Yitzhaq*, lies the traditional association of each of the patriarchs with different character traits. On the basis of Micah 7:20, Abraham is correlated with *hesed*, a complex word that comes in rabbinic literature to mean kindness or benevolence. One could justify this association by pointing to biblical stories in which Abraham manifests kindness, especially his hospitality to his angelic guests and his intercession on behalf of Sodom (Gen. 18). But Hutner arrives at a deeper connection through abstract reflection on the nature of kindness. Kindness, he says, is governed by a logic of excess or overflow. The gift emerges freely out of the bond between giver and receiver, and in such a manner that the giver's capacity to give is not thereby depleted. Creation out of nothing (ex nihilo), for Hutner, is the paradigmatic expression of kindness, because it occurs without prior motivation, and yields a surplus, something more than was present before. This is the force of the phrase in Psalm 89:3 that the rabbis and their successors render: "the world was built [through] hesed." The closest analogy to creation ex nihilo in this world is fertility, where something new comes into being through love, and without evident depletion of the parent. Abraham, observes Hutner, is the only one of the three patriarchs whose name itself incorporates the word for father (Hebrew *av* or *ab*; see Gen. 17:5). Abraham is the paradigmatic patriarch because his status as father follows from his essential character as a person of hesed. And the eternal survival of Abraham's seed is the physical expression of the dynamic of excess that constitutes Abraham's characteristic feature of kindness. For a Jew to do kindness is for her to imitate God as creator of the world, and to make manifest her belonging to the covenant that links God's creativity to its immediate human correlates, namely, the kindness and the inexhaustible seed of Abraham.

The relationship between God and Israel in Jewish theology is intimate and intense. It is a relationship with a very long past, tracing thousands of years back to Abraham, a relationship dense with joy and sorrow, a drama of nearness and distance that plays out on the stage of history, in the annual progress of the seasons and their festivals, and in the spiritual life of the individual Jew. It is a relationship that can be and has been encoded in almost any imaginable framework of meaning, from the semi-playful, storytelling mode of midrash to the liturgical language of synagogue ritual and art, to the philosophical-conceptual approach of Rabbi Hutner, and more. To appreciate this relationship's strength is to arrive at the question: But what of the gentiles? What of the world? What is their place in Jewish theology? We take up this question in the next chapter.

Further Inquiry

For a gripping introduction to midrash, using the story of Joseph as a case study, see James L. Kugel, *In Potiphar's House: The Interpretive Life of Biblical Texts* (Cambridge: Harvard University Press, 1994). One might afterward proceed to Kugel's later and larger tome, *Traditions of the Bible: A Guide to the Bible as It Was at the Start of the Common Era* (Cambridge: Harvard University Press, 1998). Another important starting point—more theoretical, and with comparison to early Christian exegesis—is Daniel Boyarin, *Intertextuality and the Meaning of Midrash* (Bloomington: Indiana University Press, 1990). Benjamin D. Sommer, ed., *Jewish Concepts of Scripture: A Comparative Introduction* (New York: NYU Press, 2012), includes a number of essays addressing Jewish biblical interpretation in different periods. On the Akedah motif in Judaism and Christianity see Jon Levenson, *The Death and Resurrection of the Beloved Son: The Transformation of Child Sacrifice in Judaism and Christianity* (New Haven: Yale University Press, 1993). For the most recent comprehensive survey of ancient synagogues, including their art, see Lee I. Levine et al., eds., *Ancient Synagogues Revealed, 1981–2022* (Jerusalem: Israel Exploration Society, 2023).

●

1. A passage in a third-century CE midrashic commentary on Exodus, Mekhilta de-Rabbi Ishmael, describes the scene at the Red Sea as the Israelites stand huddled on the shore, with the Egyptian army bearing down on them. (For the biblical account, see Exod. 14:9–21, and especially 14:13–16. My loose rendering of the rabbinic passage, from *be-shallah* 3, integrates parallels.) "Rabbi Yose the Galilean said: God said to Moses: Mount Moriah is already uprooted from its place, and Isaac's altar is upon it, and the wood is as though arranged on it, and Isaac is as though bound and set upon it, and Abraham is as though with knife in hand, to slaughter his son. . . . Moses said to God: Master of the world, and me, what should I do? He said to him: You, raise up your staff. Raise up and glorify and praise and sing the thanks and praise of him to whom war belongs." Try to make sense of this striking retelling of the tense moment at the sea. What is the Akedah doing at the Red Sea, and why is it described in the way it is? Note a verbal point of contact that the rabbis point to elsewhere: the verbs "cut" in Genesis 22:3 and "divide" in Exodus 14:16 (following the NRSV) are the same in Hebrew.

2. Just as the different patriarchs each have their own significance in Jewish tradition, so likewise the matriarchs. Among the matriarchs, the most important is Rachel, who died in childbirth. The site near Bethlehem marked from the fourth century CE as Rachel's Tomb remains a major pilgrimage site, though it is likely not the original one indicated in Genesis 35:20. Jeremiah 31:15–17 describes Rachel as crying over her exiled children; God comforts her, and assures her that they will return. This verse is adduced in Matthew 2:17–18 in reference to Herod's massacre of the innocents. On the basis of the Jeremiah verses, Rachel has been understood in rabbinic literature and Jewish folk tradition to be endowed with special intercessory powers, and because she died in childbirth and cries out for her lost children, she is linked in particular to children. Prevalent today is the

practice of winding a red string seven times around Rachel's Tomb and wearing a cut from the string as a charm for childbearing. In what ways does Rachel emerge from these texts and praxes as a Mary-like figure? How is she different? For more on Rachel's Tomb and a nearby grotto connected to Mary, see Susan Starr Sered, "Rachel's Tomb and the Milk Grotto of the Virgin Mary: Two Women's Shrines in Bethlehem," *Journal of Feminist Studies in Religion* 2 (1986): 7–22.

— Chapter 9 —

Beyond Israel

In this chapter, we will survey what Jewish theology says about the world beyond Israel, from the perspective of that world and from the perspective of Israel. What expectations does God have of gentiles, either as such or in relation to Israel? What expectations does God have of Israel in relation to gentiles, or toward the world in general? By way of framing our inquiry, it will be helpful briefly to sketch the dynamic in intellectual history—though the history will be schematic in the extreme—through which the world beyond Israel entered into view as a theological concern in Judaism, and developed therein.

In the ancient Near Eastern world from which the Bible emerged, each nation had its own chief god. The god of the Moabites was named Kemosh. The Edomites worshiped Qos. And the Israelites were ruled by Yahweh. A nation's god might be the chief of a pantheon, or have pride of place therein. When nations went to war, their gods, too, warred against each other. This system of national gods, each with his own territory, is destabilized at the ideological level by the notion of creation. Naturally a nation will wish to assign to its chief god the role of creator of the world; otherwise, its god would be subordinate to a different nation's god. But if a nation's chief god created everyone, then was he really the god of this nation? Ought he not to be worshiped equally by all nations?

There are many ways that this dilemma might be solved. One might, for example, assign creation to some primordial era preceding the emergence of the national gods, in this way preventing any national god from laying claim to creation. But let us focus, for the sake of a cleaner analytical framework, on two other, typologically opposite paths toward a solution. First, a nation might cling to its god's national identity, and take the god's creator role as a ground for supremacist claim: "We, as the people of the creator god, have a special status relative to all other peoples, who belong only to minions of our god, or have no real god at all." Alternatively, a nation might fully embrace its god's identity as creator, and renounce any special status in relation to this god: "Even if we were the first to serve him, he really is, in fact, the god of all, and we will either assert his identity with other national gods, who are simply our god under different names, or we will work toward a future in which all people worship the one chief god."

Let us allow these two paths to define a spectrum. At the one extreme is an ideology of self-assertion and even domination. At the other we find a sort of self-supersession: a nation reasons its way through to renunciation of its special status. Where does Jewish theology stand on this spectrum? Of course, Jewish theology contains many distinct voices, plottable to many very different points along the spectrum, and it is not clear how one can meaningfully speak of a consensus on this question. But it is fair to say that the tendency in the modern period is to raise up voices closer to the second extreme, though rarely at that extreme, and to sideline voices closer to the first. The continuation of this chapter fills out this schematic overview from two interrelated perspectives: what Judaism has to say about God's expectations of gentiles as such and in relation to Israel (the perspective from the outside in), and what Judaism has to say about God's expectations of Israel in relation to gentiles and to the world in general (the perspective from the inside out). The last section, representing something of a subset of the latter perspective, concerns Jewish views of other religions, and Christianity in particular.

God's Expectations of Gentiles

The Bible, of course, identifies Israel's God as the creator of the world. All human beings, gentiles as much as Jews, are created "in the image of God." God makes demands of all people, and calls them to task—first Adam, then Cain, then the generation of Noah, then the people of Sodom, and so forth—when they fail to live up to these demands. How does this configuration change, if at all, when God enters into a covenant with Abraham, and then with Abraham's descendants at Sinai? What implications does the election of Israel have for the gentiles?

One response in the Bible is that the nations of the world should recognize God's relationship with Israel, and honor Israel on this account. This expectation finds especially pointed expression in the beginning of the book of Psalms. After an introductory chapter, to which we will return, the book of Psalms opens, in Psalm 2, with a scene in which the "nations" and "peoples," the "kings of the earth," plot to free themselves from the dominion of "the Lord and his anointed." God laughs mockingly at them, and follows with anger: "I have set my king on Zion, my holy hill." The speaker then recounts what God has said to Israel's king: "You are my son; today I have begotten you. Ask of me, and I will make the nations your heritage, and the ends of the earth your possession. You shall break them with a rod of iron, and dash them in pieces like a potter's vessel." The kings are therefore urged to submit to God, and perhaps (but the Hebrew is difficult) to kiss the feet of his anointed.

This psalm does not explain why the kings of the earth resist the rule of God and God's anointed king in Jerusalem. But it ends with the declaration, "Happy are all who take refuge in him." This declaration forms an inclusio with the first verse of Psalm 1, "Happy are those who do not follow the advice of the wicked. . . . " Psalm 1 develops a sharp contrast between, on the one hand, the happy ones who occupy themselves with God's instruction, and find deep-rooted success, like trees planted on streams, and, on the other hand, the wicked, who are as chaff driven by the wind. The linking of the first two psalms through the "happy" inclusio suggests that the nations, insofar as they struggle against the dominion of God through Israel, are the wicked, and that they only attain to righteousness when they declare fealty to God's king.

For the traditional Jew who is also a citizen of the modern world, who is thereby committed to the principles of equality, freedom, and tolerance, and sensitive to the dangers of chauvinism and nationalism, it is an uncomfortable fact that the election of Israel can find expression in this way, through images of authority and submission, of divine mockery and anger, and through the implicit association of Israel with the righteous and the nations with the wicked. I take the proper response to such discomfort to be the careful examination of it, and of the category of election, to clarify whether election can be and has been expressed in ways that are faithful to the tradition but better attuned to these modern commitments and sensitivities.

We find a similar but importantly different image of election near the beginning of the book of Isaiah (2:2–4). Isaiah's vision is set "in the days to come," when "the mountain of the Lord's house shall be established as the highest of the mountains." "All the nations shall stream to it," to "the house of the God of Jacob," to learn God's ways, "that we may walk in his paths." God will judge between nations, so that they can resolve conflicts peaceably: "Nation shall not lift up sword against nation, neither shall they learn war anymore." The center of this vision, like that of Psalm 2, is Zion, and all the nations turn their eyes to the "God of Jacob" who dwells there. But they do so of their own will, drawn to it by the wisdom and the promise of peace that they find there. Moreover, this vision is immediately followed by the prophet's injunction for Israel to do the same: "O house of Jacob, come let us walk in the light of the Lord" (Isa. 2:5). This injunction suggests that Israel, too, is on the move with the nations, even if, unlike the nations, they are already affiliated with the God who is their goal. Relatedly, the vision of Isaiah 2, unlike that of Psalm 2, does not explicitly subordinate the nations to Israel; they seem to come to God directly.

From the perspective of rabbinic Judaism, which is centered at Sinai, in the Torah, the joining of the nations to the God of Israel could occur, in principle, in at least three ways. Gentiles might be called to become Jewish (i.e., to convert to Judaism). Or they might be called to follow the Torah but *as* gentiles, without conversion. There are isolated voices in the Jewish tradition that support one or another of these possibilities, but by far the most prominent view in rabbinic Judaism is that God's covenant with Israel does not substantially change God's expectation of gentiles. According to a view articulated explicitly in rabbinic literature (Bavli Sanhedrin 56a), though with roots tracing to the Second Temple period, gentiles are party to God's covenant with Noah. This covenant commits them to observance of the "laws of the children of Noah," or the Noachide laws, typologically seven in number, involving exclusive allegiance to the one true God (thus, not worshiping other gods besides the God of Israel nor blaspheming against God), alongside basic moral obligations (administering justice, and refraining from murder, adultery, robbery, and cruelty in consumption of animals). Within this framework, importantly, the religious meaning of a gentile's life, from the perspective of Judaism, does not depend on Israel. The gentile, as gentile, stands in direct relation to God. The model of the Noachide laws is thus much closer to Isaiah 2 than to Psalm 2.

Now, there is no shortage of statements in rabbinic and post-rabbinic writings that echo Psalm 2. They revel in an imagined future in which the historical roles of the powerful and the powerless are reversed, and can even suggest that gentiles ought properly to serve Israel. In part, such statements were historically conditioned by the circumstances of anti-Jewish exclusion and discrimination in which they arose, but in part they reflect a danger intrinsic to the notion of election. I do not mean to suggest that a theologically coherent Judaism can envision gentiles as indifferent to God's relationship to Israel. Even if, from the perspective of the Noachide laws, the gentiles' relationship to God exists prior to and separate from Israel, surely they cannot treat as irrelevant to them such world-historical developments as God's choice of Abraham, and the covenant that God enters into with his descendants. One can hardly worship the God of Israel without looking with interest on and seeking common purpose and relations of affection with the people Israel. But there is nothing intrinsically servile in this posture. We will return to this point in chapter 17, when we take up Christian perspectives on Zionism.

Israel's Relationship to the World and to Gentiles

It is tempting to consider Judaism from an objective perspective, from what the philosopher Thomas Nagel famously called the "view from nowhere," and to ask: What is Israel's election for? What divine purpose is it meant to serve? This temptation is in fact strongest for committed Jews themselves, and in particular, for modern Jews for whom the notion of a God who chooses favorites understandably seems unseemly and uncomfortable, and whose instinct is therefore to justify God's choice by subordinating it to a broadly universalist end. The fact that this question can arise from discomfort does not mean that it is a bad or an unimportant question; on the contrary, the question must be asked. But it is important to appreciate that this question is secondary in Jewish theology. When a person in a loving relationship begins to reflect on that love, the first question that arises is not the purpose of the love. There is indeed a sort of "why" that immediately arises, but it is the "why" of "why me," or "lucky me," or "how fortunate I am."

It is this reaction, this sense of wonderment, that we must dwell on first, if we are to be able to put any question of mission or purpose in its proper place. The mode in which this sense of wonderment finds expression is the exclamation, and the exclaimed word is one that we have already encountered in this chapter, albeit in a different context, namely, "happy." In the Bible, the exclamation of happiness can incorporate a martial element, as in the conclusion to Moses's blessings of Israel before his death: "Happy Israel! Who is like you, a people delivered by the Lord, your protecting shield, your sword triumphant! Your enemies shall come cringing before you, and you shall tread on their backs" (Deut. 33:29). But characteristically in rabbinic Judaism, the sense of wonder at being God's chosen people finds more irenic expression, in the experience of being in intimate relation with God and in the perception of this relation as an undeserved gift. As we will see in the next chapter, one of the building blocks of the daily liturgy is the sequential declaration of two verses beginning with the word "happy." First: "Happy are they who dwell in your house; they forever praise you" (Ps. 84:5). And then: "Happy the people who have it so; happy the people whose God is the Lord" (Ps. 144:15). The experiential posture of wonder is reinforced by the conceptualization of the people Israel as the children of Abraham, because on this conceptualization, Israel is the object of God's love neither immediately, nor on account of any virtue of its own, but rather by a fortunate accident of birth, by which it is the heir of a spiritual giant. Relatedly, the sense of good fortune is intrinsically communal, as the distinctive relationship of God is to the people Israel; it extends to the individual Jew only through her membership in the people.

Derivative from the experiential posture of wonderment, the question of purpose or mission can properly arise. Insofar as the question arises in this way, its proper formulation is, "to what purpose can God's love be put," which preserves the axiological priority of God's love, rather than, "what is the purpose of God's love," which transforms such priority, improperly, into the merely chronological precedence of means to end. The Bible itself, in passages like Isaiah 2, suggests that the ultimate destination of Israel's election lies in the illumination of the entire world, and passages like Exodus 19:6 and Leviticus 25:42, taken up in the previous chapter, position Israel as servants, joined to a God who faces outward toward the world. Modern Jews have drawn on such passages in framing a notion of Jewish mission. For Hermann Cohen (1842–1918), the great neo-Kantian German Jewish philosopher, Jews bear witness to "ethical monotheism," that is, the notion that there is only one God, and that this unique God is the condition for perceiving the common humanity of all people, and thus, for morality.

More recently, the watchword of a mission-oriented Judaism, especially in the more liberal denominations, has become *tikkun* (or *tiqqun*) *olam*. This term, which literally means something like "fixing the world," is first attested in the Mishnah (Gittin chs. 4–5), where it indicates the norm of human civilization and especially a functional social order. This norm, according to the Mishnah, can justify new legal enactments. Thus, for example, according to one view in the Mishnah, a master cannot be permitted to liberate his slave halfway. Although the realm of property law could in principle give force to such an arrangement—the half-liberated slave would work for his master one day, and for himself the next—it would leave this individual without a legal path to having children, because according to the halakhah, slaves may procreate only with other slaves, and free people with free people. Since tikkun olam requires that the world be populated, we compel the master who has half-liberated his slave to liberate him fully. Or again, the Mishnah rules that, on account of tikkun olam, it is forbidden to pay an excessive ransom, presumably because doing so would encourage further kidnapping.

The term *tikkun olam* has acquired other theological nuances over the centuries, but today, it is predominantly used as the Hebrew equivalent of social justice. In other words, it is used to make the claim that social justice is a Jewish value. And indeed there is no doubt that social justice, or more generally, care for the poor and downtrodden, is deeply rooted in Jewish theology. The law code in Exodus, for example, insists that "if you take your fellow's cloak" to guarantee a loan, the impoverished borrower must be allowed to retrieve the cloak every evening, "for it is his only clothing, the sole covering for his skin. In what else shall he sleep? And when he cries out to me, I will listen, for I am compassionate" (Exod. 22:26–27[25–26]). Likewise, again, the Israelite farmer is enjoined to leave the corner of his field unharvested, and to refrain from collecting fallen fruit: "you shall leave them for the poor and the stranger" (Lev. 19:10). These verses, along with many others, and the teachings that have accrued around them in the tradition, orient Judaism strongly toward social justice.

But in reckoning with the sources of Jewish teaching on social justice, a complication lies in the identification of the object of care. The passage from Exodus refers to one's "fellow." The verse just prior (Exod. 22:25[24]) likewise prohibits charging interest on a loan to the poor among "my [God's] people," and Deuteronomy 23:19–20(20–21) explicitly distinguishes between a loan to one's "brother," on which interest is prohibited, and a loan to a "foreigner," to which the prohibition does not apply. But in the passage obligating the farmer to leave from the harvest for the poor, the "stranger" is included with the poor. What is the content of these categories "fellow," "brother," "foreigner," and "stranger," and why does the Bible distinguish among them?

It is helpful to consider, in this context, the modern category of citizenship. We readily understand that a country's social safety net is designed to benefit its citizens. A citizen of another country who visits America can expect that the government will protect her and her property from harm, but she is not eligible to receive government benefits intended for the poor or the elderly or the like. Between citizen and foreigner is the non-citizen resident. The extent to which a non-citizen resident should benefit from the government's social services is often a matter of debate. Everyone understands that the distinction between citizen and non-citizen—even, within limits, to the degree that it discriminates against resident non-citizens—follows legitimately from the very notion of territorially bounded countries.

The Bible likewise, envisioning a Jewish society in the land of Israel, distinguishes between Jewish inhabitants ("fellows" and "brothers"), residents of other lands ("foreigners"), and non-Jews residing in the land of Israel ("strangers"). As a default, demands for special care for the poor and downtrodden—the return of a security for the need of the impoverished borrower; interest-free loans to the poor; leaving the corner of the field unharvested—envision fellow Jews as beneficiaries, to the exclusion of foreigners. Often, as in the case of the corner of the field, the Bible includes resident aliens in the scope of the injunction. The exclusion of foreigners from the class of beneficiaries no more implies hostility toward non-Jews than does the restriction of a country's social services, in the first instance, to its own citizens and residents, nor should it erode the sense of universal fellow-feeling that follows from the notion that all human beings are the image of God.

Of course, every religion, including Christianity, produces a distinction between adherents and non-adherents, a distinction to which the adage that charity begins at home can be and is reasonably applied. The case of Judaism is different only, but importantly, in that in Judaism, the distinction incorporates an ethnic element and, paradigmatically, a territorial element. The cultivation of an intense in-group ethic of care can tend, in practice, to yield a stance of indifference toward outsiders. The desire to counter this tendency evidently underlies the famous parable of the good Samaritan in Luke 10:25–37, which seems to critique a strictly ethnic understanding of the biblical "fellow"; below we will note similar interventions in rabbinic literature that give expression to the same desire. But an intense in-group ethic of care can also, on the contrary, enable a refined and powerful moral impulse that overspills its boundaries and washes over the world. Arguably, this impulse can be more intense than any that might emerge from a context that does not recognize, even in the first place, a distinction between insider and outsider.

Let us return, in this connection, to the category of the "stranger" or resident alien, in Hebrew *ger*. We have already seen that, according to Leviticus 19:10, the resident alien is entitled to glean after the harvest with the Jewish poor. The continuation of the chapter includes the famous injunction to love one's "fellow"—that is, one's fellow Jew—as oneself (Lev. 19:18), but it also introduces the resident alien into the same circle of love: "When a stranger resides with you in your land, you shall not oppress him. The stranger who resides with you shall be to you as the native-born among you; you shall love him as yourself, for you were strangers in the land of Egypt" (Lev. 19:33–34). This passage is especially striking because it calls on Israelites to find in the foundational experience in their historical memory—the enslavement in Egypt—a ground for identification with the stranger. At work here is a powerful movement of sympathy outward, and it is important to appreciate that the context for this movement in the Bible is a Jewish society on its land. The injunction to love the stranger is the response to the presence of the stranger among Jews.

But a Jew need not live in a Jewish society in the land of Israel to feel the force of this injunction. It is enough for a Jew to feel at home, as Jews have generally felt, to lesser or greater degrees, in the modern world, as free citizens of the countries in which they live. In the premodern world, this was not the case. As we will discuss in chapter 16, in the premodern context Jews were themselves strangers, neither endowed with collective responsibility for others nor, in general, invited to identify with a common good beyond their communities. In these circumstances, the very meaning of the word *ger* transformed. For the rabbis, it no longer indicated a "stranger," a resident alien living in a Jewish state, but a convert, a gentile who chose to become Jewish. Even further, the rabbis ceased, in general, to think in political terms, and the word *goy*, which in the Bible indicates a nation—Israel, too, can be characterized as a *goy* in the Bible (e.g., 2 Sam. 7:23)—came among the rabbis to designate an individual gentile. (Both of these semantic shifts, in the words *ger* and *goy*, have somewhat earlier roots, in the late Second Temple period.) This change, coupled with the broader social circumstances of discrimination and persecution that enabled it, darkened the discourse about gentiles in rabbinic sources. Consider, for example, how different it is to speak, with Psalm 2, of a messianic future in which *goyim* (the plural of *goy*) accept Israel's authority, when the word refers not to nations but to gentiles as individuals; an image of fealty in an international political setting can become an image of personal servitude.

At the same time, the rabbis preserve and in various ways expand the Bible's affirmations of common humanity and its universalist values. By way of example, if, with the transformation of the biblical "stranger" from a resident alien to a convert, Leviticus 19:10 ("you shall leave them for the poor and the stranger") no longer supports the inclusion of gentiles in biblical poverty legislation, the rabbis nevertheless insist that "one may not object to the gentile poor collecting gleanings, forgotten sheaves, and the unharvested corner, on account of ways of peace" (Mishnah Gittin 5:8). A teaching cited in the Bavli (Gittin 61a) goes further: "We support the gentile poor along with the Jewish poor, we visit the gentile sick along with the Jewish sick, and we bury the gentile dead along with the Jewish dead, on account of ways of peace." This principle of "ways of peace" evidently derives from Proverbs 3:17, understood as a reference to the Torah: "its ways are ways of pleasantness, and all her paths are peace." The rabbinic principle of "ways of peace" can be understood—is likely best understood in its original context, in fact—in limited pragmatic terms, as reflecting a concern to avert enmity and friction, but the principle does ultimately encode, through its biblical basis, a universalist vision of peace, and many Jews in the modern period have embraced this principle as an expression of such a vision.

Judaism and Other Religions

In part because of its tendency to divide the world into Jewish and gentile, without considering divisions among gentiles, Judaism does not have a well-developed theology of other religions. Modern Jewish theologians, however, by drawing on a range of traditional sources, have made some strides in this area. Alon Goshen-Gottstein, a scholar whose work I draw on heavily for the discussion below, observes that the interests and criteria of a Jewish theology of other religions will necessarily diverge, though inevitably not totally, from those of the Christian theology of other religions, which tends to define the field. The Christian theology of other religions centers chiefly on soteriology, or the doctrine of salvation. It asks: Can an adherent of a given religion be saved in virtue of her adherence to that religion? Secondarily, the Christian theology of other religions is concerned with revelation: Can another religion be a vehicle of divine revelation, or does it constitute "only" a form of human seeking of God? The question of soteriology does not arise as such in Judaism, which does not think of human beings as in need of salvation. The question of revelation can enter, as we will note below, though it is not central.

For Goshen-Gottstein, the central issue for a Jewish theology of other religions should be legitimacy or validity; the question is whether a given religion is pleasing to God. The tradition of the seven Noachide laws incumbent upon gentiles creates a halakhic or legal framework within which to evaluate a religion's validity. Especially significant, in this respect, is the Noachide law demanding exclusive worship of the one true God. The jurist will ask: Is a given religion's conception of the divine close enough to the "true" one that its worship can be deemed as directed toward God, rather than as a form of what halakhah calls "foreign worship" (colloquially: idolatry)? But the halakhic framework of the Noachide laws need not be the only arbiter of a religion's legitimacy. Nor is it necessary to come to a single, generalized conclusion about a religion: it can be pleasing to God in some respects, and not pleasing in others.

To turn from other religions generally to Christianity in particular, perhaps the most famous traditional statement concerning other religions is Maimonides's judgment on Christianity. Maimonides, a towering medieval jurist and philosopher whose thought we will take up in chapter 13, classifies Christianity as foreign worship in a number of places in his writings, though he never clearly indicates the basis for this classification. It could lie in his understanding of the doctrine of the Trinity or incarnation, or the practice of Christian iconography. In any case, we should appreciate that Maimonides's characterization of Christianity as foreign worship represents, in the first instance, a halakhic decision, with halakhic implications for both gentiles and

Jews. (For gentiles, the implication is that a Christian violates the Noachide law mandating worship of the one true God, and would do better to conceive of God in the manner of Islam, which Maimonides classifies as non-idolatrous. For the Jew, for example, the Mishnah prohibits engaging in commerce with an idolater close to an idolater's festival, lest, by doing so, the Jew supplies a reason for the idolater to thank his god on the festival. On Maimonides's view, this prohibition applies to Christianity.) But, as Goshen-Gottstein notes, this halakhic characterization is not the end of the story for Maimonides. Elsewhere (*Mishneh Torah*, Law of Kings, 11:3), Maimonides tentatively ventures that the rise of Christianity and Islam should be understood as God's providential means to bring the knowledge of the Torah and of the one God to the world, that it might become unified in true worship. Elsewhere still (Responsum 149 [Blau edition]), Maimonides rules that one may teach a Christian but not a Muslim about the mitzvot in an attempt to persuade him of the truth of Judaism, because Christians acknowledge the divinity of the Jewish Bible according to the traditional text, while Muslims do not. Maimonides's view of Christianity is thus more nuanced than it might appear if the field of vision of a Jewish theology of other religions were confined to the halakhic criteria supplied by the Noachide laws.

On the whole, premodern Jews living in Christendom tended to view Christianity and Christians negatively, and sometimes very negatively. Christianity came to be identified with the Roman empire, and thus with the exile that began with the destruction of the second temple by Rome, so that to pray for redemption was to pray for the end of Christian political power. The cross became a symbol of persecution and oppression. Jews from the Talmud forward wrote parodies about Jesus that ridiculed Christian beliefs in sharp and often crude ways. With the Enlightenment and the integration of Jews into western society, warmer relations began to develop in some circles, and the possibility for a distinctive Jewish theology of Christianity emerged. Especially in recent decades, gestures of support and friendship from a wide range of Christians, including Catholics moved by the spirit of Vatican II and evangelical Protestants supportive of the state of Israel (on which more in chapter 17), have inspired Jewish attempts to consider Christianity as a category in Jewish theology, and to engage in theological dialogue with Christians out of the assumption (among others) that, sharing with Christians a scriptural canon and a complex, intertwined past, Jews can gain better insight into their own faith by learning about Christianity. Pioneering in this regard is *Dabru Emet: A Jewish Statement on Christians and Christianity*, issued by Jewish thinkers in the academic world in the year 2000, and an associated book, *Christianity in Jewish Terms.*[1]

Jewish theology can indeed be greatly enriched by engaging with Christianity, on two general grounds at least. First, such engagement is a matter of recovering something lost: due to the efforts of both Jews and Christians over the ages to guard the boundary between the two faiths, some concepts with deep Jewish roots came to be marked as Christian, and therefore, at least within certain frameworks and under certain rubrics, off-limits for Jews. Grace is one example; faith, in some ways, is another. (This process of course operated in the same way in the other direction, with similar impoverishing consequences for Christian theology.) By studying Christian theology, Jewish theologians can learn to recover such concepts in a distinctively Jewish garb. Second, engagement with Christian theology is a matter of drawing inspiration from a biblically rooted religious formation whose distinctive experience with Christ led it to insights about the Bible that the Jewish tradition, shaped by its own distinctive and productive experiences, may have missed.

And yet it is important to recognize a certain theological limit to these new engagements with Christianity. The limit lies in the basic asymmetry between Christianity and Judaism, which we remarked on in chapter 1. Christianity, arising as it does out of Judaism, must grapple with Judaism, must come to an understanding of Judaism, in order to understand itself. A post-supersessionist Christianity embraces, at the theological level, the historical fact of its origin in Judaism, and is driven by this recognition to embrace Jews. But Judaism has no structural dependence on Christianity, nor does it, as traditionally understood, call upon Jews in a theologically specific way to embrace post-supersessionist Christians, beyond the general injunction to respond to kindness with kindness. This asymmetry is something that must be grappled with in modern Jewish-Christian dialogue and theology.

1. The statement appeared in *The New York Times*, September 10, 2000, p. 23, New England edition. Online, see, e.g., https://ccjr.us/dialogika-resources/documents-and-statements/jewish/dabru-emet. On the corresponding book, see the "Further Inquiry" section at the end of this chapter.

How far might a Jewish theology troubled by this asymmetry go? How far could it attempt to as it were embed Christianity in Judaism? Could it go any further than Maimonides, beyond viewing Christianity, along with Islam, as part of God's providential plan to spread belief in the God of Israel among the nations? Traditional Judaism takes prophecy to have ended near the beginning of the Second Temple period, corresponding to the closing of the biblical canon, but it does recognize the continuing possibility for inspiration of a lesser sort, and one could imagine the inclusion of Jesus and Paul under this rubric. More significantly, the biblical category of the ger, the stranger, could be recovered as a framework for conceptualizing Christians from a Jewish perspective. As noted above, the ger is in origin a gentile who resides among Jews in a Jewish state in the land of Israel. By extension, the term could describe Christians who conceive of themselves, insofar as they are Christians, as attaching themselves to the Jewish people in the manner envisioned by Paul, as understood along the lines laid out in chapter 5. When the Bible enjoins Jews to love the stranger, it grounds this obligation in the fact that the stranger is a foreigner, residing in a land not his own, without the social network and safety net that the native enjoys. Obviously, this is not the case for Christians as such in a literal sense, but could Jews not conceive of Christians who yoke their religious identity to a people to whom they do not belong, who take as the word of God a set of books written in the language of that people and about them, who refuse the comfort of inhabiting a religious space that they might call fully their own, as strangers in a like sense? There is a contrast on this score between a post-supersessionist Christianity and Islam. While Islam is an "Abrahamic religion," it does not, as a rule, assign special theological significance to the Jewish people, nor does it deem the Jewish Bible sacred. While Islam, on this approach, would belong to the general category of other religions, with which Judaism must of course engage thoughtfully and with respect, the Christian would have the distinct status, from the Jewish perspective, of a ger.

Conclusion

In chapter 5 we examined Romans 9–11, Paul's anguished reflection on the fact that his own people, Israel, especially beloved of God, had, in the main, said no to Christ. One could imagine a modern Jew, who understands herself to be a member of a people chosen by God and is also committed to the universalist ethical principles that are the bedrock of liberalism, writing an anguished analogue, seeking to come to terms with the tension between these two truths. The questions and answers surveyed in this chapter, concerning both the perspective of Judaism from the inside out—on how Jews ought to relate to gentiles and to the world—and the perspective of Judaism from the outside in—on how gentiles are supposed to relate to the God of Israel and God's people—would find their way into such a reflection, but the conclusion might, like Paul, acknowledge the mystery: "O the depth of the riches and wisdom and knowledge of God! How unsearchable are his judgments and how inscrutable his ways! 'For who has known the mind of the Lord? Or who has been his counselor?'" (Rom. 11:33–34).

Further Inquiry

I have often asked students, in connection with the topics covered in this chapter, to watch Menachem Daum's 2004 documentary, *Hiding and Seeking: Faith and Tolerance After the Holocaust*. The documentary broaches the question of tolerance toward and engagement with gentiles among Orthodox Jews within the yeshiva world (first and foremost, Daum's own family), and the ways in which this question intersects with the memory of the Holocaust. The canned history at the beginning of the chapter echoes musings of Yehezkel Kaufmann in his *Exile and Estrangement: A Socio-Historical Study of the Issue of the Fate of the People Israel from Ancient Times until Today* (Tel Aviv: Dvir, 1930). On Jewish theologies of election, see especially Joel S. Kaminsky, *Yet I Loved Jacob: Reclaiming the Biblical Concept of Election* (Nashville: Abingdon Press, 2007). For the Noachide laws and other rabbinic perspectives on non-Jews, see Marc Hirshman, "Rabbinic Universalism in the Second and Third Centuries," *Harvard Theological Review* 93 (2000): 101–15; Adi Ophir and Ishay Rosen-Zvi, *Goy: Israel's Multiple Others and the Birth of the Gentile* (Oxford: Oxford University Press, 2018); Holger M. Zellentin, *Law Beyond Israel: From the Bible to the Qur'an* (Oxford: Oxford University Press, 2022). On Jewish social justice teachings, see Jill Jacobs, *There Shall Be No Needy: Pursuing Social Justice Through Jewish Law & Tradition* (Woodstock: Jewish Lights, 2010); Aryeh Cohen, *Justice in the City: Toward a Community of*

Obligation (Brighton: Academic Studies Press, 2012). Uri L'Tzedek, an Orthodox social justice organization, also offers extensive online material at utzedek.org. For the approach of Alon Goshen-Gottstein discussed above, see his "Jewish Theology of Religions," in Steven Kepnes, ed., *The Cambridge Companion to Jewish Theology* (Cambridge: Cambridge University Press, 2020), 344–71. On the most famous compilation of Jesus parodies in the Jewish tradition, *Toledot Yeshu* ("the story of Jesus"), see Daniel Barbu and Yaacov Deutsch, *Toledot Yeshu in Context: The Jewish "Life of Jesus" in Ancient, Medieval, and Modern History* (Tübingen: Mohr Siebeck, 2020). The book emerging from *Dabru Emet*, mentioned above, is Tikva Frymer-Kensky et al., eds., *Christianity in Jewish Terms* (Boulder, CO: Westview Press, 2000). The body of each chapter, written by a Jewish scholar, takes up a theological topic of importance to Judaism and Christianity. This essay is followed by two responses, one from a Jewish scholar and one from a Christian scholar. On contemporary Jewish approaches to Christianity, including in the state of Israel, see part II of Karma Ben-Johanan, *Jacob's Younger Brother: Christian-Jewish Relations after Vatican II* (Cambridge: Harvard University Press, 2022).

●

1. Other than Maimonides's *Guide to the Perplexed*, which we will take up in chapter 13, the most famous medieval work of Jewish philosophy is the *Kuzari* ("Khazar") of Yehudah Halevi (ca. 1075–1141). The *Kuzari*, which one might also call anti-philosophical, is a Platonic-like dialogue conducted mainly between a Jewish sage and the king of the Khazars that eventually leads to the king's conversion to Judaism. In the course of the discussion (e.g., essay 1, sections 31–43, 95, 101–3, 115), the Jewish sage, standing for Halevi, claims an ontological difference between the Jewish people and other human beings: the former have a quasi-angelic character, as heirs to a divine essence tracing from Adam but descending only through a particular line. This notion is of course immediately disquieting and fraught with danger, though it constituted less a danger than a psychological balm at a time when Judaism was, as indicated in the full title of the work (loosely: "an apology for a despised religion"), disempowered and beleaguered. Wherein, precisely, does the difference lie between Halevi's view, on the one hand, and the standard conception of a people chosen by God and perpetuated via birth? Why does Halevi's view seem more problematic?

2. In chapter 1 I suggested that Judaism can be called a world religion insofar as it puts forward "a religious vision in which everyone in the world finds a place, albeit not the same place: Jews should worship God as Jews, and gentiles as gentiles." We have fleshed out this vision in this chapter. Consider now: Does Judaism, conceptualized as a world religion in this way, differ categorically from a post-supersessionist Christianity that envisions the church as composed of Jews, as Jews, alongside gentiles?

3. While the more liberal Jewish denominations today, as noted, frame Jewish mission in terms of tikkun olam, more traditional Orthodox Jews tend instead to speak of *qiddush hashem*, an obligation to "sanctify God's name" by behaving in an exemplary way toward and among non-Jews: with politeness, consideration, and punctilious morality. The point is to make manifest the wisdom and beauty of the Jewish way of life, not in order to inspire conversion, but to model a set of values, and to proclaim Israel's God as the source and measure of morality. (The notion of being a "light unto the gentiles," from Isa. 49:6, is also cited for the same purpose.) How is this conception of Jewish mission similar to and different from the conceptualization of Jewish mission as tikkun olam?

— Chapter 10 —

Prayer and the Synagogue

THIS CHAPTER AND THE NEXT TWO CONCERN the most prototypically "religious" praxes in Judaism: prayer, the synagogue, sabbath, the festivals, and life-cycle rituals. In this chapter we survey the basics of Jewish prayer, with a focus on the theological content of major prayer texts. This chapter also briefly examines the most important locus of prayer, the synagogue. The next chapter takes up the festival calendar, with a particular focus on the weekly day of holiness, the sabbath, while chapter 12 addresses the life-cycle rituals, with particular attention to the topics of marriage and sexuality. When I introduce prayer texts in the discussion below and elsewhere, I draw on the Ashkenazi tradition, with translations (sometimes modified) and page numbers from a prayer book (*siddur*, "arrangement," pl. *siddurim*) popular in modern Orthodox circles, the Koren siddur.[1]

Blessings

The fundamental unit of Jewish prayer is the blessing (*berakhah*, pl. *berakhot*). A blessing begins with the words "Blessed are you, Lord our God, king of the universe," and then proceeds to the specific content of the blessing. If the blessing is longer than one sentence, then it inevitably extends for several sentences, and concludes by returning to the formula, "Blessed are you, Lord," followed by a relative clause that summarizes the key theme of the blessing. Such blessings structure the main units of the fixed thrice-daily prayers, which we will describe below, but they also occur separately from these prayers. Thus,

1. *The Koren Siddur: Nusaḥ Ashkenaz* (Jerusalem: Koren Publishers, 2009).

for example, a blessing is recited before the performance of a commandment, like eating unleavened bread on the night of Passover.

Let us enter into some detail concerning the most important context for blessings outside the daily prayers, namely, the pair of actions that define us as living beings: ingestion and excretion. The Bavli (Berakhot 35a) requires that one make a blessing prior to "deriving benefit from this world," by which is meant, first and foremost, eating and drinking. Rabbi Levi makes the point sharply by setting two verses against each other. Psalm 24:1 assigns the earth to God: "the earth and all its fulness are the Lord's." Yet Psalm 115:16 puts it in the possession of human beings: "the heavens are the Lord's heavens, and the earth he gave to humankind." The solution to this contradiction is the blessing. By acknowledging God as the ultimate source of his food, a person obtains God's permission to transfer the food into his possession and thus makes it permissible to eat. To eat without first blessing God would be, as it were, to steal from God. Likewise, Jewish law recognizes an obligation to bless God after eating, on the basis of Deuteronomy 8:10: "and you shall eat and be sated, and you shall bless the Lord your God for the good land that He has given you."

The words of the blessings are not left to the individual to determine. Rather, in keeping with the conceptualization of food blessings as legal obligations, the formula, or rather formulas, are fixed in advance. There is one blessing for fruits—"Blessed are you, Lord our God, king of the universe, who creates the fruit of the tree" (994)—another for vegetables, and others, respectively, for grain-based foods (e.g., a muffin), for bread, for wine and grape juice, and for foods that do not fit into any of the above categories. It can be complicated to determine the appropriate blessing over a food that seems to cut across categories, or that contains multiple ingredients; in fact, many traditional Jewish schools host "*berakhah* bees," on the model of spelling bees, to encourage mastery of the blessings over common and obscure foods. There are also fixed blessing formulas for after eating (974–96), whose content and length depend on whether one has eaten a less substantial food, a more substantial food, or, most significantly, a meal with bread.

The system of food blessings encodes, through their content and through the categories that structure them, an array of theological commitments. Here I will mention only one, which is of particular relevance for the continuation of this chapter and for subsequent chapters: an attachment to the land of

Israel. In the case of the blessing after eating, a "substantial" food is defined as a grain-based food, wine or grape juice, or one of the other fruits that the Bible associates (most significantly, in Deut. 8:8, just before the verse that is the source of the obligation to bless after eating) with the land of Israel: figs, pomegranates, olives, and dates. Likewise, the texts of the blessings after substantial foods and after a meal with bread both devote extensive attention to the land of Israel, praising God for giving it to the people of Israel and praying for the return of the Jews to their land, the installment of a Davidic messiah on his throne, and the rebuilding of the temple. The blessing system thus refracts every substantial moment of eating—even by a Jew in America, eating food grown in America—through the biblical vision of God's people dwelling in the promised land.

Excretion of food, too, demands a blessing of praise. After exiting the bathroom—because God's name is too holy to be pronounced in the bathroom itself—one recites the following text.

> Blessed are you, Lord our God, king of the universe, who fashioned people with wisdom, and wrought in them manifold spaces, manifold hollows. It is a fact patent and well-known before your throne of glory that if even one of them were to rupture or be blocked, it would be impossible to endure and stand before you. Blessed are you, Lord, who heals all flesh, and does wondrously. (1005)

The blessing voices a mundane but theologically profound paradox about the human body. It is a marvel of complexity that attests to the creator's wisdom. In this respect, the human body is a mark of God's presence. And yet the human body's very complexity renders it unstable, always prone to failure, and thus a mark of difference from God. In order to maintain this fragile thing, we retreat to the bathroom, and in doing so remove ourselves from God's presence.

Daily Prayer

Rabbinic law mandates three daily prayers: the morning prayer (*shaharit*), the afternoon prayer (*minhah*), and the evening prayer (*ma'ariv*). The text of these prayers is fixed, and can be found in any siddur. A religious Jewish home will inevitably contain multiple *siddurim*, and they line the bookshelves of the synagogue. Prayer ideally occurs in a synagogue, in the midst of a congregation that stands for the people Israel. But in principle and often in practice, a person will pray on his own, and in any place that he finds himself when the time for prayer has arrived: at home, in an airport, etc. Importantly, however, the major units of the fixed prayers are written in the first-person plural. Thus, even one who prays by herself prays, implicitly, with Israel.

At the center of each of the three daily prayers is the *Amidah* ("standing"), so called because one recites it in a standing position, since this prayer occurs, in a special way, in God's presence. For this reason, too, one takes three steps forward before beginning the prayer, by way of approaching God, and three steps backward after, to take one's leave. Likewise, unlike almost all other prayers, the Amidah features bowing—not full prostration but from the waist—at the beginning and end. The Amidah consists of a series of nineteen blessings. (For the text see the Koren siddur, 108–34.) The first three blessings feature declarative statements praising God: for entering into a relationship with the patriarchs and thus with Israel; for wondrous deeds that give life to the world, especially the seasonal rains and the future resurrection of the dead; and for God's sanctity, or for what we might call God in Godself. The fourth blessing transitions the Amidah into a new unit, a series of fourteen blessings devoted to requests. The request blessings hover between the immediate and the distant future. On the one hand, they seek a life of material and spiritual bounty: wisdom, health, prosperity, justice, forgiveness for sins. On the other hand, the request blessings express hope for the messianic end time. They call on God to fight on Israel's behalf and redeem them; to gather the exiles to the land of Israel; to restore Jerusalem to its former glory and dwell therein in a rebuilt temple; to establish in Zion a justly administered state governed by an anointed king—the messiah—from the house of David; and to condemn the wicked and reward the righteous. While the blessings focused on the immediate future are concentrated in the first half of the request sequence, and those oriented toward the distant future in the second, there is no sharp dividing line between them, and some requests, such as that for forgiveness of sins, seem to have both futures in mind. The request sequence thus blurs the near and the distant horizons of expectation and suggests that mundane prosperity in the present is a sign of future redemption. The request sequence concludes with two request blessings calling on God to accept Israel's prayers. This double conclusion tracks the two vectors of the request sequence. The first one is general, and concerns, by implication, the prayers for a prosperous present, while the second one incorporates a request that Israel's prayers be supported by the restoration of the major form of divine worship envisioned by the Bible, namely, the sacrificial rites in the temple. After the request sequence, the Amidah concludes with a blessing of thanksgiving and a prayer that God bestow peace on Israel.

Like the blessings after substantial foods, then, the Amidah envisions the messianic redemption. This theological orientation is reinforced by spatial orientation. One is supposed to pray the Amidah facing toward the Temple Mount in Jerusalem, which means, for Jews in the West, facing east. The orientation toward redemption in these key liturgies makes manifest a central aspect of Jewish theology with which we have not yet engaged in depth: a strong exilic consciousness. Ever since the destruction of the temple at the hands of the Romans in 70 CE, if not earlier, the people of Israel are not where they should be, and more generally, the world is not as it should be. Israel hopes for a return to the biblical vision of a people on its land, surrounding a rebuilt temple in Jerusalem, and ruled by the messiah. And it hopes for something more: for universal recognition of Israel's God, for the perfection of the world, for an end to evil.

While Judaism's vision of redemption involves the messiah, it does not center on the messiah's person. At some point, from somewhere, a person will emerge who is recognized as a descendant of David, and this person—a human being in every respect, like David himself—will be enthroned in Jerusalem, presumably to be succeeded by his offspring. But Jewish messianic expectation does not typically imagine him as having a decisive role in effecting Israel's redemption. The chief agent of Israel's redemption is, rather, God. The assignment of agency to God means that, despite the prominence of exilic consciousness and despite the fervor and centrality of the hope for redemption, traditional Judaism is on the whole quietist: it is up to God, not to human beings, to change Israel's status in the world, and to perfect the world. However, when Judaism encountered modernity, its powerful redemptive impulse, no longer constrained to the same degree by quietist piety or by social exclusion, moved Jews to attach themselves to an array of ideologies and movements within the Jewish world and without, seeking a better world for Jews and others. The elevation of ethical monotheism and tikkun olam, described in the previous chapter, belong in part to this dynamic; we will turn to other expressions of it in chapter 16.

Because the Amidah is the central Jewish prayer, it is the paradigmatic site in the modern period for liturgical reform among non-traditional denominations. Let us examine how prayer books published within Reform Judaism have modified the first two blessings. Here is the text of the first blessing of the Amidah in the Reform prayer book, *Gates of Prayer*, from 1975.

> We praise You, Lord our God and God of all generations: God of Abraham, God of Isaac, God of Jacob; great, mighty, and awesome God, God supreme. Master of all the living, Your ways are ways of love. You remember the faithfulness of our ancestors, and in love bring redemption to their children's children for the sake of Your name. You are our King and our Help, our Savior and our Shield. Blessed is the Lord, the Shield of Abraham.[2]

This formulation represents a loose but generally faithful translation of the traditional Hebrew text. There is only one important theological change: in the traditional formulation, God will bring a *redeemer* to Israel, but in the Reform version, God will bring *redemption*.

This seemingly minor change—with roots in the early nineteenth century, at the birth of Reform Judaism—reflects the core commitments of this denomination at its inception. As an offspring of the Enlightenment in Central and Western Europe, Reform Judaism sought to reimagine the tradition in ways that made it more compatible with Enlightenment rationalism and universalism. This theological motivation dovetailed with a practical one, to which we will return in chapter 16: Christian Europe was opening up to the possibility of integrating Jews as citizens of their respective countries, but Jews needed to counter the prevalent objection that Judaism was backward, superstitious, and hostile to outsiders. For Reform Judaism, this meant, among other things, a different answer to the question of: What do we hope for? Reform Judaism rejected the vision of a return of the Jewish people to Zion

2. Chaim Stern, ed., *Gates of Prayer: The Union Prayerbook, Weekdays, Sabbaths, and Festivals; Services and Prayers for Synagogue and Home* (New York: Central Conference of American Rabbis, 1975), 60.

under the rule of a messianic king. This traditional expectation seemed to frame Jews as permanent outsiders in their countries, *in* them but not *of* them, ultimately loyal to a different political order, even if that order was as yet unrealized. Reform Judaism did not renounce the very notion of a horizon of expectation, but it generalized it, from one in which a "redeemer"—a messianic king—figures prominently, to a more universal hope for "redemption," for Israel and indeed for the entire world. Relatedly, Reform Jewish prayer books beginning in the late nineteenth century reformulated the second blessing of the Amidah so that it eliminated reference to the resurrection of the dead, which was taken to be contrary to reason. Instead of the traditional concluding formula, "Blessed are you, Lord, who resurrects the dead," the *Gates of Prayer* version has: "Blessed is the Lord, the Source of Life."

The Western world today is not what it was in the early nineteenth century, or in 1975, and neither is Reform Judaism. With the waning of universalism and the rise of skeptic challenges to the coherence and ambition of a universalist conception of human reason; with the decline of the melting-pot model of political life in favor of one that permits and indeed encourages the assertion of hyphenated affiliation; with the birth of the state of Israel and the attachment to it among Jews worldwide; with the emergence of gender, race, and sexual orientation as sites first for the redressing of grievances and then for the cultivation of identity, the commitments and with them the liturgy of Reform Judaism have changed. The Central Conference of American Rabbis produced a new prayer book in 2007, entitled *Mishkan T'filah: A Reform Siddur.*[3] The name itself reflects Reform Judaism's movement back toward tradition: The subtitle describes the work not as a "prayer book" but as a "siddur," and the title, likewise, is exclusively in Hebrew, the language both of traditional prayer and of the modern state of Israel. (*Mishkan T'filah* means: "a tabernacle of prayer.") Likewise, in a departure from *Gates of Prayer*, the book is oriented from right to left, following the Hebrew paradigm, rather than from left to right. The conclusion of the second blessing reads: "Blessed are You, Adonai, who gives life to all (revives the dead)." The formulation "who gives life to all" retains the "traditional" Reform rejection of resurrection, but an alternative,

3. Elyse D. Frishman, ed., *Mishkan T'filah: A Reform Siddur* (New York: Central Conference of American Rabbis, 2007). For the quotations below, see pp. 76 and 78.

parenthetical formulation is given that affirms resurrection. Note too that "Lord" is replaced by the Hebrew original, *Adonai*.

While these revisions mark a return to tradition, in other respects the 2007 version of the Amidah affirms new, non-traditional norms. Here is the first blessing of the Amidah according to *Mishkan T'Filah*.

> Blessed are you, Adonai, our God, God of our fathers and mothers, God of Abraham, God of Isaac, and God of Jacob; God of Sarah, God of Rebecca, God of Rachel, and God of Leah; the great, mighty and awesome God, transcendent God who bestows lovingkindness, creates everything out of love, remembers the love of our fathers and mothers, and brings redemption to their children's children for the sake of the Divine Name. Sovereign, Deliverer, Helper and Shield, blessed are you, Adonai, Sarah's helper, Abraham's Shield.

This version introduces the matriarchs alongside the patriarchs, both at the beginning of the blessing and in the concluding formula. The appearance of the matriarchs underscores the depth of the commitment to gender equity in Reform Judaism today. Gender equity is not conceptualized as a matter of concession to modern norms, but rather as a genuinely Jewish value.

We turn now from the Amidah to the two other major components of thrice-daily prayer. One of them is a collection of psalms, along with other biblical passages praising God. The psalms component features in the morning and afternoon prayers. In the case of the afternoon prayer, the psalms component is extremely concise: Psalm 84:5 ("Happy [*ashre*] are they who dwell in your house; they forever praise you"), then the last verse of Psalm 144 ("Happy the people who have it so; happy the people whose God is the Lord"), followed by the entirety of Psalm 145, an alphabetical acrostic. (See in the Koren siddur, 206–8.) This unit of two verses plus Psalm 145 is called Ashre, after its first word. In the morning, the psalms component is greatly expanded. It centers on Ashre, but also incorporates other psalms, as well as verses from elsewhere in the Bible.

The third major component of daily prayer is the *Shema* liturgy, which is recited in the morning and evening prayers. The core of this liturgy is a sequence of three passages from the Pentateuch that enjoin Israel to study, observe, and recall God's word always, upon getting out of bed and when lying down to sleep, at home and on the road: Deuteronomy 6:4–9 (which begins with the word *shema*, "hear," giving its name to the liturgy as a whole); Deuteronomy 11:13–21; and Numbers 15:37–41. It is the fact that these passages refer to rising from and returning to bed that destines the Shema liturgy for the morning and evening prayers specifically. The sequence of biblical passages is introduced and followed by blessings. The first blessing praises God in relation to the time of day: light is the theme of the version designated for the morning, and the end of day for the evening version. The second blessing, immediately preceding the biblical passages, introduces them by thanking God for giving Israel the Torah and the commandments, as the ultimate expression of God's love for Israel. While the Shema liturgy centers the Torah and the commandments, it too, like the Amidah and the blessings after substantial foods, orients itself toward the redemption of Israel; this is the topic of the blessing that follows the biblical passages.

The morning service consists, in sum, of an extended psalms component, followed by the Shema liturgy and the Amidah; all told, it is an affair of roughly thirty or forty minutes. The afternoon service and evening service are shorter, each taking roughly ten to fifteen minutes to complete. The afternoon service includes a short psalms component followed by the Amidah, while the evening service is composed of the Shema liturgy followed by the Amidah. A traditional synagogue schedules, at a minimum, two gathering times per day: in the morning, for the morning service, and around sunset, for the afternoon service just before sunset, and then the evening service just after sunset. A synagogue with a large membership might schedule two morning services, an early one for those who must begin the workday early and a later one for those without such a time constraint.

Communal Prayer and the Synagogue

When a quorum (Hebrew *minyan*, "count") has gathered, prayer takes on a congregational form, coordinated by the prayer leader (*hazzan*, also called the *sheliah tsibbur*, or "emissary of the congregation"). Traditionally, and still in Orthodox Judaism, a quorum consists of ten males over the age of halakhic adulthood, that is, thirteen (corresponding roughly to puberty). In the liberal denominations today, the quorum is gender-blind. Anyone, male or female, who has reached the age of halakhic adulthood, counts toward the quorum. Certain especially holy prayers are only recited in a quorum, because the quorum represents the congregation of Israel, and God is understood to be present in a special way when Israel assembles. Most importantly, in the presence of a quorum the Amidah is recited twice, first by each individual to himself, and then by the hazzan, on behalf of the congregation as a whole. In the repetition of the Amidah, in the third blessing, whose topic is God's sanctity, the congregation recites the *qedushah* ("sanctity"), a liturgy centered on the praises of God that the biblical prophets attribute to the angels: the trisagion of Isaiah 6:3 ("Holy, holy, holy is the Lord of hosts; the whole earth is full of his glory") and the cry from the chariot in Ezekiel 3:12 ("Blessed is the glory of the Lord from his place"). The opening of the qedushah articulates its underlying logic, that the community of Israel joins itself to the angelic host in singing God's praises: "We will sanctify your name in the world just as they sanctify your name in the heavens above" (112).

Other than fluency in the prayers and a passable chanting voice, there are no special qualifications to be a prayer leader; anyone who counts for the quorum can serve as a prayer leader. It is worth noting, in particular, that there is no ex officio role for a rabbi in congregational prayer. Congregational rabbis play vital roles as teachers of Torah and halakhah, as moral exemplars, as pastoral counselors, but they serve no ritual function whatsoever. They are, of course, eligible to serve as prayer leaders, and they can and typically do officiate at other ceremonies, like weddings (one of the topics we will take up in chapter 12) and funerals. But they do so only in virtue of their knowledge and experience, not in virtue of any distinct, intrinsic status, and a layperson with the requisite knowledge can officiate just as well. In this respect, then, rabbis differ sharply from Catholic priests.

Though congregational prayer, like individual prayer, can occur anywhere, the paradigmatic place for congregational prayer is the local synagogue. (The Hebrew word for a synagogue is *bet keneset*, literally "house of assembly"; note that the same Hebrew word is used for Israel's parliament, the Knesset. Traditional Ashkenazi communities commonly call the synagogue by its Yiddish name, *shul*.) As noted above, a synagogue typically hosts at least two services, in the early morning and around sunset. These services draw crowds on the sabbath and festivals, but attendance is considerably sparser on weekdays. (In an Orthodox community, weekday attendees are mainly men.) Why would a person refrain from coming on a weekday? The prayer time could conflict with the work commute, or with school drop-offs and pick-ups. Or praying in a minyan might simply not be a high priority for that person. Those who do attend the daily service might do so out of a sense of obligation, both to God and to the community; they might also enjoy it as a social practice. One important segment of daily minyan-goers is mourners. For a year after the death of a parent, the child is supposed to recite a special prayer—the mourner's *kaddish* ("holy"), sanctifying the name of God—that can occur only in a minyan.

The heart of the synagogue building is the sanctuary, the space in which communal prayer occurs. The heart of the sanctuary, in turn, is the ark, a box or closet (in Hebrew *aron*)—typically fixed in place in the middle of the front wall of the sanctuary, and richly adorned with carvings—that contains one or more Torah scrolls; it is the presence of these scrolls, in part, that sanctifies the space. The ark remains closed in general, but during the morning service on the sabbath and festivals, and every Monday and Thursday, a congregant opens it and removes a Torah scroll from it. The scroll is set down on a raised table (the *bimah*, or platform) in the middle of the synagogue, and a reader chants verses from it in Hebrew. The sabbath Torah reading is extensive, designed so that, over the course of a year, the congregation completes the entire Pentateuch. The Monday and Thursday Torah readings are much shorter, consisting only of the very beginning of the coming sabbath's reading. After the reading, the Torah scroll is returned to the ark.

In Orthodox synagogues the sanctuary includes one other major structural feature besides the ark and the bimah: a barrier (*mehitsah*) between men and women. The mehitsah is often an important signifier of where a synagogue situates itself within the Orthodox spectrum. In more traditional Orthodox synagogues the women's section is set off behind the men's section, or in a balcony above it. In more progressive Orthodox synagogues, the mehitsah runs down the middle of the sanctuary. Besides the location, the height and opacity of the mehitsah can also vary across the Orthodox spectrum. Among the liberal denominations today, by contrast, seating is mixed.

A synagogue is of course not just a structure; it is a community. Indeed, although a local Jewish Federation chapter or a Jewish community center can play an important coordinating function for social events and the provision of social services, the synagogue remains, in America, the basic unit of Jewish community: it is a place for making and meeting friends, and the main destination for classes and holiday events and charity undertakings. It is also often an important site for children's Jewish education. In Israel, where the public sphere is Jewish, it is rarer for a synagogue to serve as the substrate of community. One sometimes finds that a secular Israeli Jew with no connection to a synagogue in Israel will, upon moving to America for a period of time, affiliate with a local synagogue and attend services, drawn in the first instance by the community that it enables.

Conclusion

The literature of prayer in the Jewish tradition is vast and various, and this chapter has only touched on the basic features of some of its principal components. Nor has it addressed in any detail the complex topic of the experience of prayer, or points of comparison with Christian liturgy. To partially remedy these gaps, I include after the chapter more than the usual number of starting points for further inquiry. I also conclude here with a personal perspective that broaches aspects of the corpus of Jewish prayer not mentioned above.

Everyone who prays regularly has favorite prayers, prayers that speak to them in some distinctive way; I will mention two of mine. The first occurs in *tahanun* ("plea"), a liturgy following the Amidah that seeks God's grace and forgiveness despite our sins. One section of this liturgy is a short poem, whose first strophe runs as follows: "Guardian of Israel, / guard over the remnant of Israel, / that perdition not befall Israel, / who say 'Hear, O Israel'" (154). Each brief line of the strophe ends with the word "Israel." This poetic constraint insistently draws God's attention to Israel. God is called upon to be who God is, the guardian of Israel, and to save the Jewish people in their broken, perilous state. After all, the last line recalls, Israel, though not sinless, is the nation that declares, through the Shema, the oneness of God. This prayer can stand as an example of many others in the siddur that derive their rhetorical force from their poetic character.

The second among my favorite prayers is recited in connection with the removal of the Torah from the ark. While most prayers are written in Hebrew, this one is in Aramaic, a cousin of Hebrew; it is in fact an excerpt from the *Zohar*, a medieval mystical work that we will encounter in chapter 14. In the prayers that we have discussed above, the first person, where it occurs, is always in the plural. The plural has its own power: even one who prays alone can, through it, perceive himself as part of the Jewish people. But it comes at the cost of a certain alienation from oneself, and from one's individual relationship with God. But the siddur does incorporate, here and there, some first-person singular prayers, typically beginning with or including the formula "may it be your will," and this is one of them.

> I am a servant of the Holy One, blessed be He. Before him and before his glorious Torah I bow at all times. Not in any mortal do I trust, nor on any angel do I rely, but on the God of the heavens, who is a God of truth, whose Torah is truth, and whose prophets are truth, and who abounds in acts of goodness and truth. In him do I trust, and to his holy and honored name I offer praises. May it be your will to open my heart in Torah, and to fulfill the wishes of my heart, and the heart of all your people Israel, for good, for life, and for peace. (161)

The first-person singular enables a remarkable directness, and a very personal confession of faith. The prayer is also striking for its affirmation of the centrality of the Torah. To be a servant of God is to bow both to God and to God's Torah, and to seek a heart open to understanding it.

Further Inquiry

A helpful introduction to the content, forms, and theology of Jewish prayer is Lawrence A. Hoffman, *The Way into Jewish Prayer* (Woodstock: Jewish Lights Publishing, 2000). Hoffman is also the editor of a ten-volume series, *My People's Prayer Book* (Woodstock, VT: Jewish Lights Publishing, 1997–2007), which prints the prayer book framed by abundant and diverse modern commentary. The interested reader can also track down the books on Jewish and Christian prayer coedited by Hoffman with a scholar of Christian liturgy, Paul Bradshaw. Steven Kepnes, *Jewish Liturgical Theology* (Oxford: Oxford University Press, 2007), examines the titular topic in conversation with the canonical figures of modern German Jewish philosophy, and, following them, with attentiveness to liturgical theology as a space for interfaith engagement. On the ways in which assorted bodily aspects of the Amidah recitation—stepping forward, standing, bowing, etc.—were understood in the Talmud to signify and enable the realization of a set of relationships between the person praying and God, see Uri Ehrlich, *The Nonverbal Language of Prayer* (Tübingen: Mohr Siebeck, 2004). On the history of synagogue structures in America, see Marc Lee Raphael, *The Synagogue in America: A Short History* (New York: New York University Press, 2011).

●

1. The Shema liturgy includes verses (Deut. 6:8; 11:18) calling on Israel to bind God's word to their arms and heads. From at least the late Second Temple period, these verses were understood in a concrete sense, to require the fastening of small boxes containing these very verses, along with others, to one's body. Today, these objects—called phylacteries in Greek, as in Matthew 23:5, or *tefillin* in Hebrew, and consisting of two boxes containing compartments for pieces of parchment bearing the biblical texts, along with leather straps by which one fastens the boxes to the arm and head—are worn during the weekday morning service. Find some images of people wearing tefillin online. How might one experience and understand this practice, which literally binds the Torah to one's body? Note the custom of reciting Hosea 2:19–20 while completing the fastening: "I will betroth you to Me forever; I will betroth you to Me in righteousness and justice, loving-kindness and compassion; I will betroth you to Me in faithfulness; and you shall know the Lord" (16). What might be the meaning of this custom?

2. Genesis 19:27 reports that, having conversed with God before the destruction of Sodom, after its destruction Abraham "arose in the morning to the place where he had stood before the face of the Lord." The references to the previous conversation with God, to the morning, and to standing (*amad*, the verb underlying the word *Amidah*), together lead the rabbis (Bavli Berakhot 6b, 26b) to suppose that the verse speaks of Abraham praying the morning Amidah. In fact, they claim that Abraham instituted the practice of a morning Amidah. And not only that: the fact that he returned to the same place as before is evidence that one should "fix a place" for praying the Amidah. The halakhic literature takes this to mean that a person should, ideally, always pray in the same location in his synagogue (or in his home, if he prays at home), rather than praying now in one location, now in another. A visitor to a synagogue will therefore seek to be careful not to sit in a veteran's "fixed place." Why? What benefit comes from having a fixed place for prayer?

3. Music is a central component of the prayer experience, especially for communal prayer. For recordings of the music that one might encounter in some contemporary synagogues in America, see the Hadar Institute's online repository, https://www.hadar.org/torah-tefillah/services. You might, in particular, read through the *hallel* ("praise") prayer (732–42) along with the recordings at https://www.hadar.org/torah-tefillah/services/hallel.

4. In one respect, the closest Christian analogy to the Amidah, as the centerpiece of Jewish liturgy, is the eucharist. But from a theological perspective they are in fact very different. The Amidah is a prayer of praise, request, and thanksgiving. The eucharist, like the other sacraments, is a sign, and for many Christians, an "efficacious" sign, that is, a sign that has an actual though invisible effect in the world, through the grace of God. A better comparison to the eucharist, then, is probably the ritual law. (Recall, from chapter 3, Augustine's claim that the sacraments are a sort of "translation" of the ritual law.) But within rabbinic Judaism, the ritual law is conceptualized chiefly as commandments, not as signs, nor is there sustained interest in the question of their metaphysical effect, if any. Perhaps the closest approximation to an efficacious sacrament in rabbinic Judaism is the Day of Atonement, because the day itself is understood to effect atonement for the people Israel. The Day of Atonement is also the liturgical event in Judaism that most seeks to evoke, in a sustained way, its roots in the sacrificial rites of the temple at the time that the temple stood. This is presumably no coincidence: in Judaism, it is the Jerusalem temple that is the privileged site for the real presence of and efficacious relationship to God in the world. And even as the synagogue is a holy place that represents, in rabbinic parlance, a "minor temple," it is categorically different in this respect from the Jerusalem temple. To put the point differently, the general absence of sacraments in Judaism reflects the fact that Judaism defines the present as an era of exile—an era in which God is absent from the world—in a way that Christianity does not. Is there a categorical difference between Judaism and Christianity on this score, or does the fact that Christianity, too, recognizes Jesus's absence—situates the present between Christ's first and second coming—narrow the gap?

— Chapter 11 —

The Sabbath and the Festivals

PERHAPS THE MOST FAMOUS MODERN OBSERVATION about the sabbath (in Hebrew: *shabbat*) was penned by a man named Asher Ginsberg (1856–1927), who wrote under the pseudonym Ahad Ha'am (Hebrew for "a common man"). Ginsberg was a proponent of cultural Zionism. The prospect of a vibrant Jewish community in Palestine attracted him because he saw it as capable of serving as a vehicle for the cultural revival of the Jewish people in the modern world. For the most strident secular Zionists, the Zionist project demanded stark deviation from or even rejection of the tradition, because the tradition taught Jews to embrace lives of powerlessness and passivity in the Diaspora, to await God's redemption in its own time, to pay no mind to politics or to the great questions of the age, but instead to cultivate personal piety within an inward-turned Jewish community. Ginsberg had himself left far behind the Orthodox dogmas in which he had been educated, but he rejected a sharp opposition between Zionism and tradition. For him, Zionism should enable Jews to preserve the tradition and infuse it with new meaning, to marshal its resources toward humanistic ends appropriate to modernity.

Amid Zionist debate about whether to move the observance of the sabbath to Sunday or even dispense with it altogether, Ginsberg, not surprisingly, came down firmly in the opposition. Any such change, he wrote in an 1898 essay, "The Sabbath and Zionism," would undermine the distinctiveness of the Jewish people and facilitate assimilation. The sabbath must be preserved because it was the sabbath that had secured Israel's well-being throughout their long exile.

> Anyone who feels in his heart a true connection to the life of the people across all the generations cannot in any way . . . imagine the existence of the people

> Israel without "the Sabbath queen." One can say without exaggeration that, more than Israel kept the Sabbath, the Sabbath kept them, and had she not restored to them their "soul" and renewed their spiritual life every week, the travails of the "workdays" would have pulled them ever downward, until they would descend to the lowest level of "materiality" and of moral and intellectual debasement.[1]

"More than Israel kept the Sabbath, the Sabbath kept them." The cultural renewal that Ginsberg sought in Zionism was, in a sense, a correlate of the spiritual regeneration that was the gift of the sabbath to Israel across the ages.

This chapter is dedicated chiefly to the topic of the sabbath. It will describe the distinctive features of the rabbis' interpretation of the sabbath, and will show how the sabbath has structured and continues to structure Jewish community. At the end of the chapter we will briefly describe the other holy days that fill out the Jewish festival calendar.

Two Dimensions of the Sabbath

The roots of the sabbath lie in the Bible. According to Genesis 2:1–3, God, having spent six days creating the world, ceases from work on the seventh day, and blesses and sanctifies it. When the Israelites leave Egypt for the wilderness and begin to receive their daily manna from heaven, they learn that the manna will not fall on the sabbath. God allows them to collect a double portion on the sixth day, Friday, so that they can cook and bake in advance, and have food for the sabbath. On the sabbath, they are supposed to refrain from going out to collect manna: "Do not leave your place on the seventh day" (Exod. 16:29). Other passages from the Bible convey the severity of the labor prohibition—intentional violation thereof is a capital offense (Num. 15:32–36)—and offer some details about the sort of actions that run afoul of it, but on the whole the Bible leaves the content and contours of the labor prohibition rather vague.

The Bible also preserves an air of uncertainty around the purpose and meaning of the sabbath rest. At Sinai, within the framework of the Deca-

1. For the Hebrew text see https://benyehuda.org/read/2786.

logue (Exod. 20:8–11), God commands the Israelites to refrain from labor on the sabbath in imitation of God's rest at the creation of the world. The version of the Decalogue in Deuteronomy 5 makes no reference to the creation of the world; instead, the sabbath rest is linked to the fact that God freed Israel from Egyptian servitude. We may say, then, at a minimum, that by resting on the sabbath, a Jew affirms God as the creator of the world and the agent of the exodus. But labor also belongs to the human condition, at least from Adam's curse (Gen. 3:17–19). How might the sabbath rest be construed as speaking to the human condition? One can imagine two different approaches. The first is that the sabbath rest enjoins human beings to cease from labor so that they may enjoy the fruits of their labor. The sabbath, on this perspective, allows a person to imagine herself back in Eden, where the means to satisfy human beings' material needs are immediately at hand, with no need to break a sweat. Alternatively, the sabbath rest is a sign that human beings were made for something other than the satisfaction of their material needs, that the ends served by their labor are not ultimate ends. If on the first perspective, to which we might assign the watchword, "we have everything we need," the sabbath rest is best experienced through bodily delight, then on the second, whose watchword is "we are more than our needs," it finds its ideal expression in attentiveness to the realm of the spirit or mind.

The rabbinic sabbath combines these two approaches. More precisely, it does not see them as competing alternatives, but as complementary: cultivation of the spirit does not demand physical abstemiousness; body and spirit do not stand in stark opposition. Rabbinic Judaism does in limited ways recognize self-denial as a tool for the achievement of mastery of Torah and for the prevention and purgation of sin, a point to which we will return in the next chapter, but its vision of the sabbath exemplifies a general tendency to sideline asceticism. We can frame the point differently, in relation to God's sanctification of the sabbath (Gen. 2:3). The sanctity of the sabbath renders it something like the temple, filled with the presence of God. But "where" is the human being who observes the sabbath? Is he "inside" the temple, like a priest, who, being so close to God, may not drink wine, or defile himself in any way? On the rabbinic perspective, he is more like one who dwells outside the temple, "under his vine and under his fig tree, with no cause for fear" (Micah 4:4), basking in the presence of God, but from a distance that does not demand the suppression of his human self, but rather enables it to find its most blessed expression.

Let us see how this simultaneous commitment to the body and to the spirit plays out in the traditional celebration of the rabbinic sabbath. The halakhic day runs from evening to evening, so that the sabbath begins on Friday evening and ends on Saturday evening. More precisely, it runs from Friday at sunset to Saturday at dusk, which means that the sabbath lasts closer to twenty-five than to twenty-four hours. The reason for this anomaly lies in an uncertainty about the precise point at which the new day begins: when the sun disappears below the horizon (sunset), or when sunlight is no longer visible (dusk)? Because the rabbis take the sabbath labor prohibition with utter seriousness, the law requires that one mark the beginning of the sabbath according to the earliest possible definition of the evening, and the end of the sabbath according to the latest possible definition.

In the home, the beginning of the sabbath is signified by the lighting of candles. Candle lighting occurs just before sunset; to light the candles on the sabbath itself would be a direct violation of Exodus 35:3, "you shall kindle no fire in all your dwellings on the sabbath day." The purpose of lighting candles is to illuminate the home on Friday night, to enable enjoyment of the festive meal. Today, of course, this effect can be and is more simply achieved by turning lights on before the sabbath, but rabbinic law from the medieval period forward encodes the lighting of candles as a commandment, and so the practice is retained today. The commitment of rabbinic Judaism to candlelight on Friday night is not uncontroversial. Karaite Judaism, mentioned in chapter 1 as a form of Judaism that coalesced in the early medieval period in opposition to the authority of the rabbis and their oral law, reads Exodus 35:3 as prohibiting not only the kindling of a flame on the sabbath, but the mere presence of a lit flame in one's home. The lighting of Friday night candles in rabbinic Judaism is an expression of its embrace of the principle of bodily delight on the sabbath. (It is important not to reduce the Karaites to a foil; they too, in fact, recognize the sabbath as a day of delight, but in different ways.)

The synagogue hosts a Friday night service that consists of a liturgy for "greeting the sabbath"—more on this liturgy in chapter 15—followed by the evening prayer. Notably, the sabbath Amidah, on Friday night and at all sabbath services, is much shorter than the weekday Amidah, because it omits the entire request sequence in the middle. The abbreviated Amidah implicitly positions the sabbath as a reprise of Eden and a forestate of the eschaton; the congregation must think of itself as lacking nothing, as already redeemed.

After the service, congregants return to their homes for a festive dinner. This meal begins with a blessing over wine marking God's sanctification of the sabbath (*qiddush*), followed by the eating of bread (typically the braided loaves called *challah*), which defines the meal as a substantive one. Friday night dinner, often marked by the presence of guests, sabbath songs, and Torah study, is the first of three mandated meals consumed over the course of the sabbath. (The second is the lunch following morning services the next day, and the third, a dinner before sunset.) In mandating meals, too, the rabbis insist on a different perspective on the sabbath than the one embraced by some other Jews. There is abundant testimony, for example, that at the time of the early rabbis, the Jewish community in Rome fasted on the sabbath. Likewise, Josephus (*Jewish War* 2.147–149) reports that the Essene sect, which flourished toward the end of the Second Temple period, refrained from defecating on the sabbath, presumably because they recognized defecation to be a source of ritual defilement, and understood ritual defilement to be incompatible with the holiness of the sabbath. It is difficult to see how they could have avoided defecation on the sabbath unless they refrained from eating on that day. For the rabbis, by contrast, the holiness of the sabbath is not incompatible with eating and defecation. True, God is present on the sabbath as though in the temple, but Jews celebrate God's presence at a remove that permits recognition of their human nature.

In rabbinic Judaism, the husband is understood to have a sexual duty to his wife, just as he is obliged to provide for her material needs, and the rabbis (Bavli Ketubot 62b; Bava Kamma 82a) recommend Friday night as the ideal time for the satisfaction of this duty. This recommendation, too, marks a sharp divergence from other forms of Judaism. In the book of Jubilees, which appears to have been sacred to the Second Temple–era sect that collected the Dead Sea scrolls, lying with one's wife occurs first in the list of activities prohibited on the sabbath (50:8). For Karaite Jews, too, sexual intercourse is prohibited on the sabbath, on the ground that the ritual defilement that it generates is a profanation of the sabbath's holiness.

Sabbath morning is taken up almost entirely with a lengthy morning service in the synagogue. In addition to expanded prayers, the sabbath morning service is marked by Torah study. Torah study assumes, in the first instance, a ritualized form: the reading of an extended portion from the Pentateuch (as described in the previous chapter), followed by the reading of a related passage from the Prophets. Afterward the rabbi typically offers a homily that draws out the readings' contemporary relevance. Lunch after the service closely resembles the preceding dinner: it is a festive, drawn-out affair, with blessings over wine and challah, and often including company, song, and Torah study. Because cooking is forbidden on the sabbath, the food that is eaten on the sabbath must ordinarily be prepared in advance, though one can, within certain limitations, reheat it on Saturday morning by placing it on a hotplate or a warming tray that was set in place before the beginning of the sabbath. But there is one permitted mechanism for achieving a freshly cooked, hot meal for shabbat lunch, a mechanism that has defined the culinary experience of rabbinic Judaism throughout the ages: slow cooking. A meat stew may be set to cook slowly from Friday before sundown overnight into Saturday morning, so that it is ready to be eaten at lunch. The name and ingredients of the dish vary from community to community. Among Ashkenazim, for example, it goes by the name *cholent* (a cousin of French *chaud*, "hot") and typically contains beef, barley, beans, and potatoes, while the stew of Sephardic Jews from Morocco includes chickpeas, along with spices like nutmeg and clover, and is called *adafina* or *dafina* (from Arabic *dafana* "to bury, cover," because the pot was traditionally buried in coals). The fact that Karaite Judaism prohibits slow cooking on the sabbath presumably lies behind a famous comment by a twelfth-century Talmud commentator from Provence (*Ha-ma'or ha-qatan* to Bavli Shabbat 16b): "It is an enactment by our rabbis to make the sabbath a delight through slow-cooked stew, and anyone who does not eat slow-cooked stew should be investigated on suspicion of heresy."

Shabbat afternoon is unstructured: what defines it is the labor prohibition, which, as we will see below, precludes, for traditional Jews, more or less all weekday activities. One may not go to work or write or use a computer or phone. One may not travel anywhere by car or bus. What fills this time? Lunch can extend deep into the afternoon. One might nap or take a walk or read a book, or meet with friends in the park. Some people study Torah, whether individually or with a havruta or in a class. Children will often play ball. In general, the labor prohibition works today to disengage the traditionally observant Jew from the isolating, goal-oriented dynamic of modern life, and to nudge her toward engagement with family, community, and, at least ideally,

Torah. As the evening approaches, congregants gather in the synagogue for the afternoon service and then, with nightfall, the evening service. With the end of the sabbath, a ritual called *havdalah* ("separation"), involving wine, spices, and the lighting of a candle, marks the beginning of the new week.

The Labor Prohibition

As noted in chapter 6, in connection with the extended Talmud passage on procreation, the rabbis treat the commandments of the Bible as laws, and while exhortations to piety can and often should be left vague, laws must be precisely defined. The rabbis go about defining the labor prohibition by reflecting on the key products of human work, first and foremost food and clothing, and identifying the discrete actions needed to make them; these are the labors that are prohibited on the sabbath. Thus, for example, to make bread, one must plow a field, plant seeds, harvest, thresh, etc., and so each of these actions constitutes a category of forbidden labor. But for the rabbis, these specified labor categories, thirty-nine in all (Mishnah Shabbat 7:2), are only a starting point.

Consider, for example, threshing, or the application of weight and pressure to unloose the wheat berry from the chaff. In virtue of what is threshing prohibited? Surely, the rabbis reason, the essential labor is not connected to wheat per se; the labor lies, rather, more abstractly, in the extraction of something desirable out of an object into which it was integrated. But then, by extension, the act of squeezing the juice out of an orange must also count as "threshing," and hence forbidden. Perhaps it is even threshing to wash dishes with a sponge, because one presses the sponge so that it releases water. Perhaps even brushing one's teeth with an ordinary toothbrush should be forbidden as threshing, because the bristles release water when they are pressed against the teeth. In stores that cater to Orthodox communities one can in fact purchase non-absorbent "shabbos sponges," and even "shabbos toothbrushes" with rubber bristles. (*Shabbos* is the Ashkenazi pronunciation of Hebrew *shabbat*, as fans of the Coen brothers' 1998 film, *The Big Lebowski*, will know.) Is this picayune? Of course it is, but it follows directly and perhaps even inevitably from a commitment to the severity of the labor prohibition, and from the conviction that a community as a whole will treat a norm with utmost seriousness, will preserve it at great cost, will teach it to the next generation, only if it is assigned the force of law.

Of special importance among the thirty-nine chief labors is carrying. The roots of this prohibition are present already in the Bible, most clearly in Jeremiah 17:19–27 and Nehemiah 13:15. As the rabbis understand it, this labor involves transferring an object from a private domain into the public domain, or vice-versa, or transporting an object a certain minimal distance within the public domain. It does not matter, for the rabbis, if the object is heavy or light; labor, as they define it, is not a matter of physical exertion, but of completing a discrete action of a particular sort. This prohibition is very limiting. It prevents one, for example, from bringing food to a neighbor's house, or carrying a house key in one's pocket, or even pushing a stroller. The rabbis of late antiquity devised or inherited a workaround for this prohibition: the erection of a boundary around an entire neighborhood, consisting of a wire strung along the tops of poles. This boundary is constructively treated as a continuous series of doorways (each composed of two consecutive poles and the wire running between them) that open into the interior of a single domain, so that carrying is permitted anywhere in the enclosed neighborhood. This mechanism is called an *eruv* ("mingling"). (My account represents a drastic simplification of an extremely complex body of laws.) More or less every significant Orthodox community today is surrounded by an eruv, erected in cooperation with the municipality. Because an eruv can incorporate existing telephone poles and wires, an urban eruv blends imperceptibly into its surroundings. Karaite Judaism does not accept the validity of an eruv.

The eruv is one way in which the sabbath structures traditional Jewish community. A traditionally observant Jew who wishes to carry on the sabbath must live within the eruv. More decisively still, Orthodox Judaism forbids the use of a car on the sabbath, because, among other things, cars burn gasoline, in violation of the prohibition against igniting a flame, and are a means for the sort of long-distance travel that is forbidden on the sabbath. Therefore, a traditional Jewish community must be walkable: everyone must live roughly within walking distance of each other and of the synagogue.

Besides the internal combustion engine, the technological innovation that defines modern private life today is electricity. As electrical devices became widespread in the late nineteenth and into the twentieth century, traditional Jews generally refrained from using them on the sabbath, out of a halakhic "instinct" that to use them would not be in keeping with the principle of sabbath rest. Rabbis struggled and continue to struggle to identify a firm basis for the prohibition of electricity. In the case of an incandescent light, where the filament burns, one might construe turning on the switch as the equivalent of lighting a fire, but this analogy can be challenged. The question is still closer in the case of appliances and now of non-incandescent bulbs (fluorescent, LED, etc.). While the rabbinic consensus among both Orthodox and Conservative rabbis is that the use of electricity is generally forbidden, the uncertainty surrounding the question is grounds for lenience in cases of great need. Such uncertainty does not extend to devices like laptops and smartphones, which are understood to be clearly forbidden because, among other things, they record data, in violation of the sabbath labor of "writing."

Modern technology creates innumerable new challenges for sabbath observance, but it also offers innumerable new solutions, both to those very challenges and to other, pre-technological challenges. The Zomet Institute in Israel is at the forefront of inventing such solutions, through a combination of technological know-how and deep expertise in rabbinic law. Browse its website (zomet.org.il) and you will find everything from a device for sensing a baby's breathing that is compatible with the consensus limits on electricity use, to a halakhically sound machine for milking cows on the sabbath. (And why should milking cows pose a problem in the first place? It is an act of threshing, of course.)

Besides workarounds like the eruv and inventions like those of the Zomet Institute, there is one major exception to the sabbath labor prohibition. A foundational halakhic principle is that "saving a life pushes aside the sabbath." In fact, one is permitted to violate almost any prohibition to save a life. (One source of this principle is Lev. 18:5: "you shall keep my statutes and my ordinances; by doing so one shall live." In Bavli Sanhedrin 74a, among other places, the verse is understood to convey that the commandments should enable life and not be a cause for death. To what extent this teaching prohibits martyrdom in circumstances of religious persecution is a question taken up in that very passage.) But the scope and severity of the sabbath labor prohibition mean that, from the Second Temple period forward, the issue of balancing life and well-being against observance of the law has arisen most often in connection with the sabbath. In Matthew 12, the Pharisees object to the fact that Jesus's disciples pluck grain to satisfy their hunger. The consensus rabbinic view might permit such an action, but only if the hunger were life-threatening and only if there were no way to obtain food other than by plucking grain. In any case, when it is a matter of life and death—a life-threatening injury or illness, for example—then rabbinic law not only permits but insists on the performance of any labor required to address the danger.

The Festival Calendar

The Jewish calendar is lunisolar, that is, both lunar and solar. The months are lunar; they are linked to the phases of the moon. Each of the twelve months of the standard year begins with the new moon, and lasts either twenty-nine days (for six of the months) or thirty (for the other six), until the next new moon. The twelve months thus sum to 354 days, which is eleven days shorter than a solar year. Without any correction for this gap—that is, if the year, too, were purely lunar—the calendar would fall out of line with the seasons, which are determined by the earth's relationship to the sun. A festival that fell out on May 1 in one year would come out the next year on April 19, and the year after on April 8, and the year after at the end of March, etc., and keep on moving backward into the winter, then the fall, and so forth. The calendar of Islam works precisely this way. But in Judaism, as a corollary of the biblical vision of a people on its land, the three major festivals—known as the pilgrimage festivals—carry specific agricultural significance, and therefore must be bound to the seasons. To compensate for the difference between the lunar and the solar years—eleven days each year, or a little more than the equivalent of one lunar month every three years—it intercalates a thirteenth lunar month roughly once every three years. In this way, the first month, Nisan, always roughly corresponds to the month of April, in the beginning of the spring, and the other months follow suit. Even though Nisan, in the spring, is the first month of the year, the Jewish calendar marks the New Year at the beginning of the month of Tishre (roughly September). The explanation for this oddity lies again in the agricultural foundation of the calendar. The dry season in the land of Israel runs from roughly April to September, and the beginning and end of this season mark the two foci of the calendar.

The festivals fall into three groups. We have made reference at various points in previous chapters to the fall New Year and to Yom Kippur, the Day of Atonement, which falls out ten days after the New Year. These two festivals, both legislated in the Pentateuch, are often called the High Holidays or the Days of Awe, to convey their seriousness as occasions of annual divine judgment. A second group of festivals post-dates the Pentateuch. These festivals mark historical events of special significance for the Jewish people, for good and for ill. The book of Esther describes the founding of the festival of Purim, in Adar (March), to memorialize the salvation of the Jews of the Persian Empire in roughly the sixth century BCE from the genocidal intentions of Haman. Purim pairs with Hanukkah, in Kislev (December). This holiday celebrates the victories of Hasmonean rebels in Judea of the second century BCE over the Seleucid Empire, which promoted a policy of aggressive Hellenization. The books that describe these events, 1 and 2 Maccabees, preserved in the Catholic Old Testament, are not canonical for Judaism. Some find in this fact and in the things that rabbinic literature says and does not say about the Hasmoneans a certain ambivalence about Hanukkah, an ambivalence that is taken to manifest rabbinic quietism. Alongside Purim and Hanukkah, the Jewish calendar marks days of sorrow, fast days, commemorating key events connected with the Babylonian Empire's destruction of Solomon's temple in 586 BCE. Of these fast days, referenced in Zechariah 8:19, the most important is the ninth day of the month of Ab (August), which became over the centuries an opportunity to mourn all subsequent tragedies, from the destruction of the second temple in 70 CE at the hands of the Romans to the Holocaust.

The third group of festivals is the three pilgrimage festivals, detailed in the Pentateuch. *Pesach* or Passover is a seven-day holiday celebrated in Nisan (April). *Shavuot* or Pentecost, while counted as a second, distinct festival, also represents something like an appendix to Passover. It falls out precisely fifty days after the beginning of Passover and lasts only one day. *Sukkot* or Tabernacles, in Tishre, is another seven-day festival, with an eighth day appended immediately after. Pesach indicates the arrival of spring and the beginning of the first grain harvest, that of barley. Shavuot celebrates the wheat harvest. Sukkot, the festival of ingathering, marks the end of the harvest season and the arrival of the rainy season. Temple rituals legislated by the Pentateuch give expression to their agricultural significance; thus, for example, Leviticus 23:17 commands the offering of two bread loaves on Shavuot, while Sukkot, according to Leviticus 23:40–41, is celebrated with a temple procession with willows and other plants that evidently conveys a hope for abundant rain in the months following the festival. The Bible also connects Pesach and Sukkot to the exodus: Pesach marks the death of the firstborn and Israel's hasty departure from Egypt, while Sukkot commemorates the fact that the Israelites, upon leaving Egypt, dwelled in tents. The rabbis fill out this historical dimension of the pilgrimage festivals by linking Shavuot to the giving of the Torah at Sinai.

It would take at least a whole other book to do justice to the mass of laws and traditions that define these festivals, and the ways in which they have inspired theological insight among Jewish thinkers across the ages. In lieu of such an exposition, let me offer a personal reflection. As in the case of other religions, the festivals in Judaism—each coming only once a year, but every year, in a rhythm that seems optimized for the formation of memory—play a key role in knitting the tradition into lived experience, and lived experience into the tradition. I think in my own case, for example, of Passover. A Jewish home must have no leaven in it on Pesach: no bread, nor any food item that has brought flour into more than incidental contact with water. To ensure the eradication of leaven, the halakhah mandates a search of the house at night, prior to the first evening of Passover. Of course, the major cleaning of the house must occur long before that night, and so the search has more of a ritual character. In fact, it often becomes a game, and here is how the game played out in my youth. You don't want to come away from a search empty-handed, so someone in the family is assigned the task of wrapping little balls of bread in paper or aluminum foil and hiding them around the house. At night, all the lights are turned off, and the search for leaven proceeds, in an absurdly inefficient and therefore also very engaging way, by the light of a single candle. The rabbis teach that one should not speak during the inspection except about matters immediately related to the search, but my father, for the sake of amusing the children, takes the rule one step further and refuses to speak at all, communicating only in hmm's and ah's and aha's through the entirety of the process. The rest of us try to follow his lead. By tradition, any leaven is supposed to be swept, by means of a sturdy bird feather, into a wooden spoon, and thence into a paper bag. This, too, we do, despite and because of its inefficiency. Besides the bread balls, we look especially for chocolate and candy, and their wrappers. My mother, we know, likes to hide a chocolate stash beside her bed, or at the back of the closet of plastic bags beside the fridge.

I, too, am known as someone who will surreptitiously take a few candies to his room over the course of the year, and squirrel away the wrappers behind bookshelves and cabinets. These places, too, we must investigate, not because wrappers are leaven, really, but because crimes must out. Sometimes we do not find quite all the bread balls, but at the end of the search we recite a formula declaring the bread balls ownerless, "like the dust of the earth," so that we need not worry about them anyhow. The bread balls that we have managed to track down, we burn the next morning, and this too fascinates, in the way that fires fascinate children.

What did we know? What did we learn from this pre-Pesach ritual, or a hundred others like it, on Pesach and all the other festivals? We could not have said quite why it was important to destroy all leaven. Nor, indeed, is this commandment immediately meaningful to adults either, though moralists have long interpreted it symbolically as a matter of smoking out our inclination to sin, of casting away bloated, ingrained habits and committing ourselves anew to being better. (Recall Justin's and Augustine's explanation of this commandment in chapter 3, and see 1 Cor. 5:6–8.) Surely we were not thinking, as we stomped around the house in near darkness, about the great themes of Pesach: the bitterness of slavery and the blessing of freedom; God's care for Israel in its suffering; the imperative to love the alien as we were aliens in the land of Egypt, and so forth. What we absorbed, simply, was that this is what we do as Jews, and in this way, by means of a candle and a feather, we became bound to the tradition and to its great themes.

Conclusion

The holy days surveyed in this chapter are rich, each in its own way, with theological content, but this content is realized and even, in an inchoate way, produced and revised, through the regular experience of them. Although all of these holy days are found in the Christian Bible, and therefore belong, in their way, to the theological legacy of Christianity, they are of course far more important for the Jewish tradition, which observes them in ways directly continuous with their biblical form. But even in Judaism, their meaning cannot be determined by examination of the Bible alone. As the above portraits of Passover eve and especially the sabbath establish in detail, the Bible furnishes only a scaffolding for the holy days; it is the tradition, along divergent paths, that builds them out.

Further Inquiry

On the sabbath among early Jews and Christians, see Herold Weiss, *A Day of Gladness: The Sabbath among Jews and Christians in Antiquity* (Columbia: University of South Carolina Press, 2003); Lutz Doering, "Sabbath and Festivals," in Catherine Hezser, ed., *The Oxford Handbook of Jewish Daily Life in Roman Palestine* (Oxford: Oxford University Press, 2010), 566–86; Margaret Williams, "Being a Jew in Rome: Sabbath Fasting as an Expression of Romano-Jewish Identity," in John M. G. Barclay, ed., *Negotiating Diaspora: Jewish Strategies in the Roman Empire* (New York: T&T Clark, 2004), 8–18. For a learned and moving reflection on the sabbath by one of the most famous modern Jewish theologians, see Abraham Joshua Heschel, *The Sabbath: Its Meaning for Modern Man* (New York: Farrar, Straus and Giroux, 2005). For halakhic analysis of the question of electricity on the sabbath, see Daniel S. Nevins, "The Use of Electrical and Electronic Devices on the Sabbath" (https://www.rabbinicalassembly.org/sites/default/files/public/halakhah/teshuvot/2011-2020/electrical-electronic-devices-shabbat.pdf). On the Jewish festivals in general, see Michael Strassfeld, *The Jewish Holidays* (New York: Harper & Row, 1985); Eliezer Segal, *In Those Days, At This Time: Holiness and History in the Jewish Calendar* (Calgary: University of Calgary Press, 2007). For insight into the festival of Sukkot and contemporary religious life in Israel, see the movie *Ushpizin* (2004). It is based on a short story by S. Y. Agnon, introduced and translated in Jeffrey Saks, "S. Y. Agnon's 'The Etrog': An Introduction," *Tablet Magazine*, September 25, 2010. On the search for leaven before Passover see Katrin Kogman-Appel, "Ritualizing the Cleaning of the House before Passover in Medieval Ashkenaz: Image and Text in Illuminated Haggadot," in *Ritual Dynamics in Jewish and Christian Contexts: Between Bible and Liturgy*, ed. Claudia D. Bergmann and Benedikt Kranemann (Leiden: Brill, 2019), 28–55.

•

1. Sukkot ("tabernacles" or "booths") is so called because it is celebrated chiefly through the construction of a temporary dwelling in which the celebrant is sup-

posed to reside for the seven days of the festival, to commemorate the booths in which God had Israel dwell in the wilderness. How might one theologically interpret the experience of leaving one's home and taking up residence instead in a temporary dwelling, a dwelling with branches for a roof? Consider in this connection the most famous rabbinic statement on the booths in the wilderness, attributed to Rabbi Akiva (thus in Sifra *emor* 17:11; other passages attribute it to a different rabbi). Rabbi Akiva says that these booths were not mundane huts, but in fact "clouds of glory," clouds gathered by God to protect the Israelites from the harsh elements of the wilderness, and to straighten their path. For discussion, see Jeffrey L. Rubenstein, "The Symbolism of the *Sukkah*," *Judaism* 43 (1994): 371–87.

2. The festival of Purim is carnival-like, celebrated with costumes, humor, and feasting. There is even an obligation of sorts to drink alcohol "to the point that one does not know [to distinguish] between 'cursed is Haman' and 'blessed is Mordecai'" (Bavli Megillah 7b). (The story of Rabba and Rabbi Zera that the Talmud introduces immediately after this statement is not to be missed.) The biblical root of the Purim carnivalesque seems to lie in the motif of reversal in the story of Esther: the wicked Haman has his comeuppance, while the Jews, led by Mordecai and Esther, are saved from genocide. But one can arguably find a similar dynamic of reversal in, for example, the Passover story, featuring the downfall of Pharaoh and the Egyptians, and the deliverance of the Israelites under Moses. What makes the reversal story of the book of Esther a more apt foundation for carnival-like celebration? In what ways is it funny, in a way that the Passover story is not?

— *Chapter 12* —

Marriage, Sexuality, and the Life Cycle

Although God promises the land of Canaan to Abraham's offspring at the very beginning of his journey (Gen. 12:7), there is only one plot of land in Canaan that enters into Abraham's ownership in his lifetime: a cave in Hebron in which he buries his wife Sarah, and that thus becomes the burial plot for the patriarchs and the matriarchs (Gen. 23). Likewise, when immigrant Jews founded new communities in America and elsewhere, the first property that the community purchased was often a cemetery. The birth or materialization of the collective thus depends, in this sense, on the death of its individual members.

Death is perhaps the most highly ritualized life-cycle event in Judaism, though the main site of ritualization is not the interment but the mourning that follows. The halakhic tradition envisions a process of slow diminishment of grief. During the seven-day period following the burial, the *shiv'ah* ("seven"), the mourner—defined as someone who has lost a parent, sibling, spouse, or child—remains at home, and, sitting on a low stool, receives visitors. At the completion of the shiv'ah the mourner "rises" and resumes ordinary life, but refrains from participating in joyous events and from cutting his hair until the completion of thirty days from the interment. In the case of a parent, the restriction against attending joyous events extends for a full year.

The antithesis of the mourner's grief is the joy of the bride and groom. Just as the burial of the dead is followed by seven days of mourning, so a wedding is followed by seven days of celebration. The joy of the wedding, like the mourning period over parents, extends, in legal terms, a full year; following Deuteronomy 24:5, the new couple is supposed to remain free of communal obligations for a year, so that they can remain together at home. We will expand at length below on the wedding ceremony, but let us first note briefly the two other important life-cycle events in Judaism. One is circumcision. On the eighth day from birth, a boy's foreskin is surgically removed. This ceremony, formally the *berit milah*, or "covenant of circumcision," goes in America by the name "bris," after the Ashkenazi pronunciation of *berit*. The other life-cycle event is coming of age, when a minor becomes a halakhic adult, obligated in the commandments, thus either *bar mitzvah* ("a son of commandment") or *bat mitzvah* ("a daughter of commandment"). Traditionally, a boy becomes bar mitzvah at age thirteen, and marks it by his public participation in the sabbath morning liturgy. As women do not have a public liturgical role in traditional Orthodoxy, when a girl, at age twelve, becomes bat mitzvah, the event is not marked liturgically. In liberal Judaism today, girls too typically mark their halakhic maturity at age thirteen, and do so in the same public way that boys do. Across all the denominations, coming of age is an occasion for a party.

Below we will consider the theological content of the Jewish wedding ceremony in comparison with that of the Catholic one, and likewise compare Jewish and Catholic positions on divorce. Afterward we will turn to two topics concerning sexuality, again with a comparative focus: celibacy and homosexuality. In our discussion of homosexuality, we will also integrate Protestant teaching and enter into differences among Jewish denominations.

Marriage and Divorce

The contemporary Jewish wedding ceremony combines, under the wedding canopy (*huppah*), two distinct stages that in the past were separated by an extended period. The first is the *qiddushin* ("sanctification"), wherein the groom provides something of value—today a ring—to the bride, and they become bound to each other. This stage loosely corresponds to the modern engagement or betrothal, but from a halakhic perspective, it is the crucial step in the marriage. The second stage is the *nisu'in* ("taking"), when the groom actually "takes" his bride to live with him. Both stages are accompanied by blessings recited over a cup of wine. The following seven blessings (in the Koren siddur, 1040) mark the nisu'in; the first is the standard wine blessing, while the other six concern the wedding.

> 1. Blessed are you, Lord our God, king of the universe, who creates the fruit of the vine.
>
> 2. Blessed are you, Lord our God, king of the universe, who has created all for his glory.
>
> 3. Blessed are you, Lord our God, king of the universe, creator of mankind.
>
> 4. Blessed are you, Lord our God, king of the universe, who made humanity in his image, the image of his likeness, and out of his very self formed a building for eternity (i.e., woman). Blessed are you, Lord, creator of mankind.
>
> 5. Bring great happiness and joy to the barren one (i.e., Zion) through the ingathering of her children to her midst in joy. Blessed are You Lord, who gladdens Zion through her children.
>
> 6. Bring great joy to these loving friends, as you gave joy to your creations in the Garden of Eden of old. Blessed are you, Lord, who gives joy to the groom and bride.
>
> 7. Blessed are you, Lord our God, king of the universe, who created joy and gladness, groom and bride, happiness and jubilation, cheer and delight, love, fellowship, peace and friendship. Lord, our God, may there speedily be heard in the cities of Judah and in the streets of Jerusalem the sounds of joy and gladness, the sounds of the groom and bride, the joyous sounds of grooms from their wedding canopy, and of youths from their feasts of song. Blessed are you, Lord, who makes the groom rejoice with the bride.

The blessing over wine aside, the six wedding blessings divide into two units of three blessings each. The first unit, consisting of blessings two through four, looks backward to Adam and Eve, and positions the wedding as a realization of God's creative plan. The second unit, blessings five through seven, incorporates the precedent of Adam and Eve, but under a new rubric that defines the entire unit: joy. In these blessings, the joy of the wedding is a figure for the future redemption of Israel, whose defining experience is "the sounds of joy and gladness," and especially the raucous sounds of wedding celebrations. Soon after the recitation of these blessings, the groom stomps on a glass and shatters it. The purpose of this practice, whose roots lie in the Talmud, is to recall the sacking of Jerusalem and the destruction of the temple, and so to dampen the happiness; after all, utter joy is unfitting in an unredeemed world. Thus, the shadow of the exile darkens the wedding's joy, and yet that very joy prefigures the end of the exile.

Just as the wedding coordinates its joy to the future redemption, so the shiv'ah coordinates its grief to the current exile. Visitors who come during the shiv'ah to comfort the mourner say, upon their departure, "may the Place (i.e., God) comfort you among the mourners of Zion and Jerusalem." To mourn over the death of a loved one is to be joined to the collective mourning of a people in exile.

Joy is of course a feature of the Catholic wedding ceremony as of the Jewish one; in fact, the *Order of Celebrating Matrimony* has the priest begin by expressing how the Church joins itself to the joy of the marrying couple.[1] But the nuptial blessing in the continuation of the ceremony does not assign joy a figural power of the sort that it possesses in the Jewish wedding ceremony; indeed, it makes no reference to it.

> O God, who by your mighty power created all things out of nothing, and, when you had set in place the beginnings of the universe, formed man and woman in your own image, making the woman an inseparable helpmate to the man, that they might no longer be two, but one flesh, and taught that what you were pleased to make one must never be divided;
>
> O God, who consecrated the bond of Marriage by so great a mystery that in the wedding covenant you foreshadowed the Sacrament of Christ and his Church;
>
> O God, by whom woman is joined to man and the companionship they had in the beginning is endowed with the one blessing not forfeited by original sin nor washed away by the flood;
>
> Look now with favor on these your servants, joined together in Marriage, who ask to be strengthened by your blessing. Send down on them the grace of the Holy Spirit and pour your love into their hearts, that they may remain faithful in the Marriage covenant.
>
> May the grace of love and peace abide in your daughter N., and let her always follow the example of those holy women whose praises are sung in the Scriptures.
>
> May her husband entrust his heart to her, so that, acknowledging her as his equal and his joint heir to the life of grace, he may show her due honor and cherish her always with the love that Christ has for his Church.

1. I use the 2016 text approved by the United States Conference of Catholic Bishops.

> And now, Lord, we implore you: may these your servants hold fast to the faith and keep your commandments; made one in the flesh, may they be blameless in all they do; and with the strength that comes from the Gospel, may they bear true witness to Christ before all; (may they be blessed with children, and prove themselves virtuous parents, who live to see their children's children). And grant that, reaching at last together the fullness of years for which they hope, they may come to the life of the blessed in the Kingdom of Heaven through Christ our Lord.

The Catholic blessing assigns a figural interpretation not to the joy of the wedding but to the marriage bond: it is a "covenant" that "foreshadowed the Sacrament of Christ and his Church." Within this framework, the husband stands for Christ, and he is supposed to love his wife "with the love that Christ has for his Church." There is no parallel to this notion in the Jewish blessing sequence. While Judaism of course supposes a bond between God and Israel, the groom in the Jewish wedding is not made to stand for God, nor does the bride represent Israel. It is not the bond between the groom and the bride but rather the joy of the wedding ceremony that contains its figural power, as a sign of the joy that will accompany Israel's future redemption.

It may be that the Jewish nuptial blessings refrain from assigning theological meaning to the marriage bond itself because, in Judaism, that bond can be broken at will; Judaism permits divorce. By contrast, the Catholic nuptial blessings underscore that husband and wife become one through their marriage, and that this unity is indissoluble. Why do Judaism and Catholicism adopt different positions on divorce? The Old Testament explicitly permits divorce. A man may write his wife a bill of divorce and send her from his home, in which case she "then leaves his house and goes off to become another man's wife" (Deut. 24:1–2). In the New Testament, however, Jesus characterizes this commandment as a concession for "your hardness of heart" (Mark 10:5); in truth, "what God has joined together," through the creation of men and women, and of the mechanism of marriage through which they become one flesh, "let no one separate" (Mark 10:9).

The Catechism of the Catholic Church (sections 1609–17) interprets Jesus's words—paralleled, with differences, in Matthew 19:3–9; see also Luke 16:18; 1 Corinthians 7:10–11—as grounded in the assumption that the indissolubility of the marriage bond follows from "the original order of creation." That is, the marriage bond has not merely a legal but something like a metaphysical character. This original order was "disturbed by sin," namely, the original sin of Adam and Eve, and therefore the marriage regime of the "Law," or the Old Testament, permitted divorce as a concession to human beings' hardness of hearts. But those baptized into Jesus are given the "strength and grace" to live marriage according to the original order of creation. Is this teaching supersessionist? If the hard hearts were understood as possessed by Jews specifically, then it would evoke punishment supersession, but the Catechism clearly identifies the hard-heartedness in question as a feature of the lapsed human condition, not of Jews specifically. The teaching on divorce does suppose that Jesus enables a better form of life for those who attach themselves to him than that available through the Law, but this supposition does not in itself entail either punishment or economic supersession.

Celibacy

While the Catholic Church recognizes marriage as a sacrament, it also valorizes the celibate life, and in general demands celibacy from its priests. The Catechism (sections 1618–20) explains the logic of celibacy in a few different ways. Christ is himself a model of the celibate life, and celibacy, as an alternative to the bonds of marriage and parenthood, is a means of maintaining a wholehearted focus on Christ: one "renounce[s] the great good of marriage to follow the Lamb wherever he goes." As the Catechism describes it, celibacy orients the Christian toward Christ's second coming. It manifests "the ardent expectation of his return, a sign which also recalls that marriage is a reality of this present age which is passing away." That is, while marriage is a good, it is a lesser good than virginity, because its goodness is indexed to the present age, prior to Christ's return and to the establishment of the kingdom of God.

Celibacy occupies a much more marginal place in Judaism. It is true, as Catholic theologian Gary Anderson has observed, that Jewish and Christian theology alike recognize that sexuality, as a feature of carnal human existence, is in a fundamental way incompatible with holiness, or proximity to God. For this reason, he notes, God instructs the Israelite men not to "approach a woman" (Exod. 19:15) for three days prior to God's appearance at Sinai. When God is immediately present, human beings proximate to God must themselves become God-like so far as they can. (Recall too the case of Moses in the Bavli passage on procreation analyzed in chapter 6. Moses separates from his wife because he takes his unique prophetic status to preclude connubiality.) From this perspective, in fact, we should expect Judaism to be warier of sexuality than Catholicism is, insofar as Judaism rejects the notion of divine incarnation, and thus insists on a categorical distinction between God and the human body. When modern artists, secular and even Jewish, turn to Christian imagery, as they often do, in order to celebrate the holiness of eros, they arguably realize this very expectation.

But Christian theology toggles between the poles of the incarnation, or Christ's first coming, and the end time, or Christ's second coming. The valorization of celibacy in the Catechism is driven by the latter. The apocalyptic mindset of the earliest Christians, their sense that the kingdom of God was at hand, that the present age would soon pass away, left an indelible stamp on Christian theology, as we observed in chapter 6, and it is one of the factors that contributes to an otherworldliness that finds expression in the preference for celibacy over marriage. In Judaism, by contrast, the apocalyptic perspective never acquired anything like the same currency, and fewer reservations attach to the embrace of life in this world. The centrality for Jewish theology of the Jewish people, a category defined in the first instance by birth, likewise ensures the marginality of celibacy. Judaism therefore does not support any institutionalized praxis of celibacy, nor does it in any way envision a celibate rabbinate; on the contrary, in traditional circles, the rabbi's wife—the rebbetzin—has a well-defined social role. Even the "pietists of Ashkenaz" (in Germany of the twelfth and thirteenth centuries), famed for their asceticism, celebrated marital sex as a good.

> A person should refrain from everything related to women that brings pleasure to the body: not to see her or touch them or sit next to her or to see her fancy clothing or to hear her singing or to speak with her, whether she is married or not, with the exception of his wife, with whom he should rejoice when she is ritually pure with all his heart's passion. . . . In his own wife he should rejoice and delight, with love, at any time he wishes, for she guards him from sin. (*Sefer Roqeah*, Laws of Repentance, 20)

For the pietists of Ashkenaz, asceticism serves as a guardrail against sin, but there is no sin in marital sex itself; on the contrary, a man should take pleasure in marital sex because it prevents sin, by providing a licit forum for sexual desire.

There are some partial exceptions to Judaism's rejection of celibacy; I will mention the most important one. Given that, in one respect, the closest analogue in Judaism to Christ, the Word of God, is the Torah, God's word, we should not be surprised to find that, to some degree, just as the Catechism argues for celibacy as a means of preserving one's devotion to Christ free from any distraction, so rabbinic Judaism entertains the possibility of someone so given over to the study of Torah that he would therefore forgo marriage. In the continuation of the Bavli sugya on procreation that we analyzed in chapter 6 (Yebamot 63b), one rabbi compares a person who refrains from "being fruitful and multiplying" to a murderer, while a second rabbi says that such a person diminishes the divine image. A sage named Ben Azzai then enthusiastically affirms both positions, only to be pounced upon by his colleagues.

> They said to Ben Azzai: Some preach well and practice well, and some practice well though they do not preach well. But you preach well and don't practice well! He said to them: But what can I do, when my soul is passionate for Torah? The world can be sustained by others!

Although Ben Azzai preached the importance of producing offspring, he did not do so himself—meaning, presumably, that he remained unmarried—because his great passion for Torah would not allow it.

An extended discussion elsewhere in the Bavli (Ketubot 62b–63a) introduces what the scholar Daniel Boyarin has called the "married monk." To resolve the tension between married life and Torah study, some rabbinic circles in Babylon evidently developed the practice of having a young man first marry, then soon afterward leave home for an extended period of time to study Torah with a distant teacher or at an academy. By marrying—presumably through the effect of the act of intercourse immediately after the wedding, as well as the sexual availability, in principle, of his wife—the "married monk" could keep his sexual impulse in check, even as, by staying away from home, he was able to devote all his attention to Torah study. The Bavli describes this practice, and also critiques it for the toll that it takes on the scholar's family, especially his wife. It puts forward, as a sort of heroic ideal, the wife of Rabbi Akiva, who not only encourages him to leave for the academy for twelve years after the wedding, but also, at the end of this period, expresses the hope—in response to an old man who pities her widow-like circumstances—that he might stay away for another twelve years. (He overhears her, and does.) But the Bavli also knows to tell the sad legend of Rabbi Rehumi. The practice of this rabbi was to remain in the academy for the entire year, and return home only on the eve of the Day of Atonement (a day on which, perhaps not coincidentally, sexual intercourse is forbidden). One year, sitting on a ledge, engrossed in the study of a halakhic tradition, he delayed his departure from the academy. His wife, at home, said to herself: "Surely now he is coming, surely now." As a tear fell from her eye, the ledge on which he was sitting collapsed, and he fell to his death.

Homosexuality

Traditionally, both Judaism and Christianity prohibit homosexual intercourse and, by extension, a homosexual lifestyle. The grounds on which they do so overlap but differ, and the differences correlate in part with the above differences concerning divorce and celibacy. The framework for traditional Jewish reasoning about homosexuality is halakhah, beginning with biblical law. Leviticus 18:22, which occurs amid a list of intercourse prohibitions, mandates: "you shall not lie with a male as with a woman; it is an abomination." Leviticus 20:13 marks "lying with a male as with a woman" as a capital crime. The rabbis construe these verses, evidently in accordance with their plain sense, to refer to anal sex. But the rabbis also (e.g., in Sifra ahare mot 13) notice that other verses in the list of intercourse prohibitions (Lev. 18:6, 19) speak not only of "uncovering nakedness"—intercourse itself—but of "approaching" to uncover nakedness. On the assumption that the Torah does not waste words, the rabbis suppose that "approaching" indicates non-penetrative manifestations of sexual affection: oral sex, for example, or even intimate hugging in a sexual way. Such things, then, also become prohibited (not only between males, but between, for example, a man and a woman who is a niddah). By similar expansive exegesis of other verses, the rabbis also prohibit lesbian sex. Later legal codifiers—Maimonides and others—incorporate these prohibitions into their works.

For many Orthodox interpreters today, this legal tradition closes the case: homosexuality is altogether forbidden. Modern Orthodox and even some ultra-Orthodox communities do recognize the scientific consensus that sexual orientation is given rather than chosen, and that the case of homosexuality is therefore different from that of other transgressions of like severity. They appreciate, too, the need for pastoral support for gay Jews. But they stop there. Other rabbinic authorities at the liberal end of Orthodoxy and within Conservative Judaism go further. Consider, for example, a 2006 ruling issued by the Committee on Jewish Law and Standards of the Conservative Movement.[2] This responsum makes two key interventions. First, it distinguishes between the prohibition on male-male anal sex and the other forms of homosexual sexual interaction. In the former case, the rabbis clearly took themselves to be identifying the plain sense of the biblical text, but the latter case is ambiguous. Did the rabbis really mean to assert that the Bible prohibits the other forms of homosexual sexual interaction? Perhaps they understood that they were decreeing such things prohibited on their own authority (because, for example, sexual kissing between males might lead to anal sex, or because to permit lesbian sex would be to undermine the Bible's heterosexual norm), and were merely attaching these decrees, in an artificial way, to biblical verses. The halakhic tradition is divided on this question, and a great medieval legist, Nahmanides, for example, takes the second view. On this view, the only thing that the Bible prohibits is male-male anal sex; the other prohibitions are only from the rabbis.

Now, all things being equal, this distinction makes no practical difference for the tradition: if the rabbis prohibit something on their own authority, it is prohibited. (Note, too, from the other direction, that even a "biblical prohibition" in halakhah is not "what the Bible says" as such, but what the rabbis understood the Bible to say.) But the distinction can make a difference in cases of exigency. Exigent circumstances can license the violation or cancellation of a rabbinic law. (Some exigencies can license even the violation of a biblical law, as in the case of breaking the sabbath to save a life, but these are rarer.) Now, the halakhic tradition recognizes human dignity (*kevod ha-beriyot*) as a consideration that in exigent circumstances can constitute a reason for ignoring a rabbinic prohibition. Thus, for example, a priest—a patrilineal descendant of Aaron, brother of Moses—may not, by Torah law, defile himself

2. See https://web.archive.org/web/20070604193252/http://www.rabbinevins.org/HHH%20Dorff%20Nevins%20Reisner%20Final2.pdf.

by contact with the dead, as by walking over a marked grave plot. The rabbis also prohibit the priest, by extension, from passing through a field known to contain human remains, because he may end up traversing the part of the field where the remains are buried. But if the priest is accompanying a mourner, to comfort him, he may pass through such a field, in violation of the rabbinic prohibition. (These laws, incidentally, remain relevant, because the priestly genealogy has been preserved until today. Most Jews with the last name Cohen—from *kohen*, "priest" in Hebrew—are priests.) Thus crucially, dignity is not simply a "Jewish value"; it is a halakhic rule, capable of outweighing other halakhic rules. And here we arrive at the responsum's second key claim: to condemn a person to a life of celibacy, to deny a person the possibility of intimate spousal life, to mark them as single within a Jewish society where family life is the norm, is a serious affront to their dignity. Therefore, in the case of a person whose sexual orientation is strictly homosexual, the rabbinic extensions of the biblical prohibition on male-male anal sex are overridden by the consideration of dignity. This license does not apply, by the logic of the responsum, to someone who is bisexual, nor does the responsum license male-male anal sex itself in any circumstance.

Most Orthodox rabbis would likely disagree with this responsum. They might say that it is too bold in its application of the concept of dignity, or that it relies too heavily on minority views to distinguish biblical from rabbinic prohibitions in this area. Nevertheless, the reasoning in the responsum is recognizably traditional, and what marks it as traditional is its legalism. It identifies relevant legal rules in the tradition, determines their precise scope, and weighs competing rules against each other. Note, importantly, that it does not matter, within the legal tradition, what, say, Moses would have answered had he been asked about a homosexual lifestyle. No doubt he would have rejected it as out of bounds. What matters, rather, is what the biblical text, as received within a dynamic and evolving legal system, is understood specifically to prohibit.

Contrast the approach of the Conservative responsum to a 1998 report of the Central Conference of American Rabbis (CCAR), the organizing body of Reform Judaism.[3] This responsum goes much further than the Conservative responsum: it does not recognize a prohibition, per se, on any form of sexual

3. Selig Salkowitz, Chair, Central Conference of American Rabbis Ad Hoc Committee on Human Sexuality, "Report to the CCAR Convention, June, 1998." For the

intercourse, and it enables the recognition of gay marriage within a Jewish ritual framework. But the fundamental difference concerns not the outcome but the process. The CCAR report reasons in an entirely different way from the legalistic one characteristic of the tradition. It does not begin with the biblical prohibition, to grapple with it as a legal rule, in conversation with legal precedents. In fact, it does not cite the biblical prohibition at all. Rather, reasoning from the fact that Jewish marriage is characterized as qiddushin, or sanctification, the report uses holiness as its key criterion: Can a homosexual couple form a marriage relationship that can be called holy? The report addresses this question by reviewing what it takes to be basic Jewish sexual values: dignity, truth, health, justice, family, modesty, fidelity, joy, love, and moral striving. The report concludes that holiness can be present in a committed same-sex relationship, and that such relationships are therefore "worthy of affirmation through appropriate Jewish ritual." It leaves it to each Reform rabbi to decide his or her conscience on whether to adopt this view in practice.

Christian reasoning about homosexuality begins with the Hebrew Bible, but, just as Judaism receives the Bible through its rabbinic interpretation, so Christianity reads the Old Testament through the prism of the New. In the case of homosexuality, as Richard Hays, a New Testament scholar and Methodist minister, argues, the two testaments are continuous, but the New Testament, especially through Romans 1, introduces a new and decisive inflection. In Romans 1, Paul makes the case that God was apparent to human beings through the "creation of the world," that is, through nature. But human beings, in their sinfulness, "exchanged" God, the creator, for creatures, and worshiped images of human beings and animals. God, in turn, gave them over to "dishonorable passions," so that women "exchanged natural intercourse for unnatural," and likewise men, abandoning "natural intercourse with females," were inflamed with passion for one another. Nature figures centrally in Paul's reasoning: it is nature through which human beings ought to perceive God, and when human beings manifest blindness toward nature in rejecting God, they fall in turn into "unnatural" forms of sexual intercourse. When the Catechism of the Catholic Church (sections 2357–59) declares that "homosexual acts . . . are contrary to the natural law" and "intrinsically disordered," it fol-

CCAR's positive endorsement of the report see: https://www.ccarnet.org/ccar-resolutions/same-gender-officiation/.

lows in the path set down by Paul. Hays and the Catechism alike ultimately counsel celibacy for gay Christians. Both appreciate the heavy burden that Christian teaching, on their interpretation, imposes on them, and both underscore the need for sensitivity and pastoral care. The Catechism also finds in the cross a sort of comfort for gay Christians, insofar as they can "unite to the sacrifice of the Lord's Cross the difficulties they may encounter from their condition."

Of course, there are more liberal Christian approaches to homosexuality. Hays finds the most compelling argument for a more liberal approach to be the authority of experience, because experience shows that there are in fact many gay Christians who find God's grace in the stable, loving homosexual relationships that they maintain. But let us focus on comparison of the more traditional approaches, Jewish on the one hand and Christian on the other. The traditional Jewish approaches, taking their lead from the Bible, confront homosexuality as a legal question. The relevant legal rules—the basic prohibition, as well as the principle of dignity that the Conservative responsum invokes—have a basis in a certain conception of what might be called nature, but this conception only acquires normative force insofar as it translates into legal rules, and then these rules function as rules do, within a jurisprudential system. For the Christian approaches, by contrast, nature exerts normative force directly.

Conclusion

In the case of divorce too, the Catholic prohibition rests on a conception of marriage as a natural phenomenon, a metaphysical joining of flesh, while the Jewish license conceives of marriage as a legal relationship that can be terminated by legal means. Why does nature play a greater role in Christian reasoning about divorce and homosexuality? Let me point to two considerations. One is Christianity's apocalyptic legacy, which we have already invoked in connection with Catholicism's teaching on celibacy. Nature looms large in the apocalyptic worldview; its intense interest in the end time draws the apocalyptic worldview always back to the beginning time, to creation. Second, nature is a philosophical category, and, as we will see in the next chapter, philosophy is more foundational for Christian theology than for Jewish theology.

Thus, even as Judaism and Christianity traditionally have in common certain fundamental values bearing on marriage, divorce, celibacy and homosexuality, their distinct theological commitments become differently manifest in these areas in immediately practical ways.

Further Inquiry

On the life cycle in the Jewish tradition see Ivan G. Marcus, *The Jewish Life Cycle: Rites of Passage from Biblical to Modern Times* (Seattle: University of Washington Press, 2004). For a guide to Jewish practice and belief connected with death, see Maurice Lamm, *The Jewish Way in Death and Mourning: Revised and Expanded* (New York: Jonathan David Publishers, 2000). Shaye J. D. Cohen's book, *Why Aren't Jewish Women Circumcised? Gender and Covenant in Judaism* (Berkeley: University of California Press, 2005), approaches traditional rabbinic thought on circumcision from a surprising but illuminating angle. See Michael L. Satlow, "Slipping Toward Sacrament: Jews, Christians and Marriage," in Richard Kalmin and Seth Schwartz, ed., *Jewish Culture and Society Under the Christian Roman Empire* (Leuven: Peeters, 2003), 65–89, for an account of the conceptualization of marriage in rabbinic thought that puts it somewhat closer to the Christian one than the account I have offered. For Gary Anderson's remarks on celibacy, noted above, see the second chapter of his book, *The Genesis of Perfection: Adam and Eve in Jewish and Christian Imagination* (Louisville: Westminster John Knox, 2001). The above analysis of the married monk in the Bavli depends on Daniel Boyarin, *Carnal Israel: Reading Sex in Talmudic Culture* (Berkeley: University of California Press, 1993). On sexuality in canonical rabbinic literature see generally Michael L. Satlow, *Tasting the Dish: Rabbinic Rhetorics of Sexuality* (Atlanta: Scholars Press, 1995), and on the impulse to sin and especially the sexual impulse, see Ishay Rosen-Zvi, *Demonic Desires: "Yetzer Hara" and the Problem of Evil in Late Antiquity* (Philadelphia: University of Pennsylvania Press, 2011). For views of sexuality among the pietists of Ashkenaz, see Yishai Kiel, "The Moral and Religious Instructions of Asheknazi Pietism Between Asceticism and Sexuality," *Daat* 73 (2012), 85–101. Richard Hays's argument on homosexuality in Christianity can be found in his book *The Moral Vision of the New Testament* (New York: HarperOne, 1996), 379–406. Within Judaism, the issue of homosexuality raises the more general question of the process of halakhic change. For theological approaches to this question, see Tamar Ross, *Expanding the Palace of Torah: Orthodoxy and Feminism* (Lebanon, NH: Brandeis University Press, 2004); Benjamin D. Sommer, *Revelation and Authority: Sinai in Jewish Scripture and Tradition* (New Haven: Yale University Press, 2015).

●

1. Consider another story about a married monk, from Bavli Qiddushin 81b. "Rabbi Hiyya son of Ashi regularly would fall on his face [in prayer] and say: May the Merciful One save me from the evil inclination. One day his wife heard him. She thought: Since it has been many years since he has separated from me, what is the reason he speaks thus? One day he was studying in the garden. She adorned herself and passed back and forth in front of him. He said to her: Who are you? She said: I am a courtesan who has arrived at this place just now. He propositioned her. She said to him: Bring me the pomegranate from the top of the branch. He jumped up, went, and brought it to her. When he returned to his house, his wife was lighting the oven. He went up and sat inside it. She said to him: What is this? He told her: Such and such happened. She said to him: It was I! He said to her: Nevertheless, I intended to sin." Try to clarify the plot of the story. What does it say about sex and carnality? For a detailed analysis of the story, see chapter 3 of Jeffrey L. Rubenstein, *The Land of Truth: Talmud Tales, Timeless Teachings* (Lincoln: University of Nebraska Press, 2018). The above translation is drawn from the book, with minor changes.

2. Consider, by contrast, the following story, from Bavli Berakot 62a. It comes after two stories in which sages in training follow their masters into the bathroom in order to learn from them proper bathroom etiquette, for after all, this too is Torah. "Rabbi Kahana entered after Rav for another matter, and sat under his bed. He heard him conversing and laughing [with his wife], and satisfying his needs. He said: Rav's mouth seems as though it never tasted a cooked dish. He said to him: Kahana, is that you? Get out of here; it isn't proper. He said to him: It is Torah, and I must learn." What does this story, in itself and in its literary context, say about sex and carnality?

— Chapter 13 —

Belief and the Maimonidean God

A PASSAGE IN THE BABYLONIAN TALMUD (Yebamot 47a–b) prescribes the process of conversion to Judaism. The process begins with Jewish authorities confirming that the person in question wishes to convert despite the fact that the people of Israel are subject to persecution. Upon receiving such confirmation from him, they ask him whether he is willing to accept upon himself the commandments distinctive to Israel, which come with the prospect of reward but also with the threat of punishment. If he accepts them upon himself, he is circumcised, and immerses in a mikveh. While in the mikveh, two sages again teach him some of the commandments. When he emerges from the mikveh, he is "a Jew in all respects." Reflecting on this passage, rabbinic tradition specifies "accepting the yoke of the commandments" as the central substantive element of the conversion process, alongside the ritual processes of circumcision and immersion in water. Joining it, as first in time if perhaps second in importance, is the express desire to join the Jewish people.

Augustine, in his *Confessions* (8.2), tells how a famous pagan rhetorician, Victorinus, converted to Christianity in Rome. He was introduced to the "first sacraments of instruction," and soon after submitted his name for baptism. Presumably in connection with his baptism, "the hour came for the profession of his faith," which Victorinus made publicly. The "recitation of the creed" (*redditio symboli*) in connection with baptism is amply attested elsewhere for the Christian West in the period. Just as the jailer in Acts 16, seeking to know what he must do in order to be saved, is told by Paul and Silas, "believe in the Lord Jesus," so, within a baptismal framework, one becomes a Christian insofar as one professes a certain set of beliefs. From a structural perspective, the recitation of the creed or the profession of faith in the Christian ritual of conversion corresponds to the acceptance of the yoke of the commandments in the Jewish ritual of conversion.

This correspondence raises the question: What place do belief and the recitation of beliefs have in Judaism? Are there beliefs that a Jew must profess? Is there a Jewish creed? Do the commandments in Judaism occupy the place that Christianity reserves for belief? We will explore these questions in conversation with the great medieval jurist and philosopher, Maimonides, who is the central figure in the history of belief as a category in Jewish theology. In putting the spotlight on Maimonides, this chapter moves us chronologically forward, past the rabbinic corpus of antiquity that is the canonical foundation of Judaism, into the medieval period. We will continue in the next chapter with other major developments in medieval and early modern Jewish thought. These two chapters together will lay the foundation for chapter 15, devoted to the topic of contemporary Jewish spirituality.

Creed and Belief among the Rabbis of Antiquity

If one were to ask a traditional Jew if Judaism has a creed, she might well point to a verse we have encountered already, the opening verse of the Shema liturgy, Deuteronomy 6:4: "Hear, O Israel, the Lord is our God, the Lord alone." There is a tradition of reciting this declaration before one's death, especially in the case of a martyr's death, as during the Holocaust. This tradition has its roots in the story of Rabbi Akiva's martyrdom (Bavli Berakhot 61b), introduced at the beginning of chapter 6. Though suffering cruel torture at the hands of the Romans for teaching Torah in public, Rabbi Akiva noticed that the time for recitation of the (evening?) Shema liturgy had arrived, and he insisted on reciting the verse, giving up the ghost with the word "alone." In this way, according to the story, he fulfilled the injunction in the next verse (Deut. 6:5), to love the Lord "with all your soul," understood to mean, even if God takes away one's soul. But if Deuteronomy 6:4 is the Jewish creed, it functions in this way, as a declaration of faith, chiefly in the shadow of death. The twice-daily recitation of the Shema liturgy, by contrast, has only a loosely privileged status in relation to most other daily prayers, and is subordinate, as a prayer, to the Amidah. To be sure, Judaism recognizes the twice-daily recitation of the Shema liturgy as a biblical commandment, but it is only one among many other commandments.

A scholar of medieval Judaism, Menachem Kellner, wrote a book in 1999 whose title consists of a provocative question: Must a Jew believe anything?[1] The titular question seems absurd on its face. Judaism is replete with beliefs: about God's existence, about the creation of the world, about God's covenant with Abraham, and later, with the Jewish people at Sinai, etc. How does Kellner's question even get off the ground? Here we must keep in mind three things, the first two of which are already familiar. First, Judaism, as a hybrid of religion and ethnicity, traditionally defines membership in the category "Jew" in ethnic terms: a Jew is a child of a Jewish mother. Hence, if the question whether a Jew must believe anything is parsed to mean, must a Jew believe anything in order to be deemed a Jew from the perspective of Judaism, then the answer is plausibly and even probably "no." Second, within the framework of rabbinic Judaism, the commandments are the privileged framework for processing the notion of "must." Thus the question whether a Jew must believe anything reemerges as the question: Is there a commandment that requires that a Jew believe something? And as far as classical rabbinic literature is concerned, the most straightforward answer to this question, too, is "no." God commands actions, not states of mind. We will return to this point below.

The third consideration requires greater elaboration. A belief, as a mental state, is a philosophical sort of thing. A belief can concern concrete things (e.g., "I believe I ate eggs yesterday for breakfast"), but in itself, as a mental state, a belief involves abstraction, and thus belongs, in broad strokes, to the realm of philosophy. Besides the ethnic dimension of Judaism and the centrality of the commandments, the third reason that belief plays little explicit role in rabbinic Judaism is that rabbinic Judaism approaches God in a "pre-philosophical" way. The term "pre-philosophical" is easily misunderstood to mean "unsophisticated." I do not in any way mean to suggest that rabbinic thinking about God lacks sophistication. My point is rather that the rabbis conceptualize God, frame questions about God, in ways different from those familiar from the Greek intellectual tradition that defines philosophy as a discipline. In this respect, the rabbis are faithful heirs of the Hebrew Bible.

1. Menachem Kellner, *Must a Jew Believe Anything?* (Portland: Littman Library of Jewish Civilization, 1999).

In an essay devoted to "The God of the Rabbis," Moshe Halbertal substantiates this point by reference to a telling passage from an early rabbinic commentary on the book of Exodus (Mekhilta de-Rabbi Ishmael be-shallah). Exodus 13:21 records that "the Lord went in front of [Israel] by day in a pillar of cloud, to lead them along the way, and in a pillar of fire by night, to give them light, so that they might travel by day and by night." The commentator wonders:

> Is it possible to say such a thing? Does it not already say, "I fill the heavens and the earth" (Jer. 23:24), and it is written, "And one called out to another and said, 'Holy, holy, holy is the Lord of Hosts! The whole earth is full of his glory!'" (Isa. 6:3) . . . What, then, is the sense of "The Lord went in front of them by day"?

To what tension is the commentator pointing? Our first instinct might be to parse the commentator's question in philosophical terms: God is infinite, limitless, omnipresent, so how could Scripture characterize God as occupying a pillar of cloud or fire? But the commentator's answer reveals that his question was in fact quite different.

> Said Rabbi [Judah the Patriarch]: Sometimes Emperor Antoninus would be holding court on the dais, and it would grow dark, and his sons were with him as it grew dark. When he left the dais, he would take the lamp and cast light for his sons. And the nobles of the empire would come to him and say: We will take the lamp and cast light for your sons! And he would say to them: No. It's not that I don't have someone to take the lamp and cast light for my sons. Rather, I wish to convey to you my love for my sons, so that you should treat them honorably. Likewise, the Holy One, blessed be He, conveyed to the nations of the world his love for Israel, so that they should treat them honorably. Yet not only do they not treat them honorably, but they kill them through cruel and unusual means.

From the answer we understand that the commentator's question was not philosophical in the conventional sense. He was not concerned with the metaphysical conundrum of an infinite being confined to a limited space. His concern, rather, was with propriety: How is it fitting for the king of the world to play the role of servant to Israel, lighting the way for them in the dark? Rabbi Judah the Patriarch's answer finds in this biblical passage another instance of the dynamic described in chapter 8: God empties Godself, humbles Godself, for the sake of God's children, Israel.

The rabbis' God is not a concept defined or intimated by a set of metaphysical properties. For the rabbis, as for the Bible itself, God is a person, a relational being: a king, a father, a warrior, and many other things besides. The thing to understand, in approaching God, is not the nature of God's being, but the network of relationships in which God is embedded, and how these relationships condition the ways in which God acts, and the ways in which a person ought to act toward God. Abraham Heschel expresses this distinction with a story about a lecture that he was supposed to deliver at a conference. He had committed to presenting on "the God of Israel," but the organizers changed the title so that his lecture appeared instead as devoted to "the Jewish concept of God." A seemingly slight change, but for Heschel, a fundamental category mistake: "Realism was replaced by 'notionalism.' . . . The God of Israel is a name, not a notion. There is a difference between a 'name' and a 'notion.' . . . A notion defines, describes; a name evokes. A notion is derived from a generalization; a name is learned through acquaintance. A notion you can conceive; a name you call."[2] This relational, pre-philosophical approach to God is hostile to a centering of Jewish religious expression around beliefs, or states of mind, and represents a third reason, along with the ethnic definition of Jewish identity and the priority of the commandments, for the marginality of belief in traditional Judaism.

Like the other two factors, this third factor also distinguishes Judaism from Christianity. The Christian figures who correspond to the rabbis are the early church fathers, and while the degree of philosophical influence on the early church fathers varied, they were on the whole far more conversant with and conditioned by Greek philosophy than the rabbis. Consider, for example, Augustine's reflection on the first part of the creed, concerning belief in God "the almighty Father" (*Patrum omnipotentem*) ("Of Faith and the Creed," chapter 2). Augustine argues that those who claim that God created the world out of existing matter implicitly deny God's omnipotence, by suggesting that

2. Abraham Heschel, *Moral Grandeur and Spiritual Audacity* (New York: Farrar, Straus & Giroux, 1996), 162.

God could not have created the world out of nothing, and that there exists something not created by God. As we will see below, this sort of reasoning, revolving around existence and metaphysical dependence, enters the Jewish tradition in the medieval period, within an Islamic thought-world shaped by Greek philosophy, but one does not find it in rabbinic literature, the canonical foundation of Judaism. Judaism and Christianity diverge around belief in part because Greek philosophy impacted Christianity at a more foundational stage than in the case of Judaism: in antiquity, rather than in the medieval period. Of course, like all claims for difference, this one too must be nuanced. Contemporary Christian theologians—among them, Pope Benedict in the excerpt from *Deus Caritas Est* quoted in the first chapter—echo Heschel by insisting that the tradition demands a real rather than a notional approach to Christ: the Christ event is a real event, not reducible to an abstract principle, and likewise a Christian's relationship with Christ is a real relationship and not a mere idea.

There is one exceptional place in the Mishnah where belief enters into the realm of halakhic discourse. Tractate Sanhedrin-Makkot concerns civil and criminal procedure, including the proper punishment for various offenses. (The word "sanhedrin" is a form of Greek *synedrion*, the court that appears many times in the New Testament.) The tenth chapter of the tractate opens with a list of individuals whose punishment is loss of their portion in the afterlife: "And these are they who have no portion in the world to come: one who says, there is no resurrection of the dead; and there is no Torah from heaven; and the Epicurean." Here, then, is, arguably, a list of required beliefs: one must believe in the resurrection of the dead, in the divine origin of the Torah, and—following from the fact that Epicureans were infamous in the Greco-Roman philosophical world for denying divine providence—in the notion that God rewards good and punishes evil.

In keeping with our observation that the marginality of belief in Judaism is bound up with the relatively marginal impact of Greek philosophy on the rabbis, it is notable that the only place in the Mishnah where the notion of obligatory belief arises, also features a rare reference to a Greek philosophical school. (The Epicurean is mentioned once elsewhere in the Mishnah, in a unique tractate dedicated to comportment and ethics rather than to law. See Abot 2:14.) This exceptional passage "proves the rule" in another way. In form, the statement "These are they who have no portion in the world to come" comes in the midst of similar lists:

> These are they who are subject to stoning, etc. (7:4)
> These are they who are subject to execution by vigilante justice, etc. (8:7)
> These are they who are subject to burning, etc. (9:1)
> These are they who are subject to execution [by the sword], etc. (9:1)
> These are they who are subject to strangulation, etc. (11:1)
> These are they who are subject to exile, etc. (13:1)
> These are they who are subject to lashes, etc. (14:1)

All these lists except ours concern a punishment administered by human beings. The structure of the tractate thus strongly marks out crimes of belief as exceptions within the realm of halakhah: they have consequences, yes, but the responsibility for administering those consequences lies with God in the next world.

Creed and Belief in Modern Judaism

The marginal or perhaps more precisely the implicit role of belief in Judaism relative to Christianity encodes important structural differences between these traditions, but in the premodern period, the immediate direct implications were minor. Most Jews, like most Christians, were not philosophers, and most Jews, like most Christians, straightforwardly believed the historical claims on which their tradition rested: the existence of God; the creation of the world by God; prophecy; the exodus from Egypt; the giving of the law at Sinai, etc. Premodern Jews did not in general think of themselves as *commanded* to believe these things in the same way that they were commanded to light sabbath candles or refrain from work on the sabbath, but they took these beliefs as a given. However, with the emergence of modern science and the historical method, which have put great pressure on traditional belief, the role of belief in Judaism became a relevant and even a pressing question in Jewish-Christian discourse and among different denominations of Judaism.

How, in the wake of the theory of evolution, can one maintain a belief in the creation of the world as described in Genesis 1–2? Is it possible to believe in the miracles of the Bible in the face of modern science and its natural laws? Can the traditional notion of the Torah as a work of Mosaic prophecy withstand the evidence amassed by historians and source critics in favor of the theory that the Torah as we have it is the result of complex redaction of multiple sources, the latest of which was written many centuries after Moses (if a person of this sort ever existed)? Summarizing a very complex set of developments in a very schematic way, we may say that, confronted by these questions, modern Jews have moved in two opposing directions: in one direction, an embrace of the fact that Judaism does not in general explicitly demand belief in these historical propositions, and in the other direction, a reactionary transformation of the implicit into the explicit, and an insistence that Judaism does require belief in these historical propositions.

Today, the latter position is regnant in ultra-Orthodoxy and even, to an important degree, in modern Orthodoxy. While modern Orthodox Jews generally accept the notion of evolution, and apply a range of exegetical tools to reconcile it with the creation stories in Genesis, they tend to uphold a more or less literal belief in the foundational stories of the Bible, even the miraculous ones, and especially in the notion of the Torah as the word of God through Moses. Ultra-Orthodox Jews sometimes go further, rejecting evolution too.

The former position is favored among non-traditional Jews, including among Jews who are traditionalist in practice but non-traditionalist in their beliefs. Such Jews double down on the conception of Judaism as first and foremost a set of practices rather than a set of faith propositions, which enables them to practice Judaism more or less traditionally, "authentically," even as they animate these practices with beliefs about God and about the Jewish past that are discontinuous with those held by their forebears. The lineaments of this posture can be discerned in one of the seminal thinkers of modern Judaism, Moses Mendelssohn (1729–1786). In his essay, *Jerusalem*, Mendelssohn seeks the proper calibration between church and state. He offers that the state should govern conduct, by means of coercion when necessary, while religious institutions should seek to cultivate convictions or beliefs, and necessarily through education rather than force. Judaism, for Mendelssohn, is a model of this balance, in a way that Christianity is not, because "among all the prescriptions and ordinances of the Mosaic law, there is not a single one which says: *You shall believe or not believe.* They all say: *You shall do or not do.*"[3]

Maimonides

Paradoxically, both the reactionary and the non-traditionalist approaches to the question of belief in modern Judaism find their anchor in the same figure from the medieval period, arguably the single most prominent figure in Jewish intellectual history: Maimonides. Moses, son of Maimon, known in English as Maimonides (Greek for "son of Maimon") and in Hebrew as Rambam (an acronym for *R*abbi *M*oshe *b*en ["son of"] *M*aimon), was born in the mid-1130s in Córdoba, in Muslim Spain. He came into the world at the tail end of a period sometimes described, too rosily, as a golden age of *convivencia*, in which Andalusian Muslims, Jews, and Christians together produced a high culture of great attainment in courtly literature, theology, and philosophy. After Córdoba fell under the control of the Almohads, a conquering force from North Africa that did not tolerate the existence of non-Muslims, Maimonides's family fled, eventually settling in Egypt. Maimonides became the recognized leader of the Jewish community there, and the physician to the sultan. He died in 1204.

Maimonides's two most important works are the *Mishneh Torah* ("restatement of the Torah"), written in Hebrew, and his *Guide to the Perplexed*, written in Judeo-Arabic. Though very different in character, these two works together form a coherent pedagogical program. The *Mishneh Torah* is a synthesis of the entire trajectory of halakhah, first and foremost the Babylonian Talmud and its interpreters. Its aim is to consolidate the Oral Law into a single work, so that the student can master halakhah through study of two books alone, the Bible and the *Mishneh Torah*. While it is unclear whether Maimonides intended the *Mishneh Torah* even for learned audiences, he evidently envisioned that the most intellectually capable student, having attained to mastery of halakhah, would proceed to the subject that Maimonides deemed to be of ultimate importance: metaphysics, or the direct study of the nature of

3. See Moses Mendelssohn, *Jerusalem: Or on Religious Power and Judaism* (Lebanon, NH: Brandeis University Press, 1983), 100.

God. It is to this subject that Maimonides dedicates his *Guide to the Perplexed.* The titular perplexity lies in the apparent tension between what philosophy—especially Aristotelian philosophy—teaches about God, and what the Bible appears to say about God.

Philosophy is not absent from the *Mishneh Torah* itself, because Maimonides makes the revolutionary claim that halakhah in fact demands of every Jew a basic grasp of philosophy. Maimonides begins the work with a unit on the "laws of the basic principles of the Torah," which opens as follows: "The basic principle of all basic principles and the pillar of all sciences is to know that there is a first existence who brought every existing thing into existence."[4] Everything that exists depends on God's existence, whereas God's existence does not depend on theirs. "Knowledge of this is a positive commandment, as it says, 'I am the Lord your God' (Exod. 20:2)." Correspondingly, "whoever permits the thought to enter his mind that there is another deity besides this God, violates a negative commandment, as it says, 'you shall have no other gods before me' (Exod. 20:3)." According to Maimonides, then, the first and foundational commandments, one of them positive ("do!") and one of them negative ("don't do!"), concern states of mind about the existence and metaphysical nature of God.

The two prooftexts that Maimonides introduces come from the very beginning of the Decalogue, surely a good place to look for the basic principles of the Torah. But Maimonides's interpretation of these verses marks a radical departure from the plain sense, in two ways. Here is Exodus 20:2 in full: "I am the Lord your God who took you out of the land of Egypt." The relevant thing about God in this verse is not God's logical and chronological priority relative to all other existing things, but the fact that God took Israel out of Egypt. Moreover, the verse does not command anything, but represents a prelude to the next verse. Exodus 20:3 forbids Israel from "having other gods," but on its plain sense, this injunction forbids Jews from expressing fealty to other gods, not, as for Maimonides, from entertaining the thought of their existence.

For Maimonides, it is so important to grasp the nature of God correctly because the only way to relate to God is by calling God to mind. God is not

4. Here and elsewhere for the *Mishneh Torah* and the *Guide to the Perplexed,* I use the translation in Isadore Twersky, *A Maimonides Reader* (Springfield, NJ: Behrman House Publishing, 1972), with modifications.

to be found anywhere in the world: not in the temple, not in the sky. God has no body of any sort, for a body is divisible, while God is perfectly single, perfectly uniform, and unchanging. God is, in a sense, reason itself, and the closest thing to God in the world is the human mind, or human reason. It is in virtue of their intellectual capacity that the Bible characterizes human beings as the image of God in the world, and it is through the human mind alone that God enters the world. A person does not come closer to God by entering a certain place, or by performing certain actions. He enters into a relationship with God only by thinking about God. And the more that someone perfects his conception of God, the more he can, by dwelling on that conception, develop that relationship. If a person conjures up a body when he thinks about God, then the image of God in his mind is not God, is indeed nothing like God, and so he is not really thinking about God. To pray to such a mental image in fact represents something like worship of a false god, or idolatry.

Though stringent and severe in its way, at the heart of Maimonides's perspective is an intense passion for God. Maimonides is careful to insist that the religious goal is not philosophical knowledge of God, per se, but active mental preoccupation with God. Philosophical knowledge is necessary so as to enable a person to call to mind the proper concept of God, but if that person does not in fact call this concept to mind, and dwell on it assiduously, then he has achieved nothing.

> That intellect which overflowed from Him, may He be exalted, toward us is the bond between us and Him. You have the choice: If you wish to strengthen and to fortify this bond, you can do so; if, however, you wish gradually to make it weaker and feebler until you cut it, you can also do that. You can only strengthen this bond by employing it in loving Him and in progressing toward this, just as we have explained. And it is made weaker and feebler if you busy your thought with what is other than He. Know that even if you were the man who knew most the true reality of the divine science, you would cut that bond existing between you and God if you would empty your thought of God and busy yourself totally in eating the necessary or in occupying yourself with the necessary. You would not be with Him then, nor He with you. For that relation between You and him is actually broken off at that time. (*Guide to the Perplexed*, III.51)

It is here, in part, that the commandments of the Torah come into play. For

Maimonides, the commandments are chiefly a practical means to a contemplative end, in two ways. First, as daily rites, they enable individuals to keep God in mind even when they must devote time to "the necessary" (farming, eating, etc.). Second, they ensure a peaceful, functioning society, which is a sine qua non for the pursuit of philosophy.

Maimonides's God is utterly transcendent. God, for Maimonides, is literally indescribable; that is, any proposition about God is necessarily false. Consider, for example, the assertion, "God is good." This assertion misses the mark in two ways. First, goodness is a general property, and thus capable of being possessed, in principle, by any number of entities. By predicating goodness of God, the assertion groups God with other entities, and thus obscures the utter difference between God and everything else. Second, the division of the sentence into a subject ("God") and a predicate ("good") implies that it is possible to conceptualize God separately from God's properties, or in other words, it implies that God is composite, whereas in fact God is perfectly unified. The same shortcomings apply to all assertions about God, which is to say that one cannot formulate a true, positive statement about God. The process of apprehending God is a process of negation, of stripping away from our concept of God the dross with which our imagination inevitably clothes it. And this process is inevitably incomplete. It is an oxymoron to suppose that God could be contained in a human mind.

Like all language, the language of Scripture, when it speaks of God, speaks falsely, if we construe its words literally. God does not speak or command. God does not reward or punish. God certainly does not have an arm or a face or any other body part. Because Maimonides is committed to the inerrancy of Scripture, he is compelled to subject Scripture to an interpretive schema that construes its God-claims in other than literal ways. Some of this work is relatively easy: God's arm, for example, can be a metaphor for God's power. Other challenges are far more serious. For example, if God does not speak, what sense can be made of prophecy? Maimonides argues that prophecy emerges naturally and automatically when a person advances sufficiently far in the perfection of his intellectual and imaginative faculties. At this point he attains special insight into the divine mind, and the capacity to express the implications of this insight in terms relevant to human conduct in the world. In this area, as in others, Maimonides compromises on elegance for the sake of partial concession to tradition; he allows, in particular, that Moses's prophetic power was of a categorically different and more supernatural kind than that of other prophets.

In an extended commentary on the above passage in Mishnah Sanhedrin-Makkot 10—part of a third work, his commentary on the Mishnah—Maimonides articulates thirteen "foundations" or "principles" of the Torah. These principles include, among other things, God's existence, God's oneness, God's incorporeality, prophecy, the divine origin and eternal authority of the Torah, and the future coming of the messiah. Only one who has true faith in these thirteen foundations, says Maimonides, "enters into the category of Israel." Although Maimonides was neither the first nor the last in the Jewish tradition to formulate a list of faith principles, his is by far the best known, popularized by a rhymed hymn, Yigdal, that entered into the daily liturgy and is sung daily even today (in the Koren siddur, 24).

Conclusion

The notion that Judaism rests on a set of foundational beliefs is a natural corollary of Maimonides's philosophical interpretation of Judaism. And yet, strikingly, putting these principles into the context of Maimonides's thought, it is clear that Maimonides himself could only have construed some of them, such as prophecy, in ways very different from the literal sense, and thus very different from how most Jews have traditionally understood and understand them. Herein lies the paradox in the legacy of Maimonides.

On the one hand, Maimonides departs from Jewish tradition by assigning pride of place to belief. In this respect, he anticipates the reactionary Jewish response to modernity: in the face of science and the historical method, we must not only uphold traditional implicit beliefs, but make them explicit, and police the boundary around them. On the other hand, Maimonides adopts a radically non-traditional conception of God that sets God far beyond the miracle stories of the Bible and the concerns of a specific people (even if, for Maimonides, God is indeed, in a remote sense, connected with those miracle stories and with that specific people). In this respect, Maimonides is an inspiration for a certain authentic but non-traditional response to modernity: one can live a life densely structured by the tradition even while construing it, and the God at its center, in new ways that are informed by modern intellectual commitments.

Further Inquiry

Moshe Halbertal's essay, "The God of the Rabbis," appears in Steven Kepnes, ed., *The Cambridge Companion to Jewish Theology* (Cambridge: Cambridge University Press, 2020), 61–76. See Emanuel Fiano, *Three Powers in Heaven: The Emergence of Theology and the Parting of the Ways* (New Haven: Yale University Press, 2023), for the claim that the crystallization of a distinctive sort of theological discourse among the Christian intellectual elite of the fourth century CE played an important role in setting Christianity apart from Judaism. On the nature of this discourse see also Johannes Zachhuber, *The Rise of Christian Theology and the End of Ancient Metaphysics: Patristic Philosophy from the Cappadocian Fathers to John of Damascus* (Oxford: Oxford University Press, 2020). My account of Maimonides, especially on language, is indebted to Moshe Halbertal, *Maimonides: Life and Thought* (Princeton: Princeton University Press, 2014). Wide-ranging historical treatments of Maimonides's life and thought can be found in Joel L. Kraemer, *Maimonides: The Life and World of One of Civilization's Greatest Minds* (New York: Doubleday, 2008), and Sarah Stroumsa, *Maimonides in His World: A Portrait of a Mediterranean Thinker* (Princeton: Princeton University Press, 2009). A new English translation of Maimonides's *Guide* recently appeared, by Lenn Goodman and Phillip Lieberman, Moses Maimonides, *The Guide to the Perplexed: A New Translation* (Stanford: Stanford University Press, 2024). For historical contextualization challenging the conventional wisdom construing Maimonides's thirteen principles as orthodox dogma see Marc B. Shapiro, *The Limits of Orthodox Theology: Maimonides' Thirteen Principles Reappraised* (Oxford: The Littman Library of Jewish Civilization, 2004). On divine corporeality in the Bible and in its Jewish and Christian reception, see Benjamin D. Sommer, *The Bodies of God and the World of Ancient Israel* (Cambridge: Cambridge University Press, 2011).

●

1. What is it about the rhetorical structure and theological content of Deuteronomy 6:4 (the Shema) that makes it compelling as a credal statement? Besides the

Shema and the Maimonidean hymn Yigdal, a possible candidate for a Jewish creed is the kaddish, mentioned in passing in chapter 10 as a mourner's prayer. For the text of a longer and shorter version of the kaddish see the Koren siddur, 56–58 and 60. Read the text through. How is it similar to and different from the Shema? What makes it especially apt for a mourner? For a historical account of how the kaddish came to be associated with mourning, see David I. Shyovitz, "'You Have Saved Me from the Judgment of Gehenna': The Origins of the Mourner's Kaddish in Medieval Ashkenaz," *AJS Review* 39 (2015): 49–73. See also Leon Wieseltier, *Kaddish* (New York: Vintage Books, 1998), a hybrid of memoir of the author's year reciting the kaddish in the synagogue after the death of his father, and reflection on the sages' teachings about death, mourning, and the kaddish.

2. A corollary of Maimonides's philosophical interpretation of Judaism is a focus on the individual rather than the community, as it is through a person's mind, in the first instance, that she connects to God. In this respect, too, Maimonides marks a break from traditional Judaism. Can you nevertheless envision a role for the community within a Maimonidean framework?

3. For Maimonides, the notion that human beings were created in the image of God does not have the human body in its purview at all; only our minds bear the impress of God. What implications might this view have for the principle of human dignity, which for Jewish and Christian thinkers alike is often associated with the body and with bodily needs, and conceptualized through the notion of creation in the image of God? On this question see Daniel H. Weiss, "Iconic Theology in Classical Rabbinic Literature and Orthodox Christianity," in *Elonei Mamre: The Encounter of Judaism and Orthodox Christianity*, ed. Nicholas de Lange et al. (Lanham: Lexington Books, 2023), 89–98. Weiss compares and contrasts Maimonides's view to those of both the classical rabbis and the Eastern Orthodox theologian John of Damascus, as an exercise in theological encounter between Jews and the Orthodox Church.

— *Chapter 14* —

Kabbalah and Hasidism

The word "myth" is commonly used to mean stories set within the divine realm: stories about the births of gods, about their alliances and dalliances, about their victories and defeats. As the scholar Yehezkel Kaufmann famously observed, the Hebrew Bible is, in the main, hostile to myth, because God transcends everything, and does not depend, in an essential way, on anything. There are other divine beings, but they do not challenge God. God is not born, nor does God beget, nor does God need sustenance. Nevertheless, the very fact that God creates the world seems to suggest some need in God that the creation of the world satisfies; just as God says of the first human being, "it is not good that the man should be alone" (Gen. 2:18), so creation seems like a response to God's own desire for company. And God does call upon human beings to serve God, through sacrifice and in other ways, again suggesting divine need.

The classical rabbis, not being philosophers, did not attempt to settle this tension. Rather, as good readers, and creative exegetes, they elaborated and in certain ways intensified it. Maimonides can be understood as the Jewish thinker who completes the Bible's demythologization of God. For Maimonides, there are no stories to tell about God, not only because language is unequal to the task of describing God, but more fundamentally because God is absolutely unchanging. Alongside Maimonides, however, another theological framework arose in the medieval period that leaned precisely in the opposite direction. Kabbalah, sometimes (though not necessarily helpfully) called Jewish mysticism, posits a divine realm full of stories, full of tension and drama. Against Maimonides's transcendent God, Kabbalah imagines God in a manner compatible with the presence of God within the world. As in the case of every pair of opposites, the opposition between Maimonides and the

Kabbalists presupposes a close similarity between them. Like Maimonides, the Kabbalists, in their interest in the metaphysics of God and in their systematicity, took their bearings from a philosophical impulse largely foreign to the world of the Bible and the rabbis. In this chapter we survey the basic teachings of Kabbalah, then turn to a spiritual movement originating in the early modern period that was partially inspired by it, Hasidism.

The Basics of Kabbalah

The word *kabbalah* in Hebrew means "receiving." The relevant image in our context is of a master conveying (*tradere* in Latin, the source of the word "tradition") teachings that are in turn received by his student. Kabbalah purports to represent a tradition of ancient teachings, handed down in secret from generation to generation, that describes the nature of God and God's relationship with the world. Late antique rabbinic literature attests to esoteric traditions, and works from the early medieval period describe praxes of mystical ascent to heaven and detail the dimensions of the heavens and of God's body itself. But the canonical work that would define Kabbalah from its appearance to the present is the *Zohar* ("shining"), a dense commentary on the Pentateuch written in Christian Spain, in Castile, in the second half of the thirteenth century. Moses de León, the author of the main body of the *Zohar*, attributed its teachings to Rabbi Shimon bar Yohai, a sage of the second century CE to whom the Talmud ascribes supernatural powers.

The *Zohar* presumes a complex conceptualization of God centered on the *sefirot* (sg. *sefirah*), literally "numerals," reflecting the importance of numbers for Jewish mysticism. There is an infinite, supernal source of divinity, the Endless (*eyn sof*). From this source, in a manner familiar from Neoplatonism, emanations descend downward, toward the world. The sefirot, ten in number, can be understood as nodes of emanation, each of which manifests a different divine trait. They are arranged in an anthropomorphic way. The first and upper triad of sefirot, corresponding roughly to the divine head, begins with Crown (*keter*), from which issues divine thought, in the form first of Wisdom (*hokhmah*), and then of its mate, Understanding (*binah*). Wisdom and Understanding are marked, respectively, as male and female, and instantiate the motif of sexual union, which, as we will see, is of central importance for the

Zohar. The upper triad generates the lower seven sefirot. Paired like arms, delicately balanced against each other, are Kindness (*hesed*) and Power (*gevurah*), reflecting God's governance of the world, sometimes through punishment and sometimes through grace. Beneath them, integrating them, at the center of the divine body, is Splendor (*tif'eret*). Below them is another triad, replicating the one above it: Eternity (*nesah*) and Glory (*hod*) stand as legs at the bottom of the torso, and between them, integrating them, Foundation (*yesod*), which is the divine phallus. The upper nine sefirot as a whole, configured as male around the central node, Splendor, reach out through the phallic vehicle of Foundation toward the tenth and final emanation, the paradigmatically female aspect of God, Kingdom (*malkhut*) or Dwelling (*shekhinah*), which is located below Foundation, set apart from the upper nine sefirot.

So conceptualized, God becomes, in Kabbalah, a dynamic and rather tenuous lattice. When the lattice can hold itself together, as a unified whole, divine Abundance (*shefa*) flows downward from the Endless, through the sefirot and into the sublunar world, sustaining it. But the lattice is ever threatening to fall out of balance. God's mercy and God's justice tug and pull at each other, and the yearning of the male and female aspects of God for each other does not necessarily find fulfillment. The story of God becomes even stormier in light of the existence of an entire negative lattice, ten evil sefirot of the Other Side (*sitra ahra*) that correspond to the above ten sefirot. The dramatic interest of the Kabbalists lies especially in the figure of Dwelling. The word "dwelling" is found in rabbinic literature as a term for God, especially with respect to God's indwelling among Israel, but in Kabbalah it becomes the term specifically for the female aspect of the divine. Set apart from the upper nine sefirot, she lives in exile, with Israel, and seeks to return to her husband. Or, in a different image, informed by chivalric romance, she has been taken captive from the divine palace, and must be rescued. Dwelling can also be conceptualized as the moon, occupying the nearest sphere to earth according to medieval astronomy. She does not produce her own light, but when the spheres are properly aligned, she can reflect the light of the highest sphere, the sun, down upon our world.

How does the divine lattice maintain its stability? What enables the male and female aspects of God to unite, and produce the Abundance that fructifies our world? The answer is encoded into the fact that the sefirot together take a human shape.

> The blessed creator made man and established him in the upper pattern so that man would be complete in [the creator's] attributes and would recognize his creator. . . . He is the supernal level above everything else which is beneath the sphere of the moon, and beneath him is set this world, and his essence lies in observing the commandments so that he may live. . . . The maintenance of the world rests upon man. . . . As man is the pillar of the world, he should seek to pursue his creator through his Torah and his commandments day and night.[1]

Human beings, insofar as they occupy the supernal position in the sublunar world, replicate in themselves the entire sefirotic structure. As such, through adherence to the commandments and to Torah study, human beings bind the world below to the world above. Of special importance in this dynamic is the righteous person, the *tsaddik*. According to Proverbs 10:25, on the rabbis' understanding of the verse, "the [tsaddik] is the foundation of the world." Within the kabbalistic framework, this verse identifies the tsaddik with Foundation, the divine phallus. Through their good deeds, the righteous become the Foundation, or phallus, that enables the sexual union of Splendor with Dwelling, the divine male with the divine female. For Kabbalah, then, observance of the commandments is not just an expression of covenantal loyalty, or a way of life with God in the world. The commandments acquire cosmic significance; they are the means of effecting unification within God and beyond God, and thus sustaining the world.

In the same way, the Bible no longer simply tells a history of the world from creation forward. The Bible is rather the cosmic drama of God's very self, in its own terms and also projected into the human realm. By way of example, consider some comments by the *Zohar* on the story of Noah.[2] The Bible introduces Noah thus (Gen. 6:9–10): "These are the offspring of Noah. Noah was a righteous man [tsaddik]. . . . And Noah had three sons: Shem, Ham, and Japheth." Although the reference of the phrase "the offspring of Noah," according to the plain sense, is to Noah's sons, or more generally, to the story of Noah, the *Zohar* is taken by the juxtaposition of

1. Elliot R. Wolfson, *The Book of the Pomegranate: Moses de León's* Sefer Ha-Rimmon (Atlanta: Scholars Press, 1988), 88.

2. I rely on the translation and commentary by Daniel C. Matt in *The Zohar: Pritzker Edition, Volume 1* (Stanford: Stanford University Press, 2004), 339–41.

this phrase to the characterization of Noah as a tsaddik. This juxtaposition evokes the role of the tsaddik in producing divine seed, by embodying the divine phallus. The *Zohar* links this idea to the fact that the entrance into the ark has the goal, according to Genesis 7:3, of "keeping seed alive on the face of all the earth." The ark, as a vessel, represents the female. Noah's entrance into the ark, then, is not just a practical means of ensuring a survivor of the flood. Through Noah's righteousness, it serves as an enactment of divine sexual union of a sort that produces seed or offspring, or in other words, that sustains the world.

Here and elsewhere, the *Zohar* draws on the close reading methods of classical rabbinic midrash, but its distinctive hermeneutics, powered by the intricate symbolic system of the sefirot, yield new and often shocking results. Recall, from the conclusion of chapter 8, Rabbi Isaac Hutner's identification of Abraham with hesed, or kindness. Hutner follows the kabbalistic tradition of mapping the three patriarchs onto the three sefirot of the second triad: Abraham with Kindness, Isaac with Power, and Jacob, who is also named Israel, and thus stands also for the people Israel, with Splendor. With this set of symbolic correspondences in hand—and there are countless others, all correlating with each other, creating an effect of infinite regress like two facing mirrors—the entire Bible can become an endlessly complex cosmic drama.

And yet, for all its hermeneutic boldness and theological daring, Kabbalah is, at heart, deeply conservative. It not only preserves the centrality of the basic commitments of rabbinic Judaism—the chosenness of Israel, the Torah, and the commandments—but strengthens them, by imbuing them with new and fundamental significance. Kabbalah, in short, is an audacious mystical interpretation of Judaism that grounds a very traditional Jewish piety. Maimonides is far more radical in this respect, because he subordinates the covenantal relationship between God and Israel, along with the commandments that define it and the Torah that narrates it, to the ultimately solitary pursuit of knowing and contemplating God. It is for this reason that Kabbalah would have much greater influence on Jewish life and practice than the philosophical vision championed by Maimonides. We will take up below one major vector of influence, namely Hasidism, but we must first briefly trace a set of post-medieval developments in kabbalistic thought.

Lurianic Kabbalah

If the God of Maimonides is transcendent, is the God of medieval Kabbalah immanent? Yes, but only in a limited way. Kabbalah does recognize a transcendent Endless, and the sefirotic apparatus is situated beyond the world, even as it is tied to the world. But the homology between the divine and the human, realized in the capacity of human beings to influence the divine realm, constitutes a sort of immanence. The question of divine immanence arose more directly among Kabbalists in Safed in the late sixteenth century. Safed, a town in the upper Galilee, then a part of the Ottoman Empire, received an influx of Jewish immigrants in the aftermath of the Spanish expulsion. Due in part to its proximity to the village of Meron, a historical pilgrimage site that came to be remembered as the burial place of Rabbi Shimon bar Yohai, the central character of the *Zohar*, Safed became in this period a center of kabbalistic thought. The greatest member of the circle of Safed Kabbalists was Rabbi Isaac Luria.

Although Luria left no writings, his students, first among them Rabbi Haim Vital, attributed to him a new cosmological myth. Its premise is the notion that God is, in principle, everywhere, and that God's omnipresence leaves no space for the world. For Luria, according to Vital, the precondition for the creation of the world was God's self-contraction (*tsimtsum*). Imagine, says Vital, a circle. God's self-contraction occurred from the center of the circle outward toward the edge. It was in the space at the center, thus emptied of God, that the world emerged. Now, was this space truly empty of God? Did God truly evacuate God's presence, or was this divine self-contraction—and with it, the existence of the world as something independent from God—only apparent? Later interpreters debate this question, but the question is, in a sense, beside the point, because the doctrine of tsimtsum takes the omnipresence of God as its starting point. Note, in this light, that in Vital's account, the self-contracted God wholly surrounds and encloses the world, so that, even if God's self-contraction is real, and God is not strictly present in the world, the world nevertheless exists in God.

Divine immanence finds expression in another cosmological myth attributed to Luria. Luria describes a process of emanation gone wrong. The divine light, emanating toward the world, was to be contained and curbed by vessels, but the light was too strong, and the vessels shattered. Our material world consists of the shards or "shells" (*qelipot*) of these vessels, which envelop sparks of this light. While the shells are evil, in their way, insofar as they imprison the sparks and prevent them from returning to their source, they also, in their way, shelter and preserve the sparks, and become sanctified by them. The myth of the "breaking of the vessels" thus posits the presence of God throughout the world. The task of human beings, against this background, is one of "fixing" (tikkun) what was broken, and liberating these sparks so that they can ascend upward. They achieve this through engagement with the material world under the auspices of the commandments. The notion of tikkun olam as social justice, discussed in chapter 9, has its most immediate roots in this Lurianic idea.

Hasidic Theology

When we turn to Hasidism (from Hebrew *hasid*, meaning "pious"), we move forward to the second half of the eighteenth century, and cast our gaze on Eastern Europe, especially the area of modern-day Ukraine and Poland. The Jewish population of Eastern Europe experienced a population boom from roughly the seventeenth century forward, fed at the beginning, in part, by the movement of exiled Jews eastward from western and central Europe. Jews in this region were almost exclusively Ashkenazi, and largely Yiddish-speaking. A passage from a British traveler's log from around 1800 conveys a sense of the prominence of Jews in this area at this time.

> We now crossed the frontier of Poland, and passed from the land of the credulous [i.e., believing Christians] to the habitations of the unbelievers, for every house we saw was in the hands of Jews. They seemed, indeed, the only people who were in a state of activity, exercising almost all the professions, and engaged in every branch of trade; millers, whitesmiths, saddlers, drivers, ostlers, and sometimes even as farmers. Their constant bustle makes them appear more abundant than they really are; and although the streets of Zytomir seemed full of them, we were informed that out of a population of 6,000, not more than one third were of this sect, . . . we could easily have imagined the contrary to have been the fact.[3]

3. The quotation is from Gershon Hundert, *Jews in Poland-Lithuania in the Eighteenth Century* (Berkeley: University of California Press, 2006), 19.

Jewish communities like this one were destroyed in the Holocaust, but for centuries prior they thrived, and Jewish life today bears the stamp of the culture that they produced. Here we focus on one especially important product of that culture, Hasidism, which persists robustly to today.

Hasidism traces its origins to a man named Israel, son of Eliezer (ca. 1698–1760), whose moniker was the Besht, an acronym for *Ba'al Shem Tov*, "master of the good Name." A "master of the Name" was someone credited with expertise in the use of theurgic means, especially the name of God, to perform healing and other miracles. Hasidism can be characterized as a kabbalistically inflected spiritual revival movement. In Hasidism, kabbalistic pietism takes a dialectical turn. On the one hand, it moves outside of relatively small, esoteric circles, and becomes democratized. Hasidism envisions the immediate presence of God in the world, and the possibility of clinging (*devekut*) to God through means accessible and appealing to the common person, like prayer, song, dance, and the cultivation of joy and other emotions. On the other hand, the kabbalistic figure of the righteous person, the tsaddik, transforms in Hasidism from a private status and an attainable if challenging ideal to a supernatural position bestowed dynastically on a public leader. Let us elaborate on this dialectic.

As we will see, Hasidism by no means speaks with one voice: There are many Hasidic sects, and even more Hasidic teachers. Nevertheless, it is possible to offer a general characterization of the theological commitments of Hasidism.[4] A prevalent Hasidic mantra insists on God's immanence: "There is no place devoid of him." According to the Besht's student, Yaakov Yosef of Polnoye, the Besht would say that common assumptions about the conditions for prayer to be effective—the notion that there are specific angels who must receive particular prayers and convey them to God, and also, we might say by extension, the rules indicating precisely how and where and when one ought to pray—are illusions, designed to encourage seeking God by making the attainment of God seem like a challenge. In fact, however, God is present everywhere, prepared to receive prayer.

God's presence in all things means that it is possible to serve God, in the words of another Hasidic mantra, "through materiality [*gashmiyut*]."

4. Because of their abundance in this section, I provide bibliographic references for specific Hasidic teachings introduced below in the "Further Inquiry" section at the end of the chapter.

Ephraim of Sudilkov, a grandson of the Besht, contends, in Lurianic fashion, that if someone engages in business or eating or even idle chatter with the awareness that all these things contain holy roots, then "he ties these things to their roots and redeems them." A characteristic exegetical instinct of Hasidism—to invert the verse's plain meaning by construing the verse as a counterfactual—is on display in a teaching on this topic from the Besht's chief successor, Dov Ber, the *Maggid* (preacher) of Mezeritch. The Maggid takes up Ecclesiastes 5:2: "God is in heaven and you are on earth; therefore let your words be few." There are those, says the Maggid, who *think* that God is on heaven and not on earth. Such people must speak only words of Torah, words that are heavenly on their face; it is their words that must be "few," then. But a person who appreciates the truth, that God is *not* only in heaven, but everywhere, can speak all sorts of words, because he appreciates that words of every sort, even idle ones, contain holiness, and he "fixes" those words, in the Lurianic sense, when he says them with the proper intention.

Joy in the service of God is a major emphasis of Hasidism. For an important student of the Maggid, Shneur Zalman of Liadi, the founder of Chabad Hasidism, on which more below, one of the sources of joy is the recognition of God's omnipresence.

> When one notices that his soul needs to be refined and illuminated through joy of heart, he should think deeply and imagine in his mind and his understanding the true conception of the oneness of Him, blessed be He, that He fills all the worlds, upper and lower, and even the fulness of this earth itself is His glory, blessed be He, and all things are esteemed as nothing before Him, and He is truly alone in the upper and lower worlds, just as He was alone before the six days of creation. . . . Consider how great is the joy of the humble common man when he approaches a king of flesh and blood who is a guest in his house; infinitely more is it when it comes to the proximity and dwelling of the king of the kings of kings, the Holy One, blessed be He. . . . Therefore they instituted that we should give praise and thanks every morning to His name, blessed be He, and say, "Happy are we! How great is our portion, etc., and how beautiful is our inheritance." . . . We must rejoice over the inheritance that our fathers bequeathed us, namely, the true oneness of the Lord, that even in the earth below, there is nothing other than Him.

For Rabbi Shneur Zalman, joy is critical for the refining of the heart, and it issues, alongside praise, from meditation on the fact that our humble home, this lowest world, is filled with the presence of the king of kings, that it is indeed nothing other than his presence.

While the mind is one path to joy, Hasidism also highlights the role of the body, and especially song and dance, in the cultivation of joy. These vehicles for the service of God figure especially centrally in the teachings of Nahman of Bratslav, a great-grandson of the Besht. In one parable, for example, Rabbi Nahman uses the figure of the dance circle to clarify a distinction between two levels of joy. The first level may be compared to a situation in which some people dance while others, more reluctant, stand off to the side. So it is when someone manages to be joyful by pushing aside melancholy thoughts. But sometimes, the dancers grab the people standing off to the side and press them into the circle. Here is the higher level of joy, when a person directly confronts the melancholy thoughts, and transforms them into joyful ones. Another teaching, attributed by Yaakov Yosef of Polnoye to the Besht, offers a kabbalistic interpretation of the Talmudic injunction to bring joy to a bride by dancing before her. The bride, says the Besht, is none other than a symbol of Presence, that is, the feminine aspect of God. It might seem inappropriate to dance before the divine bride when she is in exile, joined with Israel in its exile, and apart from her divine groom, with her garments soiled. But in fact, the raising of feet in dancing effects, theurgically, a removal of the soiled garment and a cleansing of the divine sparks from the dirt, so that they can rise upward.

Hasidism as an Institution

While to the outsider the world of Hasidism might seem like a uniform mass of black and white and curled sidelocks, this world is in fact divided into denominations or sects, which differ from each other not only in subtle matters of dress but also in theology, spiritual practices, and social norms. Each sect consists of a circle of hasidim and their master, called the *rebbe* (a Yiddish form of "rabbi") or the *admor* (an acronym for "our master, our teacher, and our rabbi"). The rebbe position is dynastic: a rebbe might be succeeded by a son or son-in-law, or in some cases by a more distant family member or a student. The sects are typically known by the place in which its founding rebbe first established his "court." Thus, for example, the Bobover sect originated in Bobowa, in Poland, under the auspices of the first Bobover Rebbe, Shlomo Halberstam (1847–1905). The sect, now centered in Brooklyn, but with branches elsewhere in the United States, Canada, Europe, and Israel, is led by this rebbe's great-great-grandson, with an offshoot headed by the previous rebbe's brother-in-law.

The rebbe is a tsaddik in the kabbalistic sense: the foundation of the world, the mediating principle between the upper and lower realms. But in Hasidism, the rebbe achieves, in relation to his followers, his hasidim, a sort of monopoly on this status. He is *the* mediating principle for them. This notion is well expressed in a teaching from Boruch of Medzhybizh: "My grandfather the Besht said: 'This is the gate of the Lord, the righteous' (Psalm 118:20). That is to say, the righteous are the gate of the Lord." Here, the Besht produces a sharp reading of Psalm 118:20—"This is the gate of the Lord, the righteous shall enter through it"—by cutting off the last words of the verse. Thus abridged, the verse conveys the notion that the tsaddik is the very gateway to God, so that the rebbe's followers can come to God only through him. A Christian will of course hear in these words the echo of Jesus's teaching in John 10:7: "Very truly, I tell you, I am the gate for the sheep." We will return to this point later.

The rebbe clings in a special way to God, and as a conduit to God for his hasidim, he must also cling to them, and they to him. On the part of the rebbe, according to one striking Hasidic teaching by Elimelekh of Lizhensk, this attachment entails great spiritual sacrifice.

> Abundance comes only through the tsaddik who is its vehicle. The tsaddik who wishes to be the vehicle of Abundance for human beings must make himself cling to them so as to bestow the Abundance that provides every good that they need. . . . But how is it possible for him to do this with a sinner, heaven forbid? And yet, even though he is a sinner, he has need of receiving Abundance and life. How, then, can the tsaddik manage to connect with him? To this the Talmud refers when it speaks of a "sin for the sake of [God's] name." The tsaddik, too, will commit one sin or another, for the sake of God's name, so that he can connect with the sinner too, and bestow goodness on him too.

The problem of sinful followers is also a familiar one from the life of Jesus, most famously in the version of the anointing story in Luke 7:36–50, though in our passage, the problem concerns not propriety (i.e., a righteous person should not keep the company of sinners) but metaphysics (i.e., a righteous person cannot serve the sinner as a vehicle of Abundance because the tsaddik and the sinner have nothing in common that would "connect" them). The claim of our passage is that a tsaddik will commit a sin of some sort intentionally so that he can thereby become, in a small way, like the sinner, and thus connect to him, and draw God's Abundance down upon the sinner. The underlying assumption, again recalling the conventional understanding of Jesus, is that in principle, the tsaddik never sins.

On the part of the follower, the hasid, clinging to the rebbe involves, first and foremost, being in the rebbe's company. A hasid might live near his rebbe, or he might undertake a pilgrimage to the rebbe's court for a sabbath or a festival. A visit to the rebbe's court typically includes a brief private consultation with the rebbe. The rebbe's advice might be sought on any and all matters, no matter how mundane. This audience might also be an occasion in which the hasid confesses his sins to his rebbe and donates "redemption" money to the rebbe's court. The highlight of the pilgrimage is the meal or meals that hasidim share with their rebbe. This event is the *tish* (Yiddish for "table"). At the tish, the rebbe distributes some of his food to his followers, sings with them, and teaches them Torah. Of particular spiritual significance is the tish of the final meal of the sabbath, which extends from the early evening, as the daylight dwindles, to past dark, after the sabbath has departed.

Chabad Hasidism and Chabad Messianism

We have noted the myriad ways in which the Hasidic rebbe functions in relation to his followers as Christ does in Christianity. The rebbe is in principle sinless. He serves as the cosmic conduit—the gate—between his followers and heaven, and plays a role in the forgiveness of sins. The conception of the messiah in classical rabbinic literature does not assign the messiah such supernatural powers, but, in a milieu informed by Christianity, the Hasidic rebbe came inevitably to be perceived as messiah-like. The messianic principle operates in a diffuse way in Hasidism, because there are many sects, and many rebbes. There is no single rebbe who might achieve the ultimate redemption; rather, each rebbe works local redemptions for his followers.

In one Hasidic sect, however, the messianic potential of the rebbe became actualized to a much fuller extent. Easily the most important Hasidic sect today is the Lubavitcher or Chabad sect. "Lubavitcher" indicates the location of the sect's court in the past: the town of Lubavitch, in Russia. "Chabad" is an acronym for the upper sefirotic triad, according to an account that differs slightly from the one presented above: *chokhmah* or *hokhmah*, *binah*, and *da'at*, that is, Wisdom, Understanding, and Knowledge. The name indicates the intellectual or study-centered character of this sect, which marked it from the first as distinctive among Hasidic sects, and is reflected in the above quotation from the work of the sect's founder, Rabbi Shneur Zalman of Liadi. In Czarist and then Soviet Russia, Lubavitcher hasidim played an important role in sustaining Jewish life under circumstances of persecution. Amid such persecution, and especially after the Holocaust, momentum developed within Chabad around the notion that the messianic era was at hand.

In the wake of the Holocaust, Chabad reestablished itself in America. Under the leadership of the seventh Lubavitcher Rebbe, Menachem Mendel Schneerson (1902–1994), a vibrant center emerged in Crown Heights, Brooklyn. From his first public discourse upon assuming his post, in 1950, Schneerson further cultivated the sense of messianic expectation among his hasidim. The starting point for this discourse is a rabbinic tradition concerning the peregrination of the divine presence.[5] With the creation of the world, the presence entered the world, but on account of the sins of Adam and his antediluvian successors, the presence departed from the earth and ascended successively, across seven generations, through the seven heavens, back to its point of origin. Abraham, however, succeeded in drawing the presence down one level, and the six lineal descendants of Abraham continued this work, culminating in Moses, who, in receiving the Torah, succeeded in restoring the presence to the earth. Schneerson links this tradition to another rabbinic statement, that "every seventh is beloved." As the seventh Lubavitcher Rebbe, thus heading the seventh generation of Lubavitcher hasidim, he takes their task to be that of Moses, of drawing the divine presence—or Presence, the seventh of the lower sefirot—

5. For the Hebrew text of the discourse, see, e.g., https://he.chabad.org/library/article_cdo/aid/3140086.

down to earth, through the vehicle of the Torah. The seventh, being an ordinal number, is defined in reference to the first, and thus the task of the seventh is to be understood by looking to the first, Abraham, who "called out in the name of the Lord" (Gen. 13:4), spreading knowledge of God in the world.

In the encounter between Judaism and modernity, Hasidism, along with other forms of Judaism that for this reason are often characterized as ultra-Orthodox, adopted a strongly insular response: building a wall between traditional life and the modern world. Hasidim in America today typically set themselves apart from the modern world by living in insular communities, by maintaining Yiddish as a mother tongue, and by dressing in very distinctive ways inherited from Eastern Europe, among other means. Though also ultra-Orthodox in its way, Chabad has taken a different path. Its dress is not quite as distinctive, it embraces the vernacular, and it encourages Torah study within certain bounds among women. Most of all, under the direction of the seventh Lubavitcher Rebbe, and inspired by its past resistance to czarist and Soviet persecution and by its messianic consciousness, Chabad has undertaken, since the 1950s, a massive project of outreach, on the model of Abraham.

The chief goal of this outreach is to bring less traditionally observant Jews closer to traditional observance. One path toward this goal is the performance of Jewish rituals in public spaces, in the hope of drawing the attention of Jews in these spaces, and of normalizing the practice of Judaism. Chabad coordinates public menorah lightings in many towns across America and elsewhere; most spectacularly, since 1979 Chabad has organized the lighting of a "National Menorah" in Washington, DC, typically attended by a White House representative. One will also often find Chabad hasidim in bus stations or at crowded intersections, asking male passersby who look Jewish but not Orthodox if they have donned phylacteries that day. For those who are willing to engage, they have phylacteries on hand, and perform the commandment with the passersby. The hope is that this engagement will spark greater interest in Judaism. But even if it does not achieve this goal, from the kabbalistic perspective of Chabad something cosmically significant is achieved by the performance of that single commandment.

Rabbi Schneerson also coordinated the dispatching of "emissaries" or "apostles" (*shelihim*) to establish outposts—"Chabad houses"—in Jewish communities but especially in places where Jews might be present on a temporary basis: among other places, major tourist destinations and college campuses. For Jewish college students or for Jews traveling as tourists, the Chabad house can offer a Jewish social context, kosher food, and prayer services. It is an odd but telling fact that in recent years a candidate for the largest Passover *seder* meal in the world is the one hosted by the Chabad house in Nepal, which attracts many hundreds of Israelis traveling in the area after their army service. Chabad emissaries also often interface with local Jewish populations by operating preschools.

Chabad's outreach work makes it a major force in Jewish life today, especially though far from exclusively in America. (It also has a major footprint in Israel and, among other places, Russia.) In not insignificant numbers over the past decades, Jews raised in secular homes or with relatively little Jewish education or practice have become more traditional, or even Orthodox; in the common parlance, these are ba'ale teshuvah (sg. ba'al teshuvah). (In chapter 1 I rendered this term in English as "penitent," but the dynamic is not one of regretting or atoning for one's upbringing, but of embracing observance of the commandments.) Chabad is one of the most important institutional engines of the ba'al teshuvah movement. Chabad does not seek converts from among non-Jews but, insofar as it performs Judaism publicly, it argues for the compatibility of Jewish and civic identity, and further, for Judaism as a force for good in the world. Its notion of mission also finds expression, to a lesser extent, in attempts to foster observance of the seven Noachide laws (discussed in chapter 9) among non-Jews. These attempts were recognized in President Reagan's proclamation 4921, marking April 4, 1982, as a "National Day of Reflection" in honor of the eightieth birthday of the Lubavitcher Rebbe, and praising the Noachide laws as "a moral code for all of us regardless of religious faith." In orienting Judaism toward the world, Chabad echoes, but in its own distinctive key, the prevailing conceptualization of Jewish identity among the non-Orthodox Jews to whom it dedicates most of its outreach efforts.

Over the course of Rabbi Schneerson's life, many of his followers came around to the view that he was himself the messiah, and he did little to discourage such speculation. Adoring crowds would sing before him a song with these lyrics: "May our lord live, our teacher and rabbi, the king messiah, forever and ever." He passed away in 1994, but many Chabad hasidim take him still to be the messiah, who will return to redeem Israel. The prevalence of this belief has exercised some in the Orthodox world. Most prominently, David Berger, a professor at Yeshiva University in New York, which houses the most important modern Orthodox rabbinic seminary in America, wrote a book charging that messianist Chabad Hasidism dissolves an all-important faith boundary between Judaism and Christianity. Judaism is committed, writes Berger, to the principle that the messiah must bring about the redemption in his lifetime; a person who departs from the world with the world yet unredeemed is by definition not the messiah. If Chabad Hasidism rejects this principle, it must be shunned as heretical, else "our children will no longer be able to tell Christian missionaries that the Jewish faith does not countenance belief in a Messiah whose mission is interrupted by death, and one of the defining characteristics of Judaism in a Christian world will have been erased.... We award victory to Christianity in a crucial aspect of its millennial debate with Judaism. We accept a fundamental revision of a cardinal principle of the faith."[6]

Berger's claim is interesting. Is it really a cardinal principle of the Jewish faith that the messiah's mission cannot be interrupted by death? If so, what is its logic? Is the concern that a messiah who could overcome death would have a god-like character that threatens a Jewish commitment to the categorical distinction between creator and creatures? But the Jewish tradition, following the lead of the Bible in Deuteronomy 34:10–12 and elsewhere, already assigns Moses a quasi-divine status. But precisely here is the rub: a supernatural messiah would have an authority equal to or greater than that of Moses, and thus could modify or annul parts of the Mosaic law, as Jesus, as understood in the Christian tradition, did. If the Orthodox world continues, despite Berger's protestation, to treat Chabad messianism mainly with indifference, it is presumably because there is (yet) no trace of such a development in Chabad. On this implicit view, so long as they adhere to the commandments, Chabad messianists remain in the fold, no matter if they espouse a messiah who comes twice.

Conclusion

Let us return, in conclusion, to considering the God of Maimonides and the God of Kabbalah together. On the one hand, they represent stark contrasts. No stories can be told about Maimonides's God, while the Kabbalists' God is

6. David Berger, *The Rebbe, the Messiah, and the Scandal of Orthodox Indifference* (Portland: Littman Library of Jewish Civilization, 2001), 31.

full of change, desire, yearning. The God of Maimonides is utterly transcendent, while the Kabbalists dwell on the multivalent interface between God and the world. And yet both Maimonides and the Kabbalists introduce, by comparison with the rabbis, a new systematicity or rigor into thinking about the nature of God. Relatedly, too, in both cases, by comparison to the rabbis, Maimonides and the Kabbalists figure God, at least in the first instance, in an impersonal way. The rabbis' God, though not human, is a person, enmeshed in personal relationships. Maimonides's God, by contrast, shares almost nothing with people, while the God of the Kabbalists, from one angle, looks less like anything animate than like a Rube Goldberg machine designed to deliver the elixir of Abundance down into the world.

And yet the theological frameworks of both Maimonides and the Kabbalists can in fact support deeply meaningful and even personal relationships, in their way, with God, even if this God is not person-like in a recognizable sense. Maimonides's vision of the ideal religious life, as one in which the philosopher always has God present in his thoughts, gives expression to this possibility. Likewise, the Kabbalists put forward the desire for unity, for clinging and attachment, as the animating force in the cosmos, bringing together, directly and analogically, the divine realm and the human. In the next chapter we will return to these observations as we take up the topic of spirituality, an amorphous category that is of great contemporary importance.

Further Inquiry

For Yehezkel Kaufmann's claim concerning the Bible's hostility to myth, see his book *The Religion of Israel, from Its Beginnings to the Babylonian Exile* (Chicago: University of Chicago Press, 1960). On the persistence of myth in the Bible and its flourishing among rabbinic interpreters, see Michael Fishbane, *Biblical Myth and Rabbinic Mythmaking* (Oxford: Oxford University Press, 2003). On pre-Zoharic mysticism, see Peter Schäfer, *The Origins of Jewish Mysticism* (Tübingen: Mohr Siebeck, 2009). The foundational scholar of Kabbalah is Gershom Scholem, and while his successors have exposed many of its flaws, the grand synthesis in his book, *Major Trends in Jewish Mysticism* (New York: Schocken Books, 1995), remains a touchstone. For the work of one such successor, addressing the reasons for and the distortive consequences of the use of the category of mysticism in

Kabbalah scholarship, see Boaz Huss, *Mystifying Kabbalah: Academic Scholarship, National Theology, and New Age Spirituality* (Oxford: Oxford University Press, 2020). My overview of the *Zohar* draws on Arthur Green's introduction in *The Zohar: Pritzker Edition, Volume 1* (Stanford: Stanford University Press, 2004), xxxi–lxxxi, and for the discussion of Lurianic Kabbalah, I depend on Christophe Schulte, *Zimzum: God and the Origin of the World* (Philadelphia: University of Pennsylvania Press, 2023). The primary sources introduced above in the discussion of Hasidic theology are Yaakov Yosef of Polnoye, *Keter Shem Tov*, 1.39, 1.147; Ephraim of Sudilkov, *Degel Mahane Ephraim, behar* 167; Dov Ber of Mezeritch, *Maggid Devarav Le-Yaakov, liqqute amarim*, 191; Shneur Zalman of Liadi, *Tanya, liqqute amarim*, 33; Nahman of Bratslav, *Liqqute Moharan*, II.23; Boruch of Medzhybizh, *Botzina di-nehora ha-shalem*, 65; Elimelekh of Lizhensk, *Noam Elimelekh, naso* 6. For a broad historical survey of Hasidism, see David Biale et al., eds., *Hasidism: A New History* (Princeton: Princeton University Press, 2018). I have benefited from the analysis of key themes in Hasidic theology and practice in Avishar Har-Shefi, ed., *Or Ḥozer: The World of Hasidism* (Ramat-Gan: Bar-Ilan University Press 2022). Hasidism has long drawn the attention of documentary filmmakers and ethnographers; two important recent examples are the film *A Life Apart: Hasidism in America* (1997), and Ayala Fader's monograph, *Mitzvah Girls: Bringing Up the Next Generation of Hasidic Jews in Brooklyn* (Princeton: Princeton University Press, 2009). On Chabad messianism and the relationship between Hasidism and Christianity, see Elliot R. Wolfson, *Open Secret: Postmessianic Messianism and the Mystical Revision of Menaḥem Mendel Schneerson* (New York: Columbia University Press, 2009); Shaul Magid, *Hasidism Incarnate: Hasidism, Christianity, and the Construction of Modern Judaism* (Stanford: Stanford University Press, 2014).

●

1. The mystical tradition identifies the people Israel with two divine figures, one male and one female. First, a corpus of mystical texts called the *hekalot* ("palaces"), much earlier than the *Zohar*, makes the claim that the face of Jacob, also called Israel, is inscribed on God's heavenly throne. According to one passage in this corpus, when Israel below recites the qedushah, the trisagion, God says, "I bend over [Jacob's face], embrace, kiss and fondle it." For the quotation, with discussion, see Rachel Neis, "Embracing Icons: The Face of Jacob on the Throne of God,"

Images 1 (2007): 41–42. Second, the *Zohar*, building on earlier sources, identifies the Presence, the paradigmatic feminine aspect of the divine, with *keneset yisra'el* (the assembly of Israel). From a theological perspective, how does the identification of Israel with divine figures differ from the more conventional identification of Israel as God's son or spouse? Compare these identifications with the ways in which Christian tradition associates the church both with Christ, who is its head, and Mary, who is its mother. On the genealogical relationship between the role of Presence in the *Zohar* and its sources, and contemporaneous Marian piety, see Arthur Green, "Shekhinah, the Virgin Mary, and the Song of Songs: Reflections on a Kabbalistic Symbol in its Historical Context," *Association for Jewish Studies Review* 26 (2002): 1–52.

2. Among the achievements of Hasidic music is the *niggun*, a relatively short, characteristically wordless tune composed so that it can be repeated over and over again. The nonverbal character of the niggun manifests the Hasidic appeal to a broad audience, but the forgoing of words is also understood to enable a distinctively powerful religious experience. Try to imagine this experience. Note that the niggun often divides into four distinct parts, corresponding to the four Hebrew letters of God's proper name.

— Chapter 15 —

Jewish Spirituality

THIS CHAPTER ATTEMPTS TO DESCRIBE SOME DIMENSIONS of the experience of God, or more broadly, "the divine," in modern and contemporary Judaism, with a focus on continuities with premodern Judaism. This topic is inevitably vague and slippery. Experiencing God is, after all, an inner state, and thus difficult to access and describe. And yet, in many ways, the experience of God is the beating heart of Judaism, as of other religions. The desire for contact with the divine, or self-transcendence, which we can loosely and provisionally identify with the word spirituality, has special prominence today, when organized religion in the West is on the wane, and the perceived capacity of a set of religious practices to enable the experience of God is a reason that many choose to adopt those practices, or to retain a commitment to them. But the desire for the experience of God should not be dismissed as the preserve of some caricature of a modern seeker, as the easy intoxicant for touchy-feely individualists engaged in self-cultivation and insensitive to notions of duty and community. The roots of the desire for the experience of God in Judaism lie in the Bible and find expression throughout the tradition.

Art Green, a contemporary Jewish theologian who articulates a Jewish spirituality rooted especially in the retrieval of Hasidic thought, says that he writes for "the many spiritually serious Jews who have turned toward Eastern spiritual paths in despair of finding anything usable in our own spiritual patrimony." It is them that he has in mind as he crafts what he calls a "seeker-friendly Judaism."[1] Why should these "spiritually serious Jews" have despaired of Judaism? In part, of course, as Green's very project implies, it is a matter of

1. Arthur Green, "A Neo-Hasidic Credo," in Arthur Green and Ariel Evan Mayse, *A New Hasidism: Branches* (Philadelphia: Jewish Publication Society, 2019), 11–12.

education. A spiritually serious Jew may have received only elementary schooling in Judaism. And here Alexander Pope's famous stricture, that "a little learning is a dangerous thing," looms large: someone whose experience of Judaism is formed mainly by a few years of weekend schooling in his childhood might easily come to think of it as childish and superficial.

But the dissatisfaction of a spiritually serious Jew with Judaism might also arise from features intrinsic to Judaism. Of course, every organized religion, in virtue of its very organization, will tend, in certain ways, to stifle the seeker. Organized religion offers familiarity, routine, answers, or in short, structure, and though it is God who animates the structure, that structure also ends up encasing God, getting in the way of encounter. But each religious formation enables and inhibits the experience of God in its own distinctive ways, and it is fair to ask how Judaism does so. We begin below with the story of one Jew's encounter with a Catholic spiritual practice that he finds moving and helpful. We will use this story as a starting point to address the above question. Then we turn to one especially powerful root metaphor in Judaism for the experience of God, namely, eros.

One might think of the medieval and early modern religious currents described in the last two chapters—the teachings of Maimonides, Kabbalah, and Hasidism—as responses to the opportunities for and obstacles to the experience of God generated by classical rabbinic Judaism, responses that draw, to lesser or greater degrees, on the classical sources themselves. Put differently, chapters 6–12 describe the basic theological framework of rabbinic Judaism, which crystallized in the first centuries of the Common Era, while this chapter, as the culmination of the previous two chapters, describes how rabbinic Jews ever since, from the medieval period to today, have understood and experienced God within this framework. The discussion below, then, will return to and nuance many of the observations about Jewish theology advanced in earlier chapters.

Brokenness

In the course of his dissertation research, Harold Braswell, a professor of medical ethics raised in a Reform Jewish community, had a powerful encounter with Catholicism. It happened when he was examining the provision of hospice care in Our Lady of Perpetual Hope Home in Atlanta. The sisters who operated this home undertook to "see Jesus," first and foremost in relation to their patients. To see Jesus in these patients meant resolving to care for them as though they were Jesus. But the nuns were not just making an ethical commitment; they were engaged in a meditative practice that involved really *seeing* the suffering Christ, making Christ visually present in their suffering patients. This practice was reinforced by the representation of Christ on the cross—crucifixes—throughout the hospice. Nor did Christ mediate only the nuns' experience of their patients' suffering; the nuns saw their own struggles too, their own crosses, through the prism of Christ, and hoped that others, too, might see them in this way. "The result was a kind of relentless reciprocity, one that tore down the usual hierarchies structuring patient care. . . . You needed others. And what you needed others for was not so much to eradicate your suffering—for that could not be done, at least here on Earth—but to make it so that our suffering might be at least a little bit more collectively borne."[2]

Braswell found himself adopting the practice, both in speaking with patients and in revisiting his own troubled relationship with his deceased mother. "I kept trying, day after day[,] to see Jesus in her: to look, and find, within her, the dying Christ. I kept coming back to her and, as I did so, I began to discover that there were many layers." Visualizing Christ in her, he discovered her anew, and found something that he could love in her.

Braswell's reflection seems to exemplify Krister Stendhal's notion of holy envy, which we described in chapter 1. He finds a deeply meaningful spiritual practice in a tradition not his own. It raises the question: How, if at all, could this practice of seeing Jesus be translated into Judaism? The practice is rooted in the redemptive character of Jesus's suffering on the cross, and the reality of this suffering depends in turn, on the incarnation of Jesus in human flesh. To see Jesus in another's suffering, or in one's own, is to redeem that suffering by joining it to an experience of the suffering God. (Recall likewise, from chapter 12, how the Catechism counsels gay Christians to join their burden to Christ's sacrifice on the cross.) As we noted in chapter 8, God in Judaism does participate in the suffering that Israel endures in their exile at the hands

2. Harold Braswell, "Coming to Jesus: How a Shocking Family Discovery and Some Time Spent at a Hospice Run by Nuns Led One Jewish Man to Reconsider Christ," *Tablet Magazine*, January 22, 2020.

of the nations of the world. But such suffering is too limited in scope to serve as the basis for a Jewish equivalent of the practice of seeing Jesus. It lacks substance, in a literal way, because Judaism rejects the notion of incarnation that enables it: God does not and never did take on human flesh. Relatedly, with rare exceptions, Judaism refrains from depicting God, suffering or otherwise, so that there is no analogue for the visual force of the crucifix, which is so central for the nuns' practice. The link between the crucifixion and the Akedah, also discussed in chapter 8, is also helpful here for the difference that it surfaces: while the Akedah is of great importance for Jewish theology (though not nearly as important as the crucifixion for Christianity), the focus in Judaism is not on Isaac's physical suffering—the knife did not touch him, after all—nor even on Isaac's or Abraham's mental anguish, but on Abraham's commitment to the service of God.

More generally, suffering in Judaism is not redemptive. To be sure, one can atone for one's sins through suffering, but, bracketing dialectical theodicies in extremis like that of the "Holy Fire," also described in chapter 8, suffering signifies, in the first instance, the absence of God, not God's presence. In keeping with its this-worldly emphasis, explored in chapter 7 and elsewhere in the preceding chapters, Judaism holds on to a vision of the fulfilled life that includes good fortune, health, and descendants. Even as Judaism turns to the world to come, and to a rich literature of theodicy rooted in the book of Job, in order to think through the case of the righteous sufferer, it remains committed to the exceptional character of this case, and to providential good fortune in this world as the rule.

One might subsume suffering as a framework for the experience of God under the general rubric of brokenness. There is the brokenness of suffering. There is also the brokenness of sin, or more generally, a sense of guilt. As we noted in chapters 6 and 7, this dimension of brokenness, too, is thematized to a considerably greater extent in Christianity than in Judaism because Judaism generally conceptualizes sin as an inclination that people can overcome, not a terminal condition from which they must be rescued. This perspective finds expression in the following passage, from Mishnah Keritot 6:3.

> Rabbi Eliezer said: One may voluntarily bring an offering of uncertain guilt on any day and at any time that one wishes. This was called the guilt offering of the pious. They said of Bava son of Butoi that he would voluntarily

> bring an offering of uncertain guilt every day, except for one day after the Day of Atonement. He said: By this lair (i.e., the temple), if they would let me, I would bring. But they say to me: Wait until you enter into uncertainty. And the Sages say: One does not bring an offering of uncertain guilt except for an offense that renders one liable for excision if committed intentionally, and for a sin offering if committed unintentionally.

A person brings an "offering of uncertain guilt" to the temple when he is uncertain whether he has sinned. For the figures named in the first half of the Mishnah—Rabbi Eliezer, Bava son of Butoi, and "the pious"—sin is an ever-present, all-consuming source of anxiety; one can never really be certain that one has not sinned. Therefore, one can and should bring an offering of uncertain guilt every day, even multiple times a day. But the Sages at the end of the Mishnah, giving voice to the mainstream view in Judaism, reject this outlook. Sin, like the suffering of the righteous, is the exception, not the rule. A person should bring an offering of uncertain guilt only if he has a concrete reason to think he has sinned, and even then, only if it is an especially severe sort of sin.

In the above quotation, Green refers to the attraction of Jewish speakers specifically to "Eastern spiritual paths," and it is notable that Buddhism, like Christianity, centers suffering—or perhaps better, discontentment—as a spiritual concern. The Jewish poet and songwriter Leonard Cohen could be counted, in some measure, among JewBus, or Jewish Buddhists; he spent a number of years in a Buddhist monastery. Cohen also draws extensively on Christian spiritual resources, as in the song "Anthem," whose first strophe is dedicated to the "holy dove," a Christian image of the Holy Spirit. The refrain of this song gives striking expression to the notion that brokenness is a path toward the experience of God: "There is a crack, a crack in everything; that's how the light gets in."

It is important not to overstate the contrast. Judaism contains the resources to support the experience of God through the brokenness of sin and suffering, and the tradition cultivates these resources. The centrality of exile in the Jewish tradition must be noted here, though insofar as it bears on the experience of God it becomes manifest chiefly as desire for unity with God, and so will be taken up below in connection with the spirituality of eros. The book of Psalms, which so informs Christian spirituality of sin and suffering, is just as much a part of the Jewish scriptural canon. The psalmist's cry echoes in Jewish responses to persecution across the ages, and even today, in moments of communal distress, Jews recite Psalm 130, the *De Profundis*, which begins: "Out of the depths I cry to you, O Lord." The liturgy is replete with confessions of sin and recognition of the need for forgiveness, throughout the year and especially during the fall penitential season that culminates in the New Year and the Day of Atonement. A passage from the Babylonian Talmud (Rosh ha-Shanah 18a) envisions the ten days extending from the New Year to the Day of Atonement as a moment when God approaches especially close, waiting for Israel to seek God out in penitence; it is of these days, says the Talmud, that Isaiah speaks when he says: "Seek the Lord while he may be found; call upon him while he is near" (Isa. 55:6). Hasidic masters like Rabbi Nahman of Bratslav elaborate on the psychology and theology of sadness and despair. We can speak, then, of a Jewish spirituality of brokenness. But in Christianity, the experience of brokenness is coordinated to a central image, indeed, *the* central image, namely, the cross, through which the suffering Christ saves from sin. Judaism lacks such an image, and conventional rabbinic teaching—on the capacity of human beings to choose well, on the vision of fulfillment in this life—implicitly marginalizes brokenness as the exception.

Before moving on to a different configuration of spirituality, let us look at two examples of the experience of God through brokenness in contemporary Judaism, two religious pop songs released in 2019 by the singer-songwriter Ishay Ribo, an Israeli of Sephardic origin, born in France.[3] The first song, "My Heart" (*ha-lev sheli*), begins as follows: "My heart is torn in two, past what a maidservant saw at the water." The thing that has torn the speaker's heart is kept vague; later strophes refer to mourning, pain, and guilt, and the listener is invited to identify with all such feelings. The words "what a maidservant saw at the water" allude to a famous rabbinic adage about the splitting of the sea in Exodus 14. The rabbis suppose that the splitting of the sea was a moment of intense divine revelation, as God entered the fray personally to wage war against the Egyptians. Even the lowly maidservant, they say, saw God at the sea in a way that Ezekiel, the prophet who had the most vivid vision of God in the Bible (Ezek. 1), could not. For Ribo, the split sea of Exodus 14 becomes

3. For the YouTube releases of these songs, see https://www.youtube.com/watch?v=6U_5KhaH6IM; https://www.youtube.com/watch?v=ECy3CMxShIQ.

a figure for the torn heart, and that torn heart, like the split sea, constitutes a locus of revelation, a path toward God, as the speaker reaches out to God in his brokenness. "Only you," he calls out to God in the refrain, "are able to turn my mourning to dance, to refine the profane." Here Ribo alludes to the dance of the women celebrating God's salvation at the sea (Exod. 15:20), and plays on the fact that Hebrew *hol* can mean both "profane" and "sand," so that the sand at the sea suggests the speaker's profane condition, which can be refined (or in a punningly concrete way, "made into glass") by God's presence.

The second song, "The Order of the Service" (*seder ha-avodah*), is built around the Mishnah's depiction of the cultic service performed by the high priest in the temple on the Day of Atonement, along with later liturgical elaborations on the Mishnah's account. The service involves, among other things, the confession of sins and the sprinkling of the sacrificial animal's blood once in one place and seven times in another—each time counted aloud: "one; one and one; one and two, . . . one and seven"—at specific locations on the altar. In Ribo's hands, these elements become a modern expression of crushing guilt.

> And so [the high priest] would say: "Please, O Name, cover over the sins and iniquities and violations that I have sinned before you, I and my household." And if a person could remember all the flaws and lacks, all the violations and iniquities, surely he would count thus: "One, one and one, one and two, one and three, one and four, one and five," and then he would despair of it, unable to bear the bitter taste of sin, the shame, the fumbling, the loss.

In the continuation, the same cultic elements are transformed again into futile attempt to count God's endless mercies and kindnesses, so that the sense of sin opens out into perception of God's goodness. The conclusion of the song describes God's forgiveness, and here the song's lens, tightly centered to this point on the high priest, corresponding to the individual sinner, widens to include the people Israel, through a resounding refrain, familiar to us already from chapters 9 and 10: "Happy the people who have it so; happy the people whose God is the Lord." This shift reflects the especially rich capacity of traditional Judaism, counting peoplehood as one of its theological foci, to enable spiritual experience through the actual or constructed presence of the community of Israel.

Mystery

Besides brokenness, another entry point into the experience of God is a sense of mystery or wonder. This sense can be occasioned by elements in nature: the vastness of the heavens or the sea, for example, which can inspire, even simultaneously, a sense of insignificance and of exaltation; or the impossibly intricate complexity of natural organisms. Theological teaching can also be a source of wonder or mystery, especially by challenging rational thought through paradox. The paradoxes of the incarnation and the trinity lie at the center of Christian theology, and Buddhism deploys koans to subvert human reason.

The moving effect of God's cosmic vastness, enshrined in such biblical texts as Psalm 8, is not neglected in the Jewish spiritual tradition. Consider, for example, the following poem, by one of the giants of medieval Iberian philosophy and poetry, Solomon ibn Gabirol (eleventh century CE).[4]

> I seek you each of my mornings and my evenings.
> I spread my palms before you, and my face.
> I pant for you with thirsty heart and seem
> Like the beggar who comes asking at my door.
> The heavens aren't space enough for you
> To dwell, and yet you have a place in my mind.
> I hide in my heart your glorious name until
> Love of you overpowers, and passes my mouth.
> And so I praise the name of my lord as long
> As my nostrils have the living breath of God.

The notion of the human mind as the ultimate residence of God in the world is familiar from the thought of the later Maimonides, though Ibn Gabirol's philosophical sources are more Neoplatonic than Aristotelian. Here, Ibn Gabirol expresses the paradox at work in this notion: God cannot be contained by the very heavens, yet God resides in the mind or heart of the very

4. For the Hebrew text and an alternative translation, with discussion, see Raymond P. Scheindlin, *The Gazelle: Medieval Hebrew Poems on God, Israel, and the Soul* (Oxford: Oxford University Press, 1999), 182–87.

human beings who importune God. For Ibn Gabirol, God's presence inside the human mind becomes like a stoppered spring, pressing outward until it forces open the poet's mouth and issues therefrom as praise of God. Related to the mystery of God's connection to human beings is the mystery of God's election of Israel, and, as I suggested in chapter 9, a posture of wonderment at election animates traditional thought on the topic. Divine election figures in the refrain of Ribo's song, "The Order of the Service," and we will return to it again momentarily.

Alongside such expressions of mystery and paradox, certain key commitments of Jewish theology tend to constrain these sources of spirituality. The most important is the covenant, which the Bible, and following it rabbinic Judaism, portray as the revelation of everything that is needful for Israel. The book of Ben Sira is not included in the Jewish biblical canon, but it was familiar to the rabbis, and they cite it sometimes. One passage in the Talmud, Hagigah 13a, introduces Sirach 3:21–22 to ground a limit to the investigation of heavenly mysteries: "Neither seek what is too difficult for you, nor investigate what is beyond your power; reflect upon what you have been commanded, for what is hidden is not your concern." (Thus the NRSV rendering of the Greek translation of Ben Sira.) The rabbis of the Talmud take a further step along this path by conceptualizing these commandments as laws. As noted in chapter 7, the rabbis do insist, in general, on locating the authority of the laws in God's will rather than in their inherent reasonableness, and they can even go so far as to celebrate the capacity for commandments to defy reason. (The law of the red heifer in Numbers 19 is the paradigmatically paradoxical law; see Pesiqta de-Rab Kahana 4.) However, the rabbinic legal system as a whole—halakhah—has its own intrinsic rationality, and indeed, the description and deployment of this rationality belongs to the very essence of the Talmudic project.

Eros and Seeking

But consider the covenantal encounter again. It is a moment with legal significance, yes, but law does not preclude love. Weddings, too, are legally significant moments. And for the rabbis, indeed, Sinai is also a wedding.

> "Daughters of Jerusalem, come out and look at king Solomon, at the crown with which his mother crowned him on his wedding day, and on the day of his heart's gladness" (Song of Songs 3:11). "On his wedding day": This is the giving of the Torah. "And on the day of his heart's gladness": This is the building of the temple. (Mishnah Ta'anit 4:8)

This passage from the Mishnah offers an interpretation of a verse from the Song of Songs. The Song of Songs describes two lovers, a man (sometimes associated in the book with King Solomon) and a woman, each in pursuit of the other. The man is a rather more distant and mysterious figure than the woman, but both passionately wish to consummate their love, and sometimes they do, but crucially, always fleetingly. Theirs is a dance of presence and absence. For the rabbis, the man is God, and the woman is the people Israel, seeking each other across the ages, drawn apart by exile but never ceasing to long for and pursue each other. It is arguably in the reception of the Song of Songs in Judaism, and through the figure of eros that animates it, and that is its own sort of mystery, that what Green calls a "seeker-friendly" Judaism—a Judaism centered on the experience of God, in God's presence and in God's absence—can perhaps most readily find expression.

In support of his vision of the contemplative life, Maimonides assigns the Song of Songs an individualist interpretation, where the man remains God, but the woman is the philosopher, whose thoughts are always upon God.

> What is the love of God that is befitting? It is to love the Eternal with a great and exceeding love, so strong that one's soul shall be knit up with the love of God, and one should be continually enraptured by it, like a love-sick individual, whose mind is at no time free from his passion for a particular woman, the thought of her filling his heart at all times, when sitting down or rising up, when he is eating or drinking. . . . This, Solomon expressed allegorically in the sentence, "for I am sick with love" (Song of Songs 2:5). The entire Song of Songs is indeed an allegory descriptive of this love. (*Mishneh Torah*, Laws of Repentance, 10:3)

The gender tension in this passage is striking: Maimonides's reading of the Song of Songs makes the lovesick woman therein (the speaker in Song of

Songs 2:5) a figure for the ideal of constant contemplation of God, but because he addresses a male audience, and takes philosophy to be the province of men, he transforms the lovesick woman into a lovesick man. But Maimonides can sometimes acknowledge the philosophical capacity of exceptional women. At the end of the *Guide to the Perplexed* (book 3, chapter 51), reflecting on the rabbinic tradition that Moses and his siblings, Aaron and Miriam, died by God's kiss, he suggests that the kiss is a figure for "the apprehension that is achieved in a state of intense and passionate love for Him." Such, says Maimonides, is the force of the opening verse of the Song of Songs (also voiced by the woman): "let him kiss me with the kisses of his mouth."

Seeking figures prominently in the above poem by Solomon ibn Gabirol. Let us take up now two other poems, both liturgical, that make use of the Song of Songs and of the tropes of love and desire. The first was written by Israel Najara, among the most famous of the Sephardic liturgical poets. Najara, whose last name—a form of Nájera, in northern Spain—marks him as a descendant of the Spanish Jewish community expelled in 1492, moved among Jewish communities in Damascus, Safed, and Gaza in the second half of the sixteenth century. His poems, often written to be sung to popular songs in Ladino (Judeo-Spanish), Turkish, and Arabic, were among the first Jewish works printed in Ottoman Palestine, and achieved great popularity.

Najara's poem, "My Lover Went Down to His Garden" (*yarad dodi legano*) is a fixture of the traditional Sephardic liturgy for Shavuot (Pentecost), the festival that celebrates the Sinai event.[5] The poem depends on the characterization of the Sinai event, as in the passage from Mishnah Ta'anit 4:8, above, as the wedding ceremony joining God and Israel. In the Jewish tradition, the wedding is accompanied by a marriage contract, a *ketubah*, which specifies the husband's obligations to the wife. Rabbinic sources invoke the ketubah in imagining the spousal relationship between God and Israel. One poignant passage (Pesiqta de-Rav Kahana 19:4), for example, compares Israel in exile to a woman whose fiancé had written her a marriage contract but then left for distant lands for many years. Her acquaintances would importune her and say: leave him, take another man while you're still young. And she would

5. For the Hebrew text and recordings of traditional recitations thereof by Persian, Lebanese, and Jerusalemite performers, see https://www.nli.org.il/he/piyut/Piyut1media_010086800369205171/NLI.

pick up her ketubah and read it, and find consolation in it. When her fiancé finally returned, he marveled at her faithfulness, and she identified the ketubah as her source of strength. Likewise, the passage continues, the nations of the world hound Israel and say: Why do you continue to endure persecution and death out of loyalty to your God? Come, be joined to us, and enjoy positions of authority. But Israel, retreating into herself and studying the Torah, finds the strength to resist them.

The central conceit of "My Lover Went Down to His Garden" is that it represents the actual marriage contract between God and Israel. Najara, borrowing the precise wording of the traditional Sephardic marriage contract, writes out a version that God might have written for Israel. Thus, the ketubah formula begins by specifying "how the groom, so-and-so [said to the bride, such-and-such: Be my wife, etc.]," and Najara accordingly devotes a strophe to expanding on this formula, through allusion to Song of Songs 5:16: "How the groom, prince of princes, leader of leaders, / Solitary and singular, matching together solitary people, / Of palate most sweet, and entirely desirable," etc. The opening strophes of the poem, introducing the text of the ketubah, tell how God proposed to Israel.

> He forsook his seraphs and his wheels, his chariot and horsemen,
> And between the beloved doe's breasts set his couch
> On his wedding day, and on the day of his heart's gladness.
>
> My love, my dove, come with me to the sanctuary hall.
> For your sake I will abandon all the throngs above and their forces,
> To betroth you forever.

These lines are a pastiche of verses, mainly from the Song of Songs (1:12, 14; 3:11; 5:2). God tells Israel that God is willing for Israel's sake to descend from heaven, to give up God's angelic retinue, and take up residence in a human house, the temple. The poem ends thus, with a familiar exclamation: "Let the groom rejoice with the bride he took as his lot. / Let the bride rejoice with the husband of her youth, and praise him: / 'Happy the people who have it so!'"

Najara rubbed shoulders with the great Kabbalists of Safed, and it is they who will lead us to the second liturgical poem on which we will focus. Kabbalah, and Hasidism in its wake, are major sources for Jewish spirituality, especially with an erotic inflection. The divine economy of Kabbalah is driven by desire, often expressed through allusion to the Song of Songs: the desire of the higher to be joined to the lower, and of the lower to the higher; the sefirotic male's longing for unity with the female, and the reverse. Our second poem focuses on the sabbath, which becomes entangled in this kabbalistic web of desire in many ways. Of particular importance for the kabbalistic reception of the sabbath is a comment on Genesis 2:3 attributed to Rabbi Shimon bar Yochai (Genesis Rabbah 11:8). What does the verse mean when it says that God "sanctified" the sabbath? Just as, later in Genesis 2, God notices Adam's loneliness and finds for him a spouse, so here, the sanctification is connected to betrothal, in Hebrew qiddushin ("sanctification"). The sabbath came to God with the concern that she was the odd one out: the six days of the week paired off with each other, but she was alone. God replied to her: the assembly of Israel will be your spouse. For God to sanctify the sabbath is, then, for God to instruct Israel, in the Decalogue (Exod. 20:8), to sanctify, that is, to betroth, the sabbath.

In the kabbalistic tradition, the sabbath as bride came naturally to be identified with the female divine figure of Presence. The Kabbalists of Safed introduced a new liturgy for Friday sundown, just before the evening prayer, to mark the entrance of the sabbath bride. This liturgy, called *kabbalat shabbat* or "greeting the sabbath," is recited today throughout the Jewish world. The liturgical poem to which we now turn, "Lord, I Pine" (*yah ekhsof*), follows in the same figural tradition. The poem, by Rabbi Aharon the Great (1736–1772), a student of the Maggid of Mezeritch and the founder of the Karliner sect of hasidim, was written to be sung at the sabbath table, to a moving melody also composed by Rabbi Aharon. A wide variety of Hasidic sects have long adopted the poem as their own, and today it is also popular outside of Hasidic circles. Here are some excerpts.[6]

> Lord, I long for the sweetness of the sabbath, which twins and unites with your treasured ones. Draw the sweetness of your awe to the people that seeks your will. Make them holy with the holiness of the sabbath, which unites

6. For the Hebrew text and some recorded performances, see https://www.nli.org.il/he/piyut/Piyut1media_010050200295805171/NLI.

> with your Torah. Open for them sweetness and desire, to open the gates of your desire. . . .
>
> You who were and are, watch over those who watch and wait for your holy sabbath. As a hart pants on streams of waters, so their soul pants to receive the holiness of the sabbath, which unites with your holy name. . . . And may your mercy roll down upon your holy people, to water those who thirst for your kindness from the river that comes from Eden. . . . Holy sabbath, my soul is sick with love for you.

The basic motifs of the poem are kabbalistic: an overpowering desire for unification, and through it, for the drawing down of divine Abundance into the world. Against the background of Rabbi Shimon bar Yohai's exegesis, the sabbath, the odd one out among the seven days of creation, acts as something like a free radical, joining itself in Rabbi Aharon's poem to Israel ("your treasured ones"), to the Torah, and to God's own name. Part of the poem's emotional potency derives from its use of the first-person singular: "Lord, I pine for the sweetness of the sabbath," or, borrowing the notion of lovesickness from Song of Songs 2:5 and 5:8, "my soul is sick with love for you." Thus, even though the song is about Israel's relationship with the sabbath, and through it, with God, it presents the experience of this relationship from the perspective of the singer as an individual, with all the intimacy thus entailed. Crucially, too, even though the poem is sung on the sabbath, it figures the sabbath as an object of longing, as though it were not yet obtained. This tension, which also contributes to the poem's potency, is theologically rooted in the association of the sabbath rest with the ultimate redemption, so that the sabbath becomes both a present experience and a passionately sought future. Through the tension of presence and absence, the sabbath becomes coordinated to the ultimate object of unfulfillable desire, God.

Conclusion

For those who take the notion of religious truth-claims seriously, it is a given that religions—or at least certain religions, including the Abrahamic ones—advance differing truth-claims that are to one degree or another incompatible with each other. The notion that different religions address human beings' spiritual needs in different ways seems likewise uncontroversial. Can we in the same way find that one religion can be better than another at addressing a particular spiritual need? Such a state of affairs seems plausible enough, and arguably, the possibility of holy envy presupposes it. Is it legitimate, against this background, for a Jew to "play"—with utter seriousness and respect—at being a Christian, and draw on Christianity's spiritual resources to enable self-transcendence in suffering, or for a Christian to reposition herself in relation to technology and community by taking on some aspects of the sabbath? Does the proximity of Judaism and Christianity enable such experiences, or make them more fraught? These questions can be a part, even an important part, of the modern Jewish-Christian encounter.

Further Inquiry

On contemporary Jewish spirituality in a neo-Hasidic vein, see the two companion volumes edited by Arthur Green and Ariel Evan Mayse, *A New Hasidism: Roots* (Philadelphia: Jewish Publication Society, 2019) and *A New Hasidism: Branches* (Philadelphia: Jewish Publication Society, 2019). For historical and sociological analysis of the attraction of Buddhism for American Jews, see Emily Sigalow, *American JewBu: Jews, Buddhists, and Religious Change* (Princeton: Princeton University Press, 2019). On the Song of Songs and Jewish theology, see Gerson Cohen, "The Song of Songs and the Jewish Religious Mentality," in *The Samuel Friedland Lectures, 1960–1966* (New York: Jewish Theological Seminary of America, 1966), 1–21; and for detailed engagement with the full range of Jewish interpretive approaches to the Song of Songs, see Michael Fishbane, *Song of Songs = Shir ha-Shirim: The Traditional Hebrew Text with the New JPS Translation* (Philadelphia: Jewish Publication Society, 2015).

•

1. In his contribution to *A New Hasidism: Branches*, referenced above, Ariel Evan Mayse introduces a Hasidic teaching that links the Hebrew word for a commandment, *mitzvah*, to the Aramaic word *tsavta*, meaning "connection." This wordplay furnishes the basis for the claim that the mitzvot work to connect human beings to God and to other human beings. How does the spiritual significance of mitzvot

conceived as connectors compare to the spiritual significance of commandments conceived (in the conventional way) as divine commands or laws?

2. In this chapter and the previous one we made passing reference to Rabbi Nahman of Bratslav or Breslov, the founder of the Breslover Hasidic sect. After Chabad, the Breslovers are the most influential Hasidic sect in the general Jewish world, with particular prominence in the ba'al teshuvah movement in Israel. Breslov Hasidism is especially famous for teaching the practice of *hitbodedut* ("isolation"): separating oneself from other people to speak directly and intently with God. In his article, "*Hitbodedut* for a New Age: Adaptation of Practices Among the Followers of Rabbi Nachman of Bratslav," *Israel Studies Review* 29 (2014): 103, Tomer Persico summarizes hitbodedut as conceived of by Rabbi Nahman in the following words: "A multistage path is laid out before us: First, the person has to physically isolate himself; after his thoughts have calmed down, he will talk frankly to God; this in turn, when done properly, should bring him to tears, and thereupon to ecstasy; this state will annul the person's self consciousness [*sic*] and feeling of self, and bring him into a mystical experience of union; finally, after returning to a more pedestrian state of consciousness, he acquires joy, and the whole world is seen by him as filled with the divine presence." How is this practice similar to and different from meditation practices familiar to you?

— *Chapter 16* —

Modernity, Zionism, and the Jewish State

SINCE THE DAWN OF MODERNITY IN THE WEST, the Jewish people and Judaism have experienced three major and interrelated upheavals. The first was the integration of Jews into the regnant cultures and emergent nation-states; the second was Zionism, leading to the founding of the state of Israel; and the third was the Holocaust. Of these, the Holocaust stands out as an event of brute violence. It had a decisive impact on Judaism insofar as it destroyed so many of the individuals and local cultures in which Judaism was embodied. The first two developments also implicated external sources of power, but Jews played in them an active role, and Jews' ideological commitments directly shaped and were shaped by them. This chapter is dedicated to these two developments. We will see how, pushed and pulled by the forces of modernity, Judaism, ever a hybrid of religion (in the paradigmatically Christian sense) and ethnicity, came to find expression in different forms, some of which assign greater weight to the religious element, and some to the ethnic element. This chapter will devote particular attention to Jewish theological responses to emergent Zionism, and the implications of Zionism and the state of Israel for Jewish theology. The next chapter will consider Christian and Jewish approaches to the theological challenge posed by the fact of Jewish power in the Jewish state, and by the particular ways in which that power has been exercised.

Enlightenment, Emancipation, and Early Zionism

At the eve of modernity, Jews in Christian lands generally lived in communities with considerable powers of self-governance in personal and civil matters, and even limited criminal jurisdiction. These communities were by no means sealed off from the larger Christian world; Jews regularly engaged with Christians economically and also, in substantial ways, culturally. But Jews nevertheless constituted a people apart, and their relationship to the state was mediated by Jewish communal structures.

A wide-ranging set of historical and ideological shifts in the eighteenth century that we can group under the rubric of the Enlightenment raised the prospect of major changes to these circumstances. The Enlightenment centered reason as a universal human endowment, the cultivation of reason through education as the task of the state, and progress as the inevitable outcome of an enlightened society. For some Enlightenment philosophers, the Jews represented the ultimate test case of their universalist commitments. It was a given, in general, that Christianity was or could be made "reasonable," but was the same true for Jews and Judaism? Were Jews not too insular, too exclusively loyal to their own? Was their religious system not too backward, too ritualistic, too superstitious? In concrete political terms, could Jews be made worthy of "emancipation," that is, the recognition of Jews, in their individual capacity, as citizens of their respective countries? The most famous of the initial Jewish responses to these questions, at the end of the eighteenth century, was Moses Mendelssohn's *Jerusalem*, which we had occasion briefly to consider in chapter 13.

Mendelssohn, a philosopher who ranked, in his day, alongside Kant, was the founding figure of an inner-Jewish Enlightenment (Hebrew *Haskalah*) that saw Jews who had been raised in very traditional households embrace vernacular languages and cultures. The *maskilim* ("enlighteners," sg. *maskil*) in the West sought in general to refashion Judaism, to lesser or greater degrees, in accordance with Enlightenment principles, and often in the image of Protestant Christianity. The modern Jewish denominations arose in Western Europe as a result of this integrationist goal. What we call today Reform Judaism altered traditional practices and beliefs in often radical ways, while what goes today by the name modern Orthodoxy introduced far more limited changes, even as it, too, in its way, embraced the Enlightenment. (We saw in chapter 10 how Reform Jews changed the Amidah to express a Judaism inflected in a more rationalist and less nationalist direction; we will take up this thread again below.) Ultra-Orthodox Jews responded to these encroachments on tradition by becoming insular and ideologically anti-modern. In support of this posture, the doctrine of *daas Torah* ("Torah wisdom") emerged in Haredi circles. This doctrine posits that the great Torah sages attain to insight that demands obedience not only in religious matters, narrowly conceived, but in all matters, including political ones.

We can define Zionism as the organized undertaking to reestablish the historical land of Israel as the home of the Jewish people, where this home might be founded and maintained, paradigmatically though not necessarily, through the exercise of Jewish sovereignty over some part of the land. When did Zionism begin? The late eighteenth and early nineteenth centuries saw the movement of small groups of pious Ashkenazi Jews to the holy land as part of the spiritual ferment that also found expression in Hasidism. But these communities, though colored by messianic expectation, had no nationalist aspirations and no political program. Zionism emerged in earnest, rather, in the late nineteenth century, both in Eastern and in Western Europe.

One of the chief motivations of early Zionists was the perception that the promise of the Enlightenment and of emancipation had been proven false by the persistence and indeed new flourishing of antisemitism. The most famous contemporaneous instance of antisemitism in Western Europe was the Dreyfus Affair, which roiled France for over a decade, beginning in 1894. A Jewish army captain, Alfred Dreyfus, was scapegoated for treason, and the French elite split among liberal Dreyfusards and conservative anti-Dreyfusards. The ranks of the latter came especially from the army and the Catholic Church. This controversy drew the attention of, among others, the man who would become the leading figure among Zionists in the West, Theodore Herzl (1860–1904). Herzl wrote of the Jewish people in 1896: "We have honestly striven everywhere to merge ourselves in the social life of surrounding communities, and preserve only the faith of our fathers. It has not been permitted to us."[1] Further east, in the Russian Empire especially, antisemitism was pervasive and often violent. Peretz Smolenskin (1842–1885), an important figure of the eastern Haskalah, saw the failure of the integrationist paradigm in a series of pogroms that began in 1881. He wrote in that year:

1. Paul Mendes-Flohr and Jehuda Reinharz, eds., *The Jew in the Modern World: A Documentary History*, 2nd ed. (Oxford: Oxford University Press, 1995), 534.

> Calamity after calamity and disaster after disaster have afflicted the Jews of Russia. . . . Many Jews have been murdered and the wounded are without number. The mob, a ravenous wolf in search of prey, has stalked the Jews with a cruelty unheard of since the Middle Ages. Perhaps most shocking of all, many supposedly decent people appeared among the makers of the pogroms. There is no end to the affliction that has already struck so many tens of thousands. . . . The actual attack on the Jews has only just begun, but it has been in preparation for many years. The real source of all this is the anti-Jewish venom which has filled most of the Russian press and periodicals for the last twenty years. Every sort of invective has been flung at us; the whole gamut of imaginable sins, deceits, and wickedness has been ascribed to us. . . . During all this time the Jewish philanthropists in Russia were preoccupied with Haskalah, in imitation of the German Jews. They, too, were foolish enough to believe that the way of enlightenment would bring them success and honor. If they would only reach a high level of enlightenment, the gentiles would accept them with respect and brotherly love, and troublemakers would no longer attack them.[2]

Smolenskin notes in the continuation that antisemites in Russia were themselves pressing for Jews to leave Russia. Why, indeed, he says, should they not, and why not, in particular, to the land of their forefathers?

Beyond concern over antisemitism, Zionism was fueled by romantic nationalism. Throughout the second half of the nineteenth century, European peoples previously absorbed into empires were beginning to assert and win recognition of their right to political self-determination. Some Jewish thinkers took them as models for imitation. True, they reasoned, the thing that has most set Jews apart from their Christian neighbors over the centuries is their distinctive religious commitments, but the Jews are also, more fundamentally, a people. Should not they, too, have a right to a state in which they might cultivate their particular national spirit? Zionists of this mind also expressed concern that the integrationist vision, despite the threat of antisemitism, might ultimately become too successful, and lead to the enervation and even the complete disappearance of the Jewish people.

2. Arthur Hertzberg, ed., *The Zionist Idea: A Historical Analysis and Reader* (Philadelphia: Jewish Publication Society, 1997), 148–49.

Consider, for example, the career of Eliezer Ben Yehuda (ca. 1858–1922). His journey began like that of a typical maskil. Born and raised in a very traditional home in Lithuania as the son of a Chabad hasid, he encountered Haskalah writings as a young man, and was inspired by them to devote himself to the question of Judaism and Jewish life in the modern world. These efforts quickly led him past Judaism, to a concern with improving the lot of humanity in general, and especially the circumstances of the Russian peasants. "With all the passion of my youthful years I became committed to the generous notion of dedicating all my life and all my mind to take part in the work of humankind in general."[3] But then came the Russo-Turkish War of 1877–78, in which Russia came to the aid of Bulgarian Serbs who were rebelling against the Ottoman Empire and seeking to attain self-rule. If a Bulgarian state carved out of the Ottoman Empire, reasoned Ben Yehuda, then why not also a Jewish one, in Ottoman Palestine? "[My thought] flew from the Shipka crossing to the Jordan crossing in the land of Israel, and I heard a strange inner voice calling to me: the resurrection of Israel and its language on the land of its fathers!"

As this last quotation indicates, Ben Yehuda became preoccupied with an aspect of the nationalist project that loomed large in nineteenth-century Romanticism: language. For romantic thinkers, the "genius" of a folk lay especially in its language. Of course, Jews did have an ancient language of their own, Hebrew. But from the Middle Ages forward, Hebrew had ceased to be the language of everyday use, and had become instead the "holy tongue," employed chiefly for prayer and the writing of Torah-study literature. The unifying mother tongue of Ashkenazi Jews was instead Yiddish. Language wars raged among Jews drawn into the Haskalah. As noted above, maskilim, especially in the West, sought to educate Jews in vernacular languages, to integrate them into their host cultures. Proponents of Reform Judaism replaced Hebrew with the vernacular as the language of prayer, while modern Orthodox Jews introduced the vernacular into the synagogue only in more limited ways. In the different circumstances of Eastern Europe, many maskilim sought to produce a distinctively Jewish enlightened culture. Yiddish was the language of choice for such a culture among some, while others labored to make Hebrew serviceable for essays and belletristic literature. Ben Yehuda

3. For the quotations from Ben Yehuda see Joseph Lang, *Speak Hebrew! The Life of Eliezer Ben Yehuda* (Jerusalem: Yad Ben-Zvi, 2008), 8–9.

went one fateful step further: Hebrew must not merely be restored as the written language of Jewish culture; it must be resurrected as the spoken language of Jewish life. He moved to Palestine and devoted himself to this goal. By isolating his son from other children he made him the first native speaker of modern Hebrew, and Ben Yehuda is remembered as no less than the father of modern Hebrew.

Early Zionism and Jewish Theology

Characteristically for Zionists from Eastern Europe, Smolenskin and Ben Yehuda came from traditional religious families but had abandoned personal halakhic observance. More typically for a Zionist from Western Europe, Herzl was not raised in a religious home, and though his turn to Zionism meant, inevitably, a greater embrace of his Jewish identity, it by no means led him to traditional religious practice. Early Zionism was in fact dominated by secular and nontraditional Jews. How did religious Jews respond to Zionism? In what ways did Jewish theology receive and shape Zionism at its inception?

Jews affiliated with Reform Judaism in Western Europe and America typically looked askance at Zionism. In 1897, two liberal German rabbis responded to news of Herzl's intended Zionist Congress by insisting in a public letter that Judaism should have no nationalist aspirations, and that antisemitism can and should be combated through local efforts.

> Eighteen hundred years ago, history made its decision regarding Jewish nationhood through the dissolution of the Jewish State and the destruction of the Temple. . . . [W]here are the Jews who do not want to assimilate? The fact that right now they are still unable to assimilate in many countries makes it precisely our duty to fight in common with the most noble and best men of all confessions for the removal of discriminatory laws.[4]

On the view expressed here, the scattering of the people Israel throughout the world with the destruction of the second temple should not be understood as a divine punishment from which Israel ought to seek relief, as an exile for

4. Mendes-Flohr and Reinharz, *Jew in the Modern World*, 539.

whose end Israel ought to pray. Rather, this momentous event clarified the true nature of Judaism, as an exclusively religious form of organization. These rabbis thus assert elsewhere in the same letter that, in relation to their non-Jewish German neighbors, "we comprise a separate community solely with respect to religion." Consider, along these lines, how the Reform Jewish liturgy of the time revised the traditional seventeenth blessing of the Amidah. In the traditional version of this blessing, the community calls on God to receive Israel's prayers and to restore the original form of divine worship, that is, the sacrificial cult in Zion. It concludes: "Blessed are you, O Lord, who restores his presence to Zion." The 1942 printing of the *Union Prayer-Book for Jewish Worship*, faithful to classical Reform theology (which was, however, even then, in part, on the wane), omits the main body of the blessing altogether, and replaces the traditional conclusion with an alternative version that makes no reference to restoration to Zion: "Praised be Thou, O God, whom alone we serve in reverence."

In contextualizing the German rabbis' opposition to Herzl's Zionist Congress, it is important to appreciate that the prospect of a Jewish state in the historical land of Israel seemed, at the time, utterly unlikely. It is not surprising that Jews invested in the project of integration—Jews who wished to make life better and richer for their co-religionists in the European countries in which they lived—were reluctant to put this project at risk by supporting a pipe dream that would only put ammunition into the hands of antisemites who sought to portray Jews as interlopers, as foreigners who could not truly be loyal citizens of the countries in which they resided because their allegiance was to another, yet unrealized state. How well-founded this concern was, and yet how powerless Jews were to allay it, becomes apparent in the most chilling way from a passage in Adolf Hitler's *Mein Kampf* in which he describes how he first became convinced of the Jews' otherness. It was settled for him, he writes, "by the opinions expressed by some of the Jews themselves."[5]

> Zionism, a great movement among them, widespread in Vienna, made a sharp claim for the national character of Judaism. It indeed seemed as though only one group among the Jews approved this claim, while the great majority con-

5. I have translated from the online edition of the Leibniz Institute for Contemporary History, vol. 1, chapter 2, 57: https://www.mein-kampf-edition.de/?page=band1%2Fp057.html.

> demned and rejected such a determination. But on closer inspection, this appearance evaporated into a foul haze of excuses made purely for reasons of convenience, not to say lies. For the so-called Judaism of a liberal mindset did not reject the Zionists as non-Jews, but only as Jews who confessed their Judaism in an impractical and perhaps even dangerous way. There was no real change in their internal solidarity.

He writes that he became "disgusted" by the alleged dishonesty of this only "apparent conflict between Zionist and liberal Jews."

Opposition to Zionism in its early stages was also widespread among traditional Orthodox Jews. Modern Orthodox Jews in Western Europe, who like Reform Jews were invested in the integrationist project, voiced similar objections to the Zionist assertion of nationalist identity. Unlike their Reform counterparts, they did not reject in principle Judaism's traditional vision of the restoration of the Jewish people to their land under the rule of a messianic king, but they insisted that this vision was for a distant future. Zionism did receive substantial support among some traditional Jews, even ultra-Orthodox Jews, especially in Eastern Europe, where the desire for integration was weaker, the prospect of integration seemed dimmer, and concerns about discrimination, poverty, and violence pressed more urgently. But in Eastern Europe too, for reasons we will detail below, most traditionalists opposed Zionism.

The conflict among traditional Jews concerning Zionism reflects the fact that, in relationship to tradition, emergent Zionism represented a paradox. On the one hand, it was deeply traditional, insofar as it sought to realize the two-thousand-year-old hope for the return of the Jewish people to the land of their ancestors. On the other hand, it was revolutionary. In taking up the romantic model of a self-determining people on its land, it centered Jewish identity on peoplehood rather than on religious practice or Torah. In seeking a state, Zionism threatened to upend the circumstances of political disempowerment in which rabbinic Judaism had crystallized and developed, and to which it had conformed itself. In dogmatic terms, Zionism broke with a foundational assumption of the rabbinic tradition, reinforced in daily prayers, that redemption would come through the agency of God.

Most of the great rabbis in the east saw Zionism in this negative light. Zionism, they said, was a modern invention that would lure Jews away from religious observance. The Zionists were presumptuous atheists who meant to wrest power from God. Some of these rabbis pointed especially to a passage in Bavli Ketubot 110b–111a that addresses the question of moving to the land of Israel from the Diaspora. The Mishnah on which the Bavli comments (Ketubot 13:11) addresses the case of a married couple where one spouse wishes to move from the Diaspora to the land of Israel, or from the land of Israel to the Diaspora, while the other does not. The Mishnah rules that the spouse who wishes to move to or remain in the land of Israel has the legal upper hand. The Mishnah thus testifies to the religious value of dwelling in the land of Israel. But the Bavli introduces a countervailing consideration: God exiled the Jewish people from the land of Israel, and so, arguably, they ought to accept their exile as punishment and remain in the Diaspora. The Bavli ends by introducing a compromise view. Jews can and even should move to the land of Israel as individuals, but not as a collective. The Bavli expresses this view through exegesis of the Song of Songs. Three times (2:7; 3:5; 8:4), the daughters of Jerusalem are adjured not to "stir or awaken love until it is ready." According to the Talmud, these verses refer to three oaths imposed by God in connection with the exile: that the Jewish people should not "ascend as a wall," that is, as a group, in force, to the land of Israel; that they should not rebel against the nations to whom God has subjugated them; and that these nations should not abuse their authority over the Jews. Now, in truth, this text is hardly a decisive prooftext against Zionism. The passage expounds the Song of Songs, not Pentateuchal law, and thus has an aggadic rather than a halakhic character; halakhic codifiers throughout the ages felt no need to include it in their works. But the passage does give forceful expression to the traditionally quietist posture of rabbinic Judaism.

Some rabbis in Eastern Europe who supported Zionism took it to be consistent with and indeed the first step toward the realization of Judaism's messianic vision. Others declined to interpret Zionism within a messianic framework altogether, and supported it for practical reasons: it could provide protection and economic opportunity to poor and persecuted Jews. A renewed Jewish community in Zion could also make it, as of old, a center of Torah study and spiritual renewal for the entire Jewish world. This vision, a religious counterpart to the cultural Zionism of Ahad Ha'am, discussed in chapter 11, inspired Rabbi Isaac Jacob Reines to found, in 1902, a religious Zionist organization, Mizrachi, that was an important social and political force in interwar Poland and in the early decades after the founding of the state of

Israel. The name *Mizrachi* means "eastern," signifying its physical orientation toward Palestine, but it is also an acronym for *merkaz ruhani* "spiritual center," signifying its particular vision of the Zionist project.

Among the famous figures of early religious Zionism was Rabbi Abraham Isaac Kook, or Rav Kook (1865–1935). A scion of the major Torah centers of Eastern Europe, including the great yeshiva of Volozhin (in modern Belarus), Kook moved to Ottoman Palestine to become the rabbi of the Jewish community in Jaffa. Here Kook engaged with halakhic questions that pressed on nascent religious Zionist communities in Palestine. Most importantly, the Bible (Lev. 25:1–24) demands observance of a sabbatical year. Every seventh year, farmers in the land of Israel must let their fields lie fallow and permit the poor to enter and pick whatever grows on its own. In addition to supporting the poor, the sabbatical law serves as a sign that the land of Israel, though granted to the people Israel, belongs ultimately to God. This law became more or less moot in the Middle Ages, when the Jewish presence in the land of Israel was small, and did not rely heavily on farming. But the Zionist movement preached an ideology of agriculture: the Jews' return to the land of Israel was also supposed to be a return to its soil, and through agricultural labor the people would both build up the land and be rebuilt by it. And yet, how could religious Zionist agricultural communities, living on the thinnest of margins, afford to cease work for an entire year? Kook supported the use of halakhic workarounds, especially the legal fiction of selling the land for the duration of the sabbatical year to a gentile. After World War I, when Palestine became a mandate territory under British control, Kook served first as the rabbi of Jerusalem, and then as the first Ashkenazi chief rabbi of mandatory Palestine. In 1924 he founded in Jerusalem the "Central Universal Yeshiva," or in its shortened Hebrew form, *Merkaz* ("center"), or *Merkaz ha-Rav* ("the center of the Rav"). This institution of higher Torah study began small, but in the 1960s it transformed into a leading religious Zionist institution in Israel.

Kook's theological writings inflect the spiritual legacies of medieval Jewish philosophy and mysticism in a direction that is at once modern and messianic. Consider, for example, an essay by Kook entitled "Pangs of Cleansing."[6] Here Kook attempts to account for the contemporaneous phenomenon of

6. See Ben-Zion Bokser, trans., *Abraham Isaac Kook: The Lights of Penitence, The Moral Principles, Lights of Holiness, Essays, Letters, and Poems* (New York: Paulist Press, 1978), 261–69.

atheism. With his characteristic inclination toward paradox, Kook, rather than condemning atheism as spiritual blindness, understands it as an inchoate expression of spiritual insight, and indeed as a necessary historical stage just prior to the messianic unfolding of God. In terms familiar from Maimonides and Kabbalah, Kook insists that "all the divine names, whether in Hebrew or in any other language, give us only a tiny and dull spark of the hidden light to which the soul aspires when it hears the word 'God.' Every definition of God brings about heresy, every definition is spiritual idolatry." Whereas in previous eras "the divine perception and feeling were prevalent in an enlightened state in full force," today among religious people the reigning conception of God is narrow and ungenerous. Spiritually sensitive people properly reject this conception; they appreciate that God, so defined, does not in fact exist. "And this is the atheism which is due to arise prior to the messianic liberation, when the knowledge of God is due to run dry in the household of Israel—and in the entire world." Although atheism is not, in metaphysical terms, any more precise than the conception of God that it challenges, its effect will be to "uproot the dross that separates man from the truly divine light, and in the ruins wrought by atheism will the higher knowledge of God erect her Temple." At the practical level, Kook's perspective on atheism facilitates religious Zionist identification and cooperation with their secular counterparts.

The Jewish State and Jewish Theology

The messianic framework within which Kook approached Zionism persisted among some religious Zionists past the founding of the state of Israel in 1948, and grew more fervent in the teaching of Kook's son, Rabbi Zvi Yehuda Kook, who assumed leadership of Merkaz in 1952. In the wake of the Six Day War in 1967 and then the Yom Kippur War in 1973, the younger Kook's students, following his teachings, founded Gush Emunim (Hebrew for "the Bloc of the Faithful"), a movement committed to establishing Jewish settlements in areas that had come under Israeli control in 1967. The movement was powered in part by the younger Kook's conviction that the settlement project represented an important step toward the messianic redemption. Far beyond those affiliated with this movement, at least a weak association of the state of Israel with the messianic era persists for religious Zionists in Israel and for the many synagogue communities in Israel and in the Diaspora that characterize Israel as "the first flowering of our redemption" in the prayer for the state of Israel that they recite in the sabbath morning liturgy (in the Koren siddur, 522).

But this association is weaker now than it was in the past. If it was most natural, in the period of emergent religious Zionism and in the state's tumultuous early decades, to think of the prospect of the return of Jews to a political existence in the land of Israel as the first stage of the redemption for which the Jewish people had always prayed, then it is easier now, with the passing of further decades and the assimilation of the state of Israel into ordinary geopolitical reality, to consider the state of Israel apart from messianism. Put differently, while a traditional Jew at the beginning of the twentieth century imagined only two eras, namely, the current world of exile and divine punishment and the messianic days of divine redemption and ingathering, the religious Jew today can think of an intermediate reality, one in which Jews have gathered from the four corners of the earth to rebuild a Jewish state, and yet the world is not necessarily any closer to redemption. (Secular Zionists, too, mutatis mutandis, recognize now that the existence of the state of Israel will not be the end of antisemitism or the utopian solution to the problem of Jewish life in the modern world.)

This does not in any way mean, of course, that the state of Israel is without religious significance for Jews today, in Israel and in the Diaspora; quite the contrary. Perhaps most straightforwardly, there is the simple fact that the tradition, founded on the Bible, envisions Jewish life as taking, ideally, the form of collective existence in the land of Israel. The archaeological record preserves everywhere the evidence of Jewish life in the land, from the biblical period forward; in Israel one can live a short driving distance from the tomb of the patriarchs in Hebron, the Temple Mount in Jerusalem, Elijah's Mount Carmel, and the Galilee synagogues of the Byzantine era. While the state of Israel protects its citizens' religious freedom, it also constructs a Jewish public sphere in which the weekend consists of Sabbath eve and the Sabbath (Friday and Saturday), the Jewish festivals are national holidays, the army serves only kosher food, Hebrew is an official language, the state educational curriculum offers at least basic literacy in the Bible and rabbinic literature, and so forth. The conditions of the state foster the production of an immensely vibrant Jewish culture, one that brims with meaning for the religious Jew. A Jewish state also enables collective Jewish action. Through Israel, contributions to the world in science and technology, in relief aid and the like, can become visible, in a distinctive way, as Jewish. Additionally, as noted above, rabbinic law encodes dwelling in the land of Israel as a religious value, and there are certain commandments, like the sabbatical law, that only apply in the land of Israel. These norms are far easier to observe now, within the framework of a Jewish state, than in the past.

For these reasons, and because the particular historical circumstances that drove the modern denominations to oppose Zionism at its inception no longer obtain, most religious (and secular) Jews today, in Israel and in the Diaspora, identify, often strongly, with the state of Israel. Many, indeed, deem it the fulfillment of a religious commandment to support the state of Israel and, if necessary, to die fighting on its behalf. The major Reform and Conservative rabbinic seminaries in America have campuses in Jerusalem to which they bring their students. (Likewise, the seventeenth blessing of the Amidah in the Reform liturgy now embraces Zion. In *Gates of Prayer: The New Union Prayer Book*, from 1975, the blessing concludes: "Let our eyes behold Your presence in our midst and in the midst of our people in Zion. Blessed is the Lord, whose presence gives life to Zion and all Israel.") Modern Orthodox American Jews typically spend a gap year in Israel between high school and college. With ultra-Orthodox yeshivot abounding in Israel, enjoying state support and drawing students in the hundreds and thousands from all corners of the Jewish world, even most ultra-Orthodox groups have come around to the view that a Jewish state is far more a boon for than a threat to Judaism, although ultra-Orthodox Israeli Jews still staunchly refrain, as a general rule, from enlisting in the army. The Satmar Hasidic sect is famous for persevering in the traditional ultra-Orthodox opposition to the state of Israel, on the ground that it substitutes peoplehood and even nationalism for God and the Torah as the foundation of Jewish identity. But even they, while hostile to the symbols of state, find themselves bound to Israel by the bare fact that a great many of their co-religionists live there today.

There is, however, a source of alienation from Israel that looms larger today than before, especially among young, progressive Jews in America: the decades-long conflict between Israel and the Palestinians. We will turn to this conflict in the next chapter, but here we may note that some contemporary Jewish theologians, moved in the first instance by the circumstances of the Palestinians, have come to embrace, in their way, the Satmar critique and to argue, in a modern key, for a diasporic or exilic Judaism of a sort that can also animate Jewish life in Israel itself. These theologians find that, especially in the crucible of military conflict and polarized politics, religious Zionism manifests a dangerous tendency to attribute holiness to the state and thus set up the state as an object of worship. They do not necessarily reject the conventional Zionist characterization of the exile as a period in which Jewish life and thought contracted and froze, but they believe that it is possible, in the modern world, to construct a more robust and engaged exilic Judaism.

The entwinement of Judaism with the state creates in Israel a range of novel practical and theological challenges and opportunities. Before entering into some illustrative examples, we may identify two general ways in which Judaism looks different in the Jewish state. First, just as the Enlightenment and the process of emancipation led, in the denominations that arose in its wake, to the downplaying of the ethnic element of Judaism in favor of the religious, to lesser or greater degrees, so, in the opposite direction, in Israel, where the state's Jewish character rests fundamentally not on Judaism per se but on the Jewish people, the ethnic element can become more prominent in the conceptualization of Judaism. Second, in a country like America that espouses a relatively stringent separation of the state from religion, multiple different sorts of Jewish communities can coexist with relatively little friction, and with little pressure to interact. A Jew who finds herself in disagreement with a particular Jewish community can simply steer clear of that community and attach herself to a different one with which she can identify. In Israel, however, the public sphere incorporates Judaism, and so its citizens must collectively make decisions about Judaism and bear the impact of those decisions. As a result, the prospect of conflict about Judaism always looms, and there is constant pressure to support expressions of Judaism that can unify rather than divide. Or to put the second point differently, for Israel to characterize and express itself as the Jewish state is for it to presuppose the possibility of democratic consensus on what Judaism is, and yet, perhaps now more than ever, consensus can be hard to find.

Take, for example, the Western Wall, the *Kotel* (Hebrew for "wall"). The Kotel is the western wall of the retaining structure that was built by Herod to support his expansion of the Temple Mount. For over a millennium, it has served as a place at which Jews gather to pray to God, and to mourn the temple's destruction; hence it is also known as the Wailing Wall. When

Israel took East Jerusalem from Jordan in 1967, the Kotel became a public prayer space, drawing Jewish (and non-Jewish) visitors from Israel and the world. It was a given at the time that the space should conform to the Orthodox standard, with distinct men's and women's sections separated by a divider, and that the prayer accoutrements that are traditionally the province of men—phylacteries, prayer shawls, and Torah scrolls—should only be made available in the men's section. But in recent decades, the status quo has been challenged both by adherents of the non-traditional denominations from America and by progressive Israelis. There have been halting attempts at a solution through the creation of a third, egalitarian prayer space, but the matter remains controversial.

Even more controversy surrounds the question, Who is a Jew? This question can provoke heated debate in America, but the stakes are higher in Israel, in part because Israel offers Jews from the Diaspora an expedited naturalization process, under a legal regime known as the Law of Return. ("Return" here indicates the emigration of Diaspora Jews to their ancestral homeland. Such emigration is also characterized as *aliyah*, literally "ascent.") Who counts as a Jew for this purpose? The case of Brother Daniel is of particular interest. Brother Daniel, born Oswald Rufeisen, was a Polish Jew and a Holocaust survivor. Prior to the war he participated in a Zionist youth association, and during the war he passed as a Pole and was able in this role to save many Jewish lives. Eventually he found safety in a convent, where he underwent a sincere conversion to Catholicism. After the war he became a Carmelite friar, with the intention of eventually relocating to the Carmelite monastery in Israel. When the opportunity to do so arose, in 1957, Brother Daniel applied for Israeli citizenship under the Law of Return, on the ground that, though he had converted to Catholicism, he did not think of himself as having thereby abandoned his Judaism. In a 1962 decision, the Supreme Court rejected his application, determining that, having converted to a different religion, he no longer counted as a Jew for the purpose of the law. This decision was encoded into Knesset legislation in 1970. Note that the Supreme Court decision should not be understood as insisting on a religious characterization of Jewish identity for the purpose of the Law of Return; an altogether secular Jew is undoubtedly eligible to make aliyah under its aegis. The point, rather, is that the law does not recognize as Jewish someone who proactively chooses to attach himself to a different religious group.

More recently, the question of Jewish identity has come to the fore in connection with the aliyah from the former Soviet Union in the 1990s. Under the 1970 clarification of the Law of Return, an individual with at least one Jewish grandparent is eligible to apply for citizenship under the Law of Return. This criterion clashes with the traditional matrilineal definition of a Jew, according to which one is a Jew if and only if one's mother is Jewish. (On the traditional definition, the only grandparent on whom one's status depends is one's mother's mother.) Due to the high rate of intermarriage among Jews in the Soviet Union, the Soviet aliyah brought to Israel a large number of individuals who became citizens under the Law of Return, and who understood themselves to be Jewish, but whom traditional Judaism does not recognize as Jewish. Now, two generations later, this group is much larger, and more or less fully integrated, from a social perspective, into Jewish Israel, and yet traditionally observant Israeli Jews still cannot recognize them as Jewish and will not marry them. Religious Zionists concerned to maintain the coherence of Israeli Judaism look at this situation with concern.

An obvious solution to this conundrum is conversion. By law, authority over conversion in Israel lies more or less exclusively with the Chief Rabbinate, which is a firmly Orthodox institution. As we noted in chapter 13, the central component of the traditional conversion process is acceptance of the yoke of the commandments. And herein lies the challenge: the vast majority of the population in question, while proud to identify as Jewish, has no interest in committing to observance of the commandments, or to the lengthy preliminary process of study of and training in the commandments. One approach to this challenge is to muddle through with a "good enough" approach: let the potential convert demonstrate some modicum of interest, and the officiating rabbi will wink at the case and give it his stamp of approval.

But some prominent Orthodox authorities have broached an alternative, more radical response. The traditional conversion process is the creation of the rabbis of the Talmud. In the Bible, by contrast, a foreigner is assimilated to Israel not, per se, by accepting the commandments, but simply by uprooting herself from her native land and joining the people of Israel in the land of Israel. The paradigmatic biblical convert is Ruth, the heroine of the biblical book named for her. A Moabite, she marries a Judean from a family that had emigrated to Moab on account of famine. Her husband dies, and when the famine ends, her mother-in-law, Naomi, decides to return to home, to the tribal land of Judah. Out of love or loyalty to her deceased husband and to Naomi, Ruth insists on going with her and remaking her life among the people of Judah: "Ruth replied, 'Do not urge me to leave you, to turn back and not follow you. For wherever you go, I will go; wherever you lodge, I will lodge; your people shall be my people, and your God my God. Where you die, I will die, and there I will be buried'" (Ruth 1:16–17).

The starting point and centerpiece of Ruth's "conversion" is her commitment to Naomi and to Naomi's people. She also pledges herself to Naomi's God, but only as a corollary of these interpersonal commitments. Not surprisingly, the rabbis (Bavli Yebamot 47b) rewrite Ruth's declaration in the image of their different conversion model, so that each phrase in the above verses indicates acceptance of a particular commandment that Naomi herself, as a Jew, observes. Thus, for example, when Ruth says, "wherever you go, I will go," she is responding to Naomi's admonition that, as a Jew, she must adhere to sabbath restrictions on travel. Likewise, "wherever you lodge, I will lodge," indicates Ruth's acceptance of the prohibition, on grounds of modesty, against being in a secluded place with a man other than one's husband.

On the bold view of some religious Zionist rabbis approaching the circumstances of the Soviet aliyah, the existence of a Jewish state demands a return, at least within the state, to the biblical model of conversion. The rabbinic model was appropriate for the Diaspora, when Jews defined themselves against their Christian and Muslim neighbors by virtue of their religious practices. But in a state of the Jewish people, the biblical model is more apt. If a person from the Soviet Union finds in her Jewish ancestry and her sense of Jewish identity sufficient grounds for her to move to Israel and throw in her lot with the Jewish state, then she should count as Jewish for all purposes, even if she does not take on observance of the commandments.

Conclusion

I am tempted to conclude this chapter by asserting that it is impossible to overestimate the importance of the state of Israel for Jewish life today, and for the development of Jewish theology. There is justification for such a rhetorical flourish, as the state of Israel is now, and has for some time been, the world center of Jewish life and Jewish theology. Today, as of old, the end-of-days vision of Isaiah and Micah can be asserted truly: "For from Zion shall go forth Torah" (Isa. 2:3; Mic. 4:2). And yet it is in fact possible to overestimate the importance of the state of Israel for Jewish life and Jewish theology. So large does it loom in the Jewish world today that one might be led to follow the lead of some early Zionists in "negating the Diaspora," and deeming it of no worth. This would be a mistake. Diaspora Jewish communities, first and foremost the American Jewish community, remain vibrant centers of Torah study and religious innovation, whose impact is felt in Israel. Nor is this by chance. The very different social circumstances of Jewish communities within and outside of Israel mean that each will arrive at different insights as they puzzle through the continuing challenge of how to be Jewish in the modern world.

Further Inquiry

For the political circumstances of Jews at the eve of and into modernity, see Jacob Katz, *Out of the Ghetto: The Social Background of Jewish Emancipation, 1770–1870* (Syracuse University Press, 1998). On Mendelsohn's thought, see Michah Gottlieb, *Faith and Freedom: Moses Mendelssohn's Theological-Political Thought* (New York: Oxford University Press, 2011). For the ways in which Judaism in Western Europe adapted itself to the category of religion, whose paradigmatic member is Christianity, see Leora Batnitzky, *How Judaism Became a Religion: An Introduction to Modern Jewish Thought* (Princeton: Princeton University Press, 2013). On the Haredi concept of *daas Torah*, see Benjamin Brown, "Jewish Political Theology: The Doctrine of *Daat Torah* as a Case Study," *Harvard Theological Review* 107 (2014): 255–89. My discussion of early ultra-Orthodox perspectives on Zionism depends mainly on Aviezer Ravitzky, *Messianism, Zionism, and Jewish Religious Radicalism* (Chicago: University of Chicago Press, 1996). On the thought of Rav Kook, see Yehuda Mirsky, *Rav Kook: Mystic in a Time of Revolution* (New Haven: Yale University Press, 2014). For a detailed, insider survey of the laws of the sabbatical year in Israel, see Yosef Zvi Rimon, *Shemita: Halacha Mimekorah—From the Sources to Practical Halacha* (New York: Ktav, 2021). On the Brother Daniel case, see Bernard S. Jackson, "Brother Daniel: The Construction of Jewish Identity in the Israeli Supreme Court," *Review internationale de semiotique juridique* 6 (1993): 115–46. The organization most associated with the attempt to enable non-traditional forms of prayer at the Western Wall is "Women of the Wall"; see their website, at https://womenofthewall.org.il/. My discussion of conversion in the state of Israel draws from Shlomo Brody, "Wink-Wink, Win-Win?" *Jewish Review of Books* (Winter 2020). On halakhic and theological trends in contemporary Religious Zionism in Israel, see Yair Ettinger, *Fraying: The Disputes Unraveling Religious Zionists* (New Milford, CT: Toby Press, 2023). Two recent attempts by American Jewish scholars to argue for a diasporic Judaism are Jonathan Boyarin and Daniel Boyarin, *Powers of Diaspora: Two Essays on the Relevance of Jewish Culture* (Minneapolis: University of Minnesota Press, 2002), and Shaul Magid, *The Necessity of Exile: Essays from a Distance* (Brooklyn: Ayin Press, 2023). An Israeli voice famous for warning against the instinct to attribute holiness to the state is Yeshayahu Leibowitz; see his collected essays, *Judaism, Human Values, and the Jewish State* (Cambridge: Harvard University Press, 1995).

●

1. Think about the implications of the revival of Hebrew as a native language for the experience of Israeli Jews. Even as Jews of the Diaspora sometimes learn Hebrew as a second language, it generally remains for them a foreign tongue, with which they engage chiefly in the contexts of prayer and Torah study. Thus, while in the Diaspora, Hebrew traditionally was, and largely still is, a means of reinforcing the distinction between the holy and the profane, in Israel it is a site for their intermingling. How different is the experience of praying in one's native language from praying in a foreign language? What does it feel like to conduct business negotiations in the language of prayer? Compare to debates in the Catholic world over the Latin Mass.

2. Mordechai Kaplan, the founder of Reconstructionist Judaism, critiqued the Reform Judaism of his day for characterizing Judaism as a purely religious category. In an essay, "Toward a Reconstruction of Judaism," published in 1927 in *Menorah Journal*, he observed: "Logical consistency demands that if Judaism is to be a religious philosophy, adherence to it should be entirely a matter of choice and not of birth," and yet Reform Judaism did not go this far, but retained the traditional notion of Judaism as something into which one is born. Reform Judaism in America today has returned to an embrace of peoplehood, in part due to the

impact of the state of Israel, but, as noted in chapter 1, it has also, in response to intermarriage, introduced a definition of who is a Jew that does in fact incorporate choice, though it also holds on to birth: outside of the case of conversion, a person is Jewish if either parent is Jewish, as long as she actively identifies with the Jewish people. Reflect on the complex confluence of different factors in the balancing of the ethnic and religious elements in the development of Reform Judaism.

— *Chapter 17* —

State Power and Theology

WITH ZIONISM CAME THE ASPIRATION FOR, and with the founding of the state of Israel the realization of, a return of the Jewish people to sovereignty, and thus to state power, after a gap of some two thousand years. As detailed in the previous chapter, there were sound practical reasons for pursuing such a return (among them, violent antisemitism), as well as a rich theological basis (inter alia, in the biblical vision of a self-governed people on its land). And yet the assumption of power came, inevitably, with a moral cost. A people that had been condemned and privileged to keep its hands clean would now have the privilege and burden of getting them dirty. Rabbinic leaders in the orbit of emergent Zionism knew the danger, of course, confronted as they were with the immensely bloody wars of the late nineteenth and early twentieth centuries. Some accepted it as the necessary cost of the Zionist project, while others responded in different ways.

Rabbi Aaron Shmuel Tamares (1869–1931), who lived and worked around Belarus and Lithuania, was initially drawn to Zionism, and served as a representative at the Fourth Zionist World Congress in London in 1900. But soon afterward he became a critic of Zionism. He insisted instead that Judaism's proper realm is the spirit, that Jews ought to work through peaceful means for the improvement of the world. In his autobiography, composed around 1926, Tamares traced the roots of his pacificist turn to the Russo-Turkish War, the very war that drew Eliezer Ben Yehuda to the cause of Zionism.

> During the Russo-Turkish War, a [gentile] neighbor received notice that his son had been killed in battle. The fallen soldier's mother wept bitterly at the news—and the little Jewish boy [i.e., Tamares himself] wept with her. From that moment on, the boy's consciousness was consumed by an awareness of the depravity of war. The same woman had a painting from the war hanging in her

> house, which depicted Russian soldiers attacking the Turks with bayonets. The boy used to stand glued to the image for hours on end, bewildered by the idea that human beings could become accustomed to such acts, and wondering how the soldiers could endure such dreadful circumstances. He was also quite astonished that the bereaved mother could tolerate having such an image in her home, compelling her always to look upon the cursed event which had left so many mothers bereaved.[1]

In the continuation, Tamares writes that, having arrived at the view that the world must be repaired "not by means of bombs but rather with 'enlightenment' and moral education," he reasoned: "Who, then, is more fit for this task than the People of the Prophets and the Tannaim [that is, the rabbis of the era of Rabbi Akiva], a people whose history is fraught with martyrology?"

Rabbi Abraham Isaac Kook featured in the last chapter as among the most important of the early religious Zionists. He, too, was troubled by the notion that a Jewish state would mean the entanglement of Judaism with politics, but his Hegelian, messianic orientation offered a solution. Writing in 1921, soon after "the war to end all wars," Kook suggested that the reemergence of the Jewish people into political life at just this moment, when war was coming to an end, represented the work of providence.

> It is not meet for Jacob to engage in political life at a time when statehood requires bloody ruthlessness and demands a talent for evil. At the beginning of our history we were granted only the foundation, the minimum that was necessary to establish a nation. After our race was weaned, our political sovereignty was destroyed, and we were dispersed among the peoples and sown in the depths of the soil, "till the time of singing is come, and the voice of the turtledove is heard in the land" (Song of Songs 2:12).[2]

Of course, subsequent history proved Kook's messianic hope premature, and the state of Israel has found it necessary to engage in conflicts for much of its history, and to maintain a universal draft.

1. Ri J. Turner, "Biography of 'One of the Sensitive Rabbis': Part 1," *In Geveb: A Journal of Yiddish Studies*, April 2017, 5.

2. Arthur Hertzberg, ed., *Zionist Idea*, 422.

While the conflicts of the first decades of the Israeli state were chiefly with surrounding countries, the heart of the matter is Israel's relationship with the native Arab inhabitants of the land, the Palestinians. The outbreak of the First Intifada in 1987 thrust this relationship into the international spotlight, and there it has remained until today, even as it intersects and overlaps with other conflicts, chiefly, today, with Iran and its allies. As I write these words, Israel is engaged in a war against the governing Palestinian body in the Gaza Strip, Hamas, in the wake of a barbaric attack by Hamas on October 7, 2023. In the context of this conflict, Yeshivat Har Etzion published a video taken in Gaza that bears on our topic.[3] Yeshivat Har Etzion is one of the original *hesder* ("arrangement") yeshivot. Ordinarily, Israelis are drafted after high school for roughly three years of army service. But under a formal arrangement coordinated with the army, a high school graduate can instead enroll in a track in which he spends roughly three and a half years studying in a yeshiva, and one and a half years in the army. (The religious Zionist community also originated a program of *mechinot*, or preparatory academies, that high school graduates can enroll in for one year prior to regular army service. Mechinot enable students to engage in the religious values, challenges, and questions implicated in army service, and teach civics more broadly.)

In the video, two soldiers in full military gear sit on salon chairs amid the rubble in Gaza. In civilian life they are students of Torah affiliated with Yeshivat Har Etzion, and they have met to discuss the weekly Torah reading: the famous story of Jacob's theft of Esau's blessing. With his arms covered by goat hair so that he would appear like the hairy Esau, Jacob approached his father, the blind Isaac. Isaac, his suspicion evidently aroused by the voice of the person before him, felt his skin, and exclaimed in puzzlement: "The voice is the voice of Jacob, and the arms are the arms of Esau" (Gen. 27:22). Traditionally, this verse has been understood to express the essence of Judaism: the imperial power—Esau, who is a figure for Rome, and by extension, for whatever foreign kingdom rules over Israel—embraces violence, but Jacob's power lies in his voice, in the sound of prayer and Torah study. The soldiers in this video assume the traditional opposition between violence and voice,

3. See https://www.youtube.com/watch?v=CZNasLKYpJU. My discussion of this video and of Rav Kook's comments after World War I is drawn from an article that I wrote for the University of Notre Dame's *Church Life Journal*: https://churchlifejournal.nd.edu/articles/the-church-the-jewish-people-and-the-war/.

but give it a novel and striking spin. Isaac, they suggest, knew that it was Jacob who stood before him, and in fact he wished from the outset to give the blessing to Jacob. But Isaac knew that Jacob would not be a fit heir until he was willing to take on the arms of Esau. He knew that Jacob would not be able to realize the blessing—God's promise to Abraham of a nation and a land—unless he was prepared to fight for it with the arms of Esau. Even as a religious Zionist might think that the setting chosen for the video is in poor taste, as insufficiently sensitive to the suffering of innocent Gazans, she would surely endorse the basic perspective voiced by these scholar-soldiers, that violence is an unfortunate necessity of statehood, and that Judaism permits and indeed demands the exercise of violence to the degree that it is necessary. Of course, the hard question, in this war and in all others, is the practical application of this standard. Israeli society, in conversation with the Jewish tradition, has long devoted careful attention to this question, at places like Yeshivat Har Etzion and at other institutions, public and private, religious and secular.

Below we will survey Christian and Jewish theological approaches to Jewish power, first and foremost in relation to the Palestinians. More broadly, we will chart the range of perspectives in Christian theology today to the Holy Land and to the state of Israel. As an entry point into these topics, we will take up the distinct but overlapping question of Christian and Jewish theological approaches to war. Our discussion in this chapter hearkens back to the survey of Christian teaching about Judaism in the first chapters of the book. In chapter 5, capping this survey, we reflected on how a post-supersessionist Christianity should read Scripture, and how it should construe the ritual law and the mission to the Jews. Here we consider Zionism and the state of Israel as another issue confronting the post-supersessionist church: How should a Christian who believes in the continuity of God's relationship with the Jewish people think about Zionism and the modern state of Israel?

War in Christian and Jewish Theology

Christian approaches to war divide, in broad strokes, into two camps. The first, more mainstream camp recognizes a category of just war in which a Christian may or indeed should take part. The other, associated with specific denominations, including the Quakers and the Anabaptists/Mennonites, but defended also by assorted theologians on common Christian grounds, insists on pacifism: a faithful Christian should never take up the sword, no matter how just the cause. Without entering into the details of these positions, or adjudicating between them, we may note that proponents of the first approach generally agree with those of the second that the New Testament furnishes a substantial basis for critique of war, and that it does so, in important ways, through contrast with the Old Testament. In the Sermon on the Mount, Jesus famously rejects the rule of "an eye for an eye and a tooth for a tooth" (cf. Exod. 21:24; Lev. 24:20) and calls for turning the other cheek (Matt. 5:39), or the "transcendence of violence through loving the enemy."[4] More importantly, Jesus embodies in himself the path of non-violence. He begins his ministry by overcoming Satan's offer of "all the kingdoms of the world and their splendor" (Matt. 4:8). When Jesus is betrayed and arrested, a companion strikes at the high priest's servant with his sword, but Jesus rebukes him: "Put your sword back in its place, for all who draw the sword will die by the sword" (Matt. 26:52). The culmination of Jesus's ministry comes with the cross, which represents the ultimate mark of Jesus's deviation from the preexisting messianic model—the model directly emerging from the Old Testament—in which the messiah's coming means victory over Israel's enemies.

In application to the relationship between Judaism and Christianity, the implication that appears to follow from these observations—that the New Testament encourages a more negative stance on war in Christianity than in Judaism—requires nuancing. The gap between Judaism and Christianity on this point is real, and bound up with the more otherworldly orientation of Christianity, but it should not be exaggerated. Christianity, too, has its just war theorists. Moreover, some of the New Testament passages that urge the "transcendence of violence" do so in continuity with the Old Testament. In Romans 12, for example, when Paul urges his readers to "bless those who persecute you" and to "not repay anyone evil with evil," he argues for this position by insisting, on the basis of Deuteronomy 32:35, that vengeance belongs to God, not to human beings. From the other side, Judaism, too, can marshal abundant resources, from the Hebrew Bible and especially from post-biblical literature, in opposition to militarism. We noted above the rabbis' association of Jacob/Israel with the voice of prayer and study, to the exclusion of the hand of violence, and their literature includes many teachings extolling peace.

4. The quotation is from Richard Hays, *The Moral Vision of the New Testament* (New York: HarperOne, 1996), 322. Hays offers a trenchant formulation of the pacifist position.

Nevertheless, recognizing a more prominent pacifist strain in Christianity, we can easily see how the sources of pacifism in the Christian tradition might be deployed by Christians to challenge specific Israeli political and military decisions, or even Zionism itself. Perhaps the most theologically ambitious critique of Zionism along Christian pacifist lines is that of the Mennonite John Howard Yoder.[5] Yoder locates the source of Jesus's renunciation of the sword in a much older Jewish pacifism that crystallized in Jeremiah's response to the Babylonian exile. For Yoder, rabbinic Judaism, insofar as it embraced quietism and remained apart from imperial power, came closer to the realization of Jesus's pacifist gospel than any Christian community in the post-Constantinian medieval world. Naturally, Yoder construes Zionism as a betrayal of rabbinic Judaism, a rejection of the call to stand apart from the world. Yoder recognized the audaciousness of his approach, which, while the contrary of supersessionism in the traditional sense, does seem to hearken back to traditional supersessionism insofar as it purports to tell Jews what their theological commitments ought to be.

And yet, insofar as Christians do recognize themselves as living in relation to a Jewish people that remains covenantally bound to the God whom Christians also worship, as belonging to a church that in its ideal form encompasses both Jews and themselves qua gentiles, and insofar as Jews welcome this new, post-supersessionist Christian perspective on Judaism, then it should be possible for Jews and Christians to speak to each other as theological siblings. Yes, they should be supportive of each other. Yes, they should act with cognizance of their complex past, which calls upon Christians especially to be sensitive to a long history of violent persecution of Jews by Christians. Christians must also, for this reason, be especially attentive to the fact that contemporary antisemitism often expresses or justifies itself as anti-Zionism. Jews and Christians should also be cognizant of their real differences, and the legitimacy of these differences. With all these qualifications in mind, they should nevertheless also, in principle, be able to call each other to account, and to suggest to each other better versions of themselves. We will expand on the contours of this stance below, but for now let me note that, while Yoder's position is especially challenging for most Jews, insofar as it calls the very notion of a Jewish state into theological question, it is saved, as it were, by Yoder's

5. See his posthumously published book, *The Jewish-Christian Schism Revisited* (Grand Rapids: Eerdmans, 2003).

methodological self-awareness, and, even more importantly, by the fact that it also challenges most Christians, who reject the absolute pacifist position.

In this respect, the common reflex among some churches, to respond immediately to outbreaks of violence between Israel and its neighbors with a formulaic call for peace, can, in its way, confront Jews as more problematic than Yoder's comprehensive rejection of Zionism. A call for peace is the easy response, and seemingly non-controversial; no one, after all, is against peace. And yet, precisely because it is automatic, precisely because it does not challenge Christians themselves, such a call can, in context, and from the perspective of the relationship between the Jewish people and a post-supersessionist church, be theologically insensitive. It can represent a failure to account for this relationship, and for the ways in which the Jewish people approach the conflict with a distinct set of stakes and, in principle, a distinctly Jewish theological calculus.

Christian Zionism

Having encountered, with Yoder, one among the range of Christian positions on Zionism and the state of Israel, let us turn now to others. As one might expect, the predominant premodern Christian perspectives on the relationship of the Jewish people to the land of Israel were supersessionist. According to the third-century CE Syriac Christian author Aphrahat, the failure of the Jewish revolt against Rome was God's mete punishment for the crime of deicide: "After the killing of Christ the King, Jerusalem became a desolation, and shall never be inhabited again; and until the fulfillment of the decree it dwells in destruction."[6] The notion of the restoration of Jewish sovereignty to Zion is, of course, precluded by the Augustinian view that the Jewish people, as Cain, are condemned by God to eternal wandering. A different approach that likewise severs the connection between the Jewish people and the land of Israel is the allegorical one, whose roots we find already in the New Testament, and which becomes well established in later centuries. On this approach, propounded by the third-century Christian thinker Origen, God's land promise to Abraham

6. The text is from *Demonstrations* 22, as translated in Robert Murray, *Symbols of Church and Kingdom: A Study in Early Syriac Tradition* (New York: T&T Clark, 2006), 58.

did not in the first place concern a specific plot of soil, but signifies, rather, a beatific state of dwelling with God, a heavenly Jerusalem. Christians in antiquity also transformed the historical land of Israel into a site of Christian pilgrimage, to mark the places where Christ and his disciples had walked the earth in the past, and where, in the future, Christ would return to establish a millennial (i.e., thousand-year) kingdom.

This vision of a future kingdom of Christ in earthly Jerusalem anticipates, though very partially, an important modern Christian perspective on the state of Israel to which we now turn: Christian Zionism. The term "Christian Zionism" could in principle refer to any sort of commitment to Zionism rooted in Christian theology, but it is commonly used, more narrowly, to describe an evangelical approach to Judaism and to Zionism that crystallized in the nineteenth century and persists, in changed form, to today. Christian Zionist theology depends on a plain-sense biblical literalism. God promised the land of Israel to Abraham's descendants, and the prophets all envisioned the return of the people Israel to their land; therefore, a Christian ought to support such a return. On the basis of Revelation 20, among other biblical texts, Christian Zionists of the nineteenth century, most famously John Nelson Darby (1800–1882), correlated the ingathering of Israel to Christ's second coming, so that Israel's restoration became a precondition for the arrival of the eschaton. Christians seeking to return the Jewish people to Zion were also moved by the poverty and persecution endured by European Jews. In the "Blackstone Memorial," an 1891 petition that the Christian Zionist William Blackstone (1841–1935) submitted to President Benjamin Harrison to gain the United States' aid in settling Russian Jews in Ottoman Palestine, he offered that this was "an appropriate time for all nations, and especially the Christian nations of Europe, to show kindness to Israel. A million of exiles, by their terrible suffering, are piteously appealing to our sympathy, justice, and humanity. Let us now restore them to the land of which they were so cruelly despoiled by our Roman ancestors."[7] Such kindness would, on the Christian Zionist view, redound to Christians' own benefit, for surely God will look kindly on those who help "God's chosen people, 'who are beloved' (Rom. 11:28), and dear unto Him as 'the apple of His eye' (Zech. 2:8)." The last quotation is from Black-

7. A scanned copy of this "memorial" is available online through the National Library of Israel: See https://www.nli.org.il/en/books/NNL_ALEPH990012469030205171/NLI.

stone's most famous work, *Jesus Is Coming*, published in 1878.[8] It is striking that a combination of biblical literalism and charity led Christian Zionists, under the banner of Romans 11, to a certain embrace of the Jewish people to which the Catholic Church would arrive—with its own very different theological commitments—roughly a century later. Among the important differences: Christian Zionists of the time were also eager to see, and made sustained efforts to secure, the conversion of Jews to Christianity, for their conversion, too, just like their return to Zion, was a necessary component of the eschatological drama.

Christian Zionists today do not necessarily embrace a millenarian perspective, that is, they are not necessarily motivated by the prospect of hastening Christ's second coming. More prominent is the theological commitment to the Jews as God's chosen people. Among the biblical verses that feature especially prominent for Christian Zionist theology today, beside Zechariah 2:8, quoted above, are Genesis 12:3 (from God's initial words to Abraham) and Psalm 122:6:

> I will bless those who bless you, and the one who curses you I will curse, and in you all the families of the earth shall be blessed.

> Pray for the peace of Jerusalem: "May they prosper who love you."

These verses, as construed by Christian Zionists, call on gentiles to support the Jewish people, as Abraham's descendants, and Jerusalem, or the state of Israel, as the homeland of the Jewish people, and promise that God will reward them with blessing and prosperity for doing so.

Let me take note of two interrelated blind spots that theological critics of Christian Zionism identify in its perspective; they will be echoed below when we turn to other Christian perspectives on Zionism and the Jewish state. First, for all their focus on Christ's second coming, Christian Zionists make too little of Christ's first coming. Genesis 12:3 and Psalm 122:6 concern gentiles in general, but Christians are not just gentiles. They are gentiles who have been brought into relation with the God of Israel through baptism into

8. See https://archive.org/details/jesusiscoming00blacgoog/page/n3/mode/2up. The quotation is from 162.

Christ's crucifixion and resurrection. This does not of course mean—the post-supersessionist Christian will grant and insist—that Christians replace the Jewish people, but surely it does mean that Christians relate to God, and to the Jewish people, within a framework more nuanced and more collaborative than that envisioned in Genesis 12:3 and Psalm 122:6. Second, critics charge Christian Zionists with ignoring other relevant biblical norms, in particular justice and goodness. Of course, Israeli society manifests justice and goodness in ways that other societies do, and in its own distinctive ways, but insofar as the policies of the state are unjust toward and inflict violence on others, first and foremost Palestinians, they violate these norms. Likewise, the church has a special care obligation toward Palestinian Christians. For critics of Christian Zionism, these considerations must, in application to contemporary Middle East politics, nuance a Christian's position on Israel.

Palestinian Liberation Theology

At the opposite extreme from Christian Zionism, and its most vocal critic, is Palestinian Liberation Theology (PLT). PLT is one instantiation of liberation theology, a direction in modern Christianity that first crystallized among post-Vatican II Catholics in Latin America and that insists on attentiveness to the ways in which sin, and specifically oppression of the poor and the vulnerable, can become a systemic feature of social and political systems. For liberation theology, a Christian's obligation to combat sin and to tend to the poor is not exhausted by evangelization efforts and charity assistance directed at individuals. Christians must also undertake organized efforts to transform existing social and political structures and to make them more just.

For Palestinian Liberation theologians like Naim Ateek, a Palestinian and an Anglican priest, the relevant unjust society is Israel, insofar as it uprooted hundreds of thousands of Palestinians from their land in 1948 (Israel's War of Independence, the Palestinians' Nakba, or "catastrophe") and continues, in different ways, to reject claims arising from this displacement, to usurp more land, and to frustrate Palestinian attempts at statehood, often by violent means. The charges that PLT lays against Israel are, of course, the subject of much controversy; supporters of Israel contest some of its historical claims, and argue that the greater share of blame for Palestinian suffering lies with rejectionist Palestinian leaders, with Palestinian and other terror groups that have killed and wounded thousands of Israeli civilians, and with hostile Middle Eastern countries that have funded these groups or have directly waged or threatened war against Israel. We will not adjudicate these disputes here, though we must appreciate the absolute importance of getting the facts and the contextual considerations right. The more a theological position rests, like PLT, on specific factual assertions, the more a Christian who is weighing it must carefully test those assertions.

A central observation of PLT is that Jesus died on the cross as an inhabitant of Roman Palestine—as a Palestinian of sorts—and at the hands of an occupying power; thus, PLT characterizes Jesus in a way that makes his suffering immediately applicable to the contemporary circumstances of Palestinians in relation to Israel. While, as noted in chapter 15, assimilation to Jesus's suffering is one of the great spiritual gifts available to Christians, and thus of course to Palestinian Christians too, the perspective articulated by PLT, framing in the way that it does the specific historical circumstances of Jesus's ministry, raises concern in a number of ways. First, the characterization of Jesus as a "Palestinian" depends on overlooking the difference between contemporary Palestinians, who are Arab Muslims and Christians, and the inhabitants of Roman Palestine in Jesus's time, who were non-Arab Jews. It thus threatens to obscure Jesus's Jewishness and lend fuel to the contemporary antisemitic charge that Ashkenazi Jews are not genealogically related to ancient Jews but are rather ethnically European. Second, the association of the Roman crucifiers of Jesus with the modern state of Israel recalls and threatens to revive the ancient anti-Jewish charge of deicide. Finally, the same association assumes that the state of Israel is an occupying power, a colonizer, a characterization that has an element of truth in it but represents a substantial and dangerous oversimplification.

Some Jews draw from the resources of their own tradition to act as vocal advocates for Palestinians. Some such Jews are Zionist, and some are not. Among the latter is Jewish Voice for Peace (JVP), which identifies itself as a "progressive Jewish anti-Zionist organization" dedicated to "solidarity with the Palestinian freedom struggle."[9] JVP understands such solidarity, and such opposition to Zionism, to be demanded by the values of Judaism. One of the

9. See https://www.jewishvoiceforpeace.org/about/#mission.

co-founders of the JVP Rabbinical Council, Rabbi Brant Rosen, is also the rabbi of Tzedek Chicago, a synagogue community dedicated to promoting a "universalist Jewish identity" that focuses on "the Torah's repeated teachings to stand with the oppressed and to call out the oppressor." It rejects Zionism on the ground that "an ethnic Jewish nation state in historic Palestine resulted in an injustice against the Palestinian people," one that continues to this day. It instead works toward "a future that includes full civil and human rights for all who live in the land—Jews and non-Jews alike."[10]

This position remains marginal among Jews in America today, most of whom are committed to the notion of Israel as a Jewish state, albeit one that protects the rights of every individual citizen. Religious Jews in the mainstream broadly agree that the Torah obligates Jews, in relation to Palestinians as to all human beings, to combat oppression, to refrain from discrimination, and to pursue peace. But they contend that these obligations do not preclude the existence of a Jewish state, that a Jewish state is desirable and indeed necessary for all the reasons described in the previous chapter, and that Israeli society, as a new permutation of Jewish tradition, manifests distinctive, admirable virtues. While internally variegated, the mainstream generally recognizes an obligation to stand with Israel as an extension of the general Jewish obligation to stand with fellow Jews, and especially when they are beleaguered. Whatever criticisms of Israel a Jew may have (and he may have many), he should, according to the mainstream, voice them from this standpoint of identification.

Intermediate Positions

Among the range of Christian perspectives on the state of Israel that recognize and seek to balance different and sometimes competing theological considerations, we may take, as an example, the view that Rowan Williams, an Anglican bishop and the former Archbishop of Canterbury, articulated in a 2004 speech to a PLT audience.[11] Williams begins with God's covenant with

10. See https://www.tzedekchicago.org/our-values.

11. Williams's speech can be found on his website: http://rowanwilliams.archbishopofcanterbury.org/articles.php/1840/lecture-to-the-5th-international-sabeel-conference-holy-land-and-holy-people-jerusalem.html.

Israel, which, embracing the post-supersessionist approach rooted in Romans 9–11, he takes to persist. Williams asks: What is the covenant "thought to be *for* in the Hebrew Scriptures," that is, what is its purpose? He finds that Israel "is called to be the *paradigm nation*, the example held up to all nations of how a people lives in obedience to God and justice with one another." God does not give the Jewish people the land of Israel outright, but "leases" it to them for the purpose of creating a society marked by exemplary wisdom and justice. Thus, Israel's identity is "missionary": "it is to manifest not God's supreme and arbitrary power in choosing and shaping a nation, but God's wisdom and justice as the pattern for human society."

Williams insists that Christianity's theological commitment to the existence of the Jewish people means that Christians should likewise be committed to the existence of Israel, as a guarantee of the Jewish people's existence in light of antisemitism. From a theological perspective, the state of Israel, because it was founded on the ashes of the Holocaust, serves as a "warning against the nightmarish extinction of political morality in modern totalitarianism." But Israel is called upon, by the circumstances of its birth and by the biblical vision that supports it, to integrate the moral vision underlying this warning into its way of life on the land. And yet this project is threatened, for Williams, by Israel's failure adequately to recognize and respond, so far as it can, to the just claims of Palestinians.

For Williams, insofar as Christians support the state of Israel on theological grounds, they have an obligation to hold Israel accountable to the moral vision inherent in those grounds. Through Jesus, Christians join with the Jews in the task of cultivating wisdom and justice, and "in the light of that, they have the freedom to call each other to account, despite their differences." Williams concedes that, when it comes to the squaring of accounts, the historical deficit lies on the Christian side, accrued through centuries of anti-Jewish discrimination and violence. Yet today, with the church having forsworn its anti-Jewish past, and with the Jewish people having reentered the realm of politics, critique in the opposite direction can become necessary. "It is essentially a matter of treating Jewish people as adults who are responsible for how they act out the calling they proclaim—not as perpetually damaged people who are too weak to be challenged, too wounded to be responsible."

Williams's perspective can be praised for its nuance, though he overlooks the robust and sophisticated culture of internal critique in Israeli society.

Theologically, too, his first step represents something of a misstep. In immediately seeking out the purpose of God's covenant with Israel, he reduces the relationship entirely to a means, a mechanism for the production of a paradigm of wisdom and justice that can serve as an example to the world. Surely the covenant does envision such an ideal result, but the Bible presents God's relationship with Israel as an end in itself, in the same way that, while a marriage typically envisions a future in which the spouses enable each other to become their best selves, and together raise kind and considerate children, the marriage is not constituted by nor dependent on this future. It rather rests, as God's relationship with Israel rests, on love. By reducing the covenant to a means, Williams ends up putting too much pressure on the end. The society that he seeks in the land of Israel is arguably beyond what can reasonably be achieved in the imperfect world within which even a nation seeking to be exemplary must operate.

A balancing approach similar to Williams's is developed within a Jewish framework by the Israeli scholar Uriel Simon.[12] For Simon, the patriarch Abraham offers the key to understanding the relationship between the Jewish people and the land of Israel. As we learn in Genesis 11–12, Abraham is not native to the land of Canaan; rather, he is promised it by God. The Jewish people are thus bound to the land of Israel not by a claim of autochthony but by divinely ordained destiny. The strength of this bond of destiny lies in the fact that the people's connection to the land can never be altogether severed; the land of Israel is always the future of the Jewish people, even when they are in exile. The weakness of the bond lies in the fact that actual residence on the land depends on adherence to God's demand for righteousness, and yet, life on the land can produce complacency and injustice. It is therefore vital, counsels Simon, for the Jewish people on their land to keep in mind that the "pendulum movement between exile and redemption, which has been our lot through our long history, has not necessarily reached its end. It could, God forbid, recur." The best hope for staving off exile is to recognize it as a possible future.

Both of these "intermediate" or balancing positions, Williams's and Simon's, center on theological interpretation of the biblical land promise, which for them grounds a calling for the state of Israel to be an exceptional state, a sign of righteousness in the world. A more minimalist balancing approach—I present here

12. "The Biblical Destinies—Conditional Promises," *Tradition* 17 (1978): 84–90.

the Christian version, but it can easily be reformulated in Jewish terms—might bracket out the land promise. Does the land promise necessarily remain in force with the coming of Christ, and even if so, does it really apply to the modern, democratic state of Israel? A post-supersessionist Christian committed to the persistence of God's covenantal relationship with the Jewish people might remain agnostic on these questions while still taking the view that this relationship demands that she be supportive of the state of Israel simply insofar as it is a home for millions of God's chosen people and a political structure that enables Jews to find security and self-determination, entirely apart from any theology of the land promise. And such support must, like any other commitment, be coordinated to other commitments, such as to human dignity and justice.

Conclusion

There is hardly a more sensitive topic within and for the contemporary Jewish community, and for contemporary Jewish-Christian relations, than the circumstances and manner in which one can or should critique the state of Israel. Around this issue, painstakingly accumulated goodwill can quickly evaporate, fissures can appear in apparently united fronts, and theological disagreements that seemed a matter of the buried past can bubble up to the surface. The prudent counsel, in this area as in others, is often silence, coupled with personal support for parties immediately involved in the conflict. But for Jewish theology, and for Christian theology in relation to Judaism, the questions arising from the expression of state power in the Jewish state are too instructive and important to ignore. In this chapter we have navigated a range of approaches, and identified strengths and weaknesses in each, in the hope of enabling responses that are equal to the topic's complexity.

Further Inquiry

In *Studies in Christian Ethics* 22 (2009), there is a response by Nigel Biggar (164–84) to the above-referenced argument by Richard Hays for a pacifist Christianity, followed in turn by Hays's response to Biggar (185–98). Biggar returns to the topic at book length in *In Defence of War* (Oxford: Oxford University Press, 2013).

On the Jewish side of the ledger, see especially Shlomo M. Brody, *Ethics of Our Fighters: A Jewish View on War and Morality* (Jerusalem: Koren, 2024). See also Reuven Firestone, *Holy War in Judaism: The Fall and Rise of a Controversial Idea* (Oxford: Oxford University Press, 2015), tracing the exegetical efforts in classical rabbinic literature to contain the idea of holy war, medieval debate around the idea, and its debated status in the modern state of Israel. A recent book by Daniel Weiss, *Modern Jewish Philosophy and the Politics of Divine Violence* (Cambridge: Cambridge University Press, 2023), fills in certain gaps in Firestone's narrative by locating in the modern German Jewish canon—the writings of Mendelssohn, Cohen, Rosenzweig, and Walter Benjamin—a sustained Jewish critique of state violence as such. A Jewish theological response to John Howard Yoder, among others, can be found in Peter Ochs, *Another Reformation: Postliberal Christianity and the Jews* (Grand Rapids: Baker Academic, 2011). On early Christian perspectives on the Holy Land, see Robert L. Wilken, *The Land Called Holy: Palestine in Christian History and Thought* (New Haven: Yale University Press, 1992). For Christian Zionism see Stephen Spector, *Evangelicals and Israel: The Story of American Christian Zionism* (Oxford: Oxford University Press, 2009); Gerald R. McDermott, *The New Christian Zionism: Fresh Perspectives on Israel and the Land* (Downers Grove: IVP Academic, 2016); and Motti Inbari and Kirill Bumin, *Christian Zionism in the Twenty-First Century: American Evangelical Opinion on Israel* (Oxford: Oxford University Press, 2023). On the Catholic side, see Faydra Shapiro and Gavin D'Costa, eds., *Contemporary Catholic Approaches to the People, State, and Land of Israel* (Washington, DC: Catholic University Press of America, 2022). For Naim Ateek's articulation of Palestinian Liberation Theology, see his book, *A Palestinian Theology of Liberation: The Bible, Justice, and the Palestine-Israel Conflict* (Maryknoll, NY: Orbis Books, 2017). On religious Jewish support for the Palestinian cause see Mikhael Manekin, *End of Days: Ethics, Tradition, and Power in Israel* (Boston: Academic Studies Press, 2023) (centered on Israeli opposition to the post-1967 occupation); and Atalia Omer, *Days of Awe: Reimagining Jewishness in Solidarity with Palestinians* (Chicago: University of Chicago Press, 2019) (more broadly critical of Zionism).

●

1. Assume a non-pacifist Christian position, that is, a Christian approach that recognizes some circumstances in which war is just, and that distinguishes between

just and unjust ways in which to wage war. Should we expect a Jewish approach to just war to be substantially different from such a Christian approach, to come out differently in meaningful ways? Or is there a coherent "Judeo-Christian" conception of justice in application to war around which both traditions would more or less coalesce? On this question consult Shlomo Brody's book, cited above.

2. Just as the final blessing of the Amidah (in the Koren siddur, 132), mirroring the final line of the priestly blessing (Num. 6:26), concerns peace, so let us end this book by reflecting on peace. One of the perennial questions about peace concerns its relationship to truth. Does peace depend on a frank, shared understanding of the truth, or on the willingness to give up on such a shared understanding? Consider the paean to peace in Sifre be-midbar 42, from an early rabbinic commentary on the book of Numbers. The paean consists of a series of statements beginning: "Great is [the work of] peace, for . . ." The first statement finds the greatness of peace in the fact that "he modified Sarah's slight," that is, though Sarah in Genesis 18:12 noted Abraham's advanced age, God, in reporting Sarah's words to Abraham in the next verse, claims that Sarah made reference to her own advanced age, so as to spare Abraham the insult. This passage might be taken to suggest that peace paradigmatically rests on distortion of the truth. Is this a good reading? If so, can domestic peace be a good model for peace between nations?

Index